Hussite Warfare

The Armies, Equipment, Tactics and Campaigns 1419-1437

Alexander Querengässer and Sascha Lunyakov

Translation by Richard Sanders

"Do not fear your enemies, nor gaze upon their number,
Keep the Lord in your hearts; for Him fight on,
And before enemies you need not flee.

Remember all of you the password which was given out.
Obey your captains and guard one another.
Stay sharp and everyone keep formation.

For greed and theft don't lose your life.
And pay no heed to the spoils of war."

*„Die Feinde aber fürchtet nicht,
und achtet ihre Menge nicht,
traget Gott in eurem Herzen,
wollen für und mit ihm kämpfen,
und vor dem Feinde weichet nicht.*

*Seid der Losung eingedenk,
die euch ward gegeben,
achtet euren Hauptmann stets,
rettet einander das Leben,
und weiche niemand aus Reih und Glied.*

*Wegen Raub, aus Gier nach Gold,
lasset euer Leben nicht,
und bei Beute haltet euch nicht auf."*

(From the Hussite War Hymn "Ye Who are Warriors of God" - *"Die da Gottes Streiter sind"* or in Old Czech *"Ktož jsú boží bojovníci"* – translation from Wikipedia.)

Author:	Alexander Querengässer
Illustrations:	Sascha Lunyakov
Maps:	Bernhard Glänzer
Translation:	Richard L. Sanders

Publisher:	Zeughaus Verlag GmbH
	Knesebeckstr. 88
	10623 Berlin, Germany
	Telephone: +49 (0)30/315 700 30
	Email: info@zeughausverlag.de
	Website: www.zeughausverlag.de

Bibliographic information from the Deutschen Bibliothek: The Deutsche Bibliothek lists this publication in the German National Bibliography; detailed bibliographic information is available at http://dnb.ddb.de

Printed in European Union
Originally published in German as "Die Heere der Hussiten"
in the Heere & Waffen series numbers 25 and 26
(Berlin: Zeughaus Verlag, 2015/2016)
© 2019 Zeughaus Verlag GmbH, Berlin, Germany

ISBN: 978-3-96360-017-3

Contents

TRANSLATOR'S NOTES

The name "Bohemian" is used interchangeably with the term "Czech" with respect to the region, language, its people, etc. It should be noted that Bohemia (German name "*Böhmen*") was ethnically mixed with a rural population that predominantly spoke Old Czech and an urban – town and city – population which included a significant proportion who were German-speaking settlers from the 12th century onward. The German-speakers were a minority in Bohemia as a whole. During the reign of King Přemysl Otakar II (Ottokar II) of Bohemia (1253-78), he founded over sixty German towns in his kingdom. Prague (Czech "*Praha*", German "*Prag*") was a significantly German city, and Czech and "Roman" King Karl (Charles) IV founded the Prague University by a deed of foundation on April 7, 1348 as a first university to the north of the Alps and to the east of Paris. Residents of Prague are known as "Prazans", a term used in this work.

Place Names: Depending on where the city or town is located as of the writing of this book, they are rendered in that language. Where Czech, Polish or Hungarian names are used, they are followed by the German name. Cities like Prague (*Praha*) and Pilsen (*Plzeň*) are shown using their common English names.

Regarding Czech or Bohemian letters,
Á á is pronounced like the "a" in "father"
Č č is pronounced "ch" like in "chat".
É é is pronounced like the long "a" in "bare".
Ě ě as in Litoměřice is pronounced like "ye" in "yes".
Í í is pronounced like the "ee" in "bee".
Ň ň is pronounced like the "ny" sound in "onion".
Ó ó is pronounced like the "oo" in "door".
Ř ř as is pronounced "rz" like the "rg" in "bourgeois".
Š š is pronounced "sh" in "ship".
Ú ú is pronounced like a long "u" like in "flute"
Ý ý is pronounced like the "ee" in "bee".
Ž ž is pronounced like the "zh" sound of the "s" in "treasure".

Quotations in the medieval German language shown in the original Middle High German (MHG) version of the work have been retained in that archaic language in the footnotes but also translated into English whenever possible. Old Czech terms and quotations are also provided whenever possible although they may not have appeared in the original German edition of this book.

When the term "Empire" is used, it refers to the Holy Roman Empire, located at the time in what is now Germany, Austria, the Czech Republic and some more far-flung territories. The terms Kaiser and Emperor are used interchangeably, but both refer to the head of the Holy Roman Empire. Where Electoral Princes are mentioned, it refers to individuals who were empowered to elect the Emperor/Kaiser. Prince Bishops were four particular bishops who were simultaneously Electors in the Empire.

German spellings with the "*Umlaut*" over a vowel have been retained but can be easily tracked as: ä = ae, ö = oe and ü = ue; where the German consonant "ß" is retained, it equates to "ss".

Throughout the original German text, the terms "*Hauptmann*" (captain, literally "head man"; Czech hejtman), "*Feldhauptmann*" (field commander, literally "field head man", Czech "*polní hejtman*") and "*Heerführer*" (literally "army leader" are used to designate military leaders. Depending upon the context, the terms may be represented in this translation as "captain", "commander", "army commander" or "military leader".

My special thanks to Dr. Zdeněk Vybíral, PhD., of the Hussite Museum (*Husitske Museum*) in Tabor, Czech Republic, for his assistance with Czech terminology and to Mr. Thomas Keleher for his English proofreading assistance.

CHRONOLOGY

1415   6 July - Jan Hus burned at the stake in Konstanz (Constance).

1419   30 July - First Prague Defenestration, beginning of the Hussite Revolution.
16 August - Death of King Wenzel IV.
2 December - Jan Žižka's victory in the Battle of Nekmíř (Nekmer).

1420   17 March - Pope Martin V issues a papal bull for a crusade against the Hussites.
25 March - Jan Žižka's victory in the Battle of Sudoměř.
12 June - Beginning of the siege of Prague by the army of the 1st Crusade under King Sigismund.
14 July - Jan Žižka's victory in battle on the Vitkov Hill.
28 July - Sigismund has himself crowned the King of Bohemia.
30 July - End of the siege of Prague.
15 September - Beginning of the siege of the Vyšehrad (High Castle) by the Hussites.
30 October - 1 November – Capture of the Vyšehrad by the Hussites.

1421   16 March – Capture and destruction of Chomutov (Komotau) by the Taborites under Jan Žižka.
Late June – Siege of Rabi Castle – Žižka blinded.
5 August - Battle of Most (Brüx). Victory of an army from Meissen under Friedrich der Streitbaren (Fredrick the Warlike) over the Prazans (citizens of Prague) under Jan Želivský.
September - 2 October – Unsuccessful siege of the town of Žatec (Saatz) by the 2nd Crusade's army.
21-22 December - Battle of Kutná Hora (Kuttenberg). Jan Žižka's victory over the 2nd Crusade's army under King Sigismund.

1422   6 January - Battle of Nebovidy. Jan Žižka's victory over the 2nd Crusade's army under King Sigismund.
8 January - Battle of Havlíčkův Brod (Deutsch Brod). Jan Žižka's final victory over the 2nd Crusade's army under King Sigismund.
10 January – Capture of Nemecky Brod (Deutsche Brod - modern Havlickuv Brod).
7 March – Execution of Jan Želivský.
17 May - Sigmund Korybut enters Prague as the kingdom's administrator.
July - 8 November – Futile siege of the Hrad Karlstejn (Karlstein Castle) by the Prazans under Sigismund Korybut. Third Crusade acts as the relief action for the castle.

1423   March - Sigismund Korybut returns to Lithuania.
20 April - Battle of Hořice (Horschitz). Jan Žižka's victory over the army of the Lords' League (Czech: panská jednota, German: Herrenbund).
4 August - Battle of Stochov (Strauchov). Jan Žižka's victory over the Herrenbund's army.

1424   7 June - Battle of Malešov (Maleschau). Jan Žižka's victory over a Herrenbund army.
29 June - Sigismund Korybut returns to Prague.
14 September – Treaty of Libeň between Sigismund Korybut and Jan Žižka.
11 October – Death of Jan Žižka.

1426   16 - June Battle of Ústí nad Labem (German: Aussig). Victory of the united Hussite armies over a Saxon army.

1427   25 March - Battle of Zwettel in Austria. Victory of a Hussite army under Andreas Prokop over an Austrian army.
4 August - Battle of Tachov (Mies). Victory of the united Hussite armies under Andreas Prokop over the armies of the Fourth Crusade.

1429-30   December 1429 – February 1430 - The "beautiful rides" (Old Czech: *spaniel jizdy,* German: *Herrliche Heerfahrt*) of the united Hussite armies under Andreas Prokop conduct raid into Saxony and Franconia.

1431   14 August - Battle of Domažlice (Taus). Victory of the united Hussite armies under Andreas Prokop over the armies of the Fifth Crusade.
14 December – Beginning of the Council of Basel.

1433   April-September – "beautiful ride" of an army of the "Orphans" (*Waisen*) under Jan Čapek into the State of the Teutonic Order (*Deutschordensstaat*)
31 May - Sigismund's coronation as the Holy Roman Emperor in Rome.
21 September - Battle of Hiltersried in Bavaria. Defeat of a Hussite army by a levy under Johann von der Pfalz-Neumarkt.
30 November – Enacting of the Acts of Compact of Prague (*Prager Kompaktakten*).

1434   30 May - Battle of Lipany. Defeat of an army of the Taborites and Orphans under Andreas Prokop by an army of the Herrenbund. Death of Andreas Prokop.

1436   5 July – Enacting of the Acts of Compact of Ilgau (*Iglauer Kompaktakten*).
23 August - Sigismund enters Prague and declares the Hussite Revolution as having ended.

1437   9 December – Death of Emperor Sigismund.

THE HUSSITE REVOLUTION

One Nation and One Reformer

In the 1420s and 1430s the Hussites spread fear and terror in Central Europe. Their mobile and strong forces defeated late medieval armies that were also powerful. So what caused these wars?

It was a remarkable linkage of social but also religious reasons that brought about the strong Hussite movement. Bohemia's colonization, which began in the High Middle Ages, was initially driven above all by German settlers. Within the kingdom, which had been in the hands of the then most powerful Luxemburg noble dynasty since the 14th century, there was already a sharp division between the rural and urban populations. Indeed, under the Luxembourgs, the flow of German settlers slackened. At the same time, a distinct Bohemian identity - based on language and culture - evolved and led to the early development of a national consciousness. Courtly literature, up to then dominated by the German language and also religious writings, almost exclusively written in Latin, were increasingly transitioned into Bohemian (Czech). These translations were predominantly done by Bohemian clerics who became the transmitters of the new social-national self-consciousness and at the same time developed a unique new grasp of religious questions.[1]

The Bohemian portion of the population in the towns and cities increased, and the lower nobility pressed to enter the Prague University that Emperor Charles had founded. After completing their studies, many young Bohemians occupied positions in the Church. The Germans in the country were thus increasingly isolated and reacted with envy and resentment.[2]

The Bohemian national consciousness got a new impetus under Charles' son, Wenzel. Wenzel, who hardly had prospects to get elected the Holy Roman Emperor, had to fight with a strong group of opposing nobles in the country in 1394. In fact, initially he could claim that his position in the country was increasingly weakening. In 1401 an army from Meissen under Saxon Margrave Wilhelm I advanced to Prague and besieged the city with the aid of an army of Bohemian rebels. However, because the opposition nobility could unite with Wenzel, the Meissen forces were forced to withdraw but left behind bitter feelings of revenge among the Bohemian population.[3]

Independent of these social upheavals but indeed closely associated with them, the first ideas for reformation of the Church arose in the beginning of the 14th century in Bohemia. The great occidental schism which led to the faithful having to finance two hostile papal courts with their tithes, the omnipresent simony that the once ascetically minded mendicant orders themselves could not stop, all placed the credibility of the Church deeply in question.

An initial critic of these contemporary conditions was the English philosopher John Wycliffe who died in 1384. He rejected the adoration of the saints, reliquaries and icons, and also criticized celibacy. His strongest criticisms were directed at the Pope, whose authority he rejected. According to Wycliffe, the faithful should rely solely on the Bible. Even though his writings were banned in England in 1382, they were widely distributed throughout Europe. Especially attentive students sat in the Prague University. One of them was Jan ("Johannes") Hus, who became familiar with Wycliffe's works around 1398 through his fellow student Hieronymus of Prague. Just four years later Hus was the professor for theology and rector of the university. He began to preach in Czech and increasingly expressed criticism of the Church's great wealth. Influenced by Wycliffe's writings, he declared the Bible as being the only authority in religious questions, by which he also challenged the Pope's authority with regard to having the final say up to that time. The demand for receiving "Communion in both kinds" was of symbolic significance. At this time, it was customary that only the priests drank wine at Communion and the remainder of the congregation only received the consecrated wafer. Hus demanded – but only shortly before his death – that everyone should have a part of the blood of Christ. Because this was handed to someone in a chalice, people began to call his followers as *"Calixtiner"* (from the Latin *"calix"* for "chalice") or also *"Utraquists"* (from the Latin *"sub ultraque parte"* = in both kinds).[4]

In 1408 the Archbishop of Prague removed Hus from his position and defrocked him as a synod preacher. Even though forbidden to do so, Hus continued his work. In 1410, the Archbishop therefore arranged to get a Bull from Pope Alexander V, one of the three (!!!) popes at that time, who banned Wycliffe's writings and their dissemination. This finally allowed him to charge Hus with heresy. The reformer was put under a Church ban (anathematized) and in 1411 expelled from Prague, which led to the first unrest in the city. But the strong popularity of Hus' ideas led to King Wenzel also giving him his protection so that he could continue to spread his teachings in

1   PALACKÝ, Der Hussitenkrieg 1419-1431, pp. 4-21;
    ŠMAHEL, Hussitische Revolution I, pp. 85-716;
    SEIBT, Die Hussitische Revolution, pp. 80-82;
    SEIBT, Entwicklung der Böhmischen Staatlichkeit, pp. 139-151.

2   HILSCH, Johannes Hus, pp. 60-103;
    PALACKÝ, Der Hussitenkrieg 1419-1431, pp. 38-46;
    ŠMAHEL, Hussitische Revolution II, pp. 717-877;
    SEIBT, Die Hussitische Revolution, pp. 82-87.

3   TRESP, Die Belagerung von Prag 1401, pp. 45-50.

4   ŠMAHEL, Hussitische Revolution II, pp. 878-917;
    RIEDER, Die Hussiten, pp. 21-50;
    MACEK, Revolutionäre Bewegung, pp. 28-36;
    SEIBT, Die Hussitische Revolution, pp. 85-87.

Bohemia. In 1414, the Council of Constance once again banned Wycliffe's teachings. In order to free the crown of Bohemia from the accusation of supporting a heretic, King Sigismund invited Hus to Constance with the promise of safe conduct. However, because Hus could not be persuaded to renounce his teaching, on 6 July 1415, he was condemned to be burned at the stake as a heretic and executed that same afternoon.[5]

The failure of Jan Hus' reform efforts, which were not dissimilar to the earlier but also later reformers like Martin Luther, was due to the scant media options in Europe around 1400. It is said that Luther could spread his teachings much more widely with the help of then modern book printing. Actually, Jan Hus' efforts presented a purely Bohemian problem. Just through the conflicts with the German population in the country by themselves alone, the efforts toward church reforms that included preaching in the Czech language became a national phenomenon that had few prospects for their further spread in the Holy Roman Empire. It would also be wrong to dismiss the Hussite movement as a peasants' and townsmen's phenomenon as happened in socialist times in central Europe. This thesis is contradicted by just the circumstance that 452 counts, lords and knights had signed a protest note against the arrest of the reformer. After the reformer's burning at the stake, his ideas spread even more extensively throughout the land, whereby along with John Wycliffe's theological concepts, Waldensian ideas entered the Hussite theology. In the meantime, according to research, the movement's radical branches blossomed especially strongly where the Waldensian influence had been greatest, like in Tabor.[6]

However, there was also a social component along with the national and the class-oriented components. The crisis events of the 14th century, i.e., the plague, the beginning of the so-called "small Ice Age" and the resulting collapse of agricultural production, led to a growing impoverishment of broad classes within the populations. In Bohemia even these classes, resting on the religious principles of Jan Hus, began to question the social order that was based on class birth.[7]

However, within these very causes also lay the insipient problems of the later reform movement, because the interests of the self-assuredly acting Bohemian nobles stood in stark contrast to the lower classes' desires for advancement. While above all the classes wanted to increase their power with regard to the central kingdom,

tensions arose between the predominantly German town and city dwellers and the impoverished rural peasant population.[8]

The First Prague Defenestration and its Effects

Bohemia continued to be ruled by King Wenzel who had supported the election of his brother as the "Roman King" and therefore wanted to protect him from the possible effects of the Hussite revolution. After the execution of Jan Hus, Wenzel attempted to force Hus' followers out of Church and state offices, which again caused the Bohemians to rise up against him. In February 1419, he closed all the Utraquist churches in Prague except for three. Many Hussite priests then left the capital and carried the movement to other Bohemian cities and towns.[9]

A group of radical representatives of the interpretation of the faith remained in Prague. They gathered around the charismatic priest Jan Želivský. On 30 July 1419, an enraged group of Prague citizens (Prazans = citizens of Prague) stormed the New Town City Hall (Czech "novoměstská radnice", German "Neustädter Rathaus") in order to free fellow believers who were jailed there. In doing so, they ran into the mayor, two councilmen, the judge's deputy, five community elders and a squire all of whom they threw out the window. The crowd assembled at the foot of the City Hall in the Charles' Square (Czech "Karlovo náměstí", German "Karlsplatz") hacked those defenestrated men to pieces using weapons they had hidden under their clothing. Shortly after that, another councilman was tortured to death. King Wenzel was so very frightened by this action that he suffered a stroke and on 16 August 1419 he died from its effects.[10]

Wenzel's death worsened the crisis even further because now the Hussites wanted to not recognize his brother Sigismund - who had assured Jan Hus safe conduct to Constance - as the king. In Prague, the reformer's followers stormed several churches and attempted to take control of the Communion with the chalice. Several churches went up in flames. The rebels profited by the circumstance that Sigismund had just equipped a large army for a campaign against the Turks in Hungary and did not want to employ it against the Hussites. Instead, his wife, Barbara of Cilli, was to temporarily take over the regency.[11]

The most senior Burggraf (Burgrave) Čeněk von Wartenberg, whom Sigismund appointed to assist the Regent, called the Bohemian nobles together for a National Assembly (Landtag). In this institution, the nobles were

5   HILSCH, Johannes Hus, pp. 30-53;
    RIEDER, Die Hussiten, pp. 51-87;
    MACEK, Revolutionäre Bewegung, pp. 37-42.

6   ŠMAHEL, Hussitische Revolution II, pp. 930-932;
    SEIBT, Die Hussitische Revolution, pp. 86-89;
    MACHILEK, Hussiten in Franken, p. 22;
    BERGER, Kampfkraft der Hussiten, p. 100.

7   KROENER, Kriegswesen, p. 9.

8   Ibid., p. 9.

9   ŠMAHEL, Hussitische Revolution II, pp. 941-950;
    RIEDER, Die Hussiten, pp. 88-94.

10 PALACKÝ, Der Hussitenkrieg 1419-1431, pp. 47-50;
    ŠMAHEL, Hussitische Revolution, pp. 1002-1020;
    RIEDER, Die Hussiten, pp. 94-99.

11 PALACKÝ, Der Hussitenkrieg 1419-1431, pp. 49-53;
    RIEDER, Die Hussiten, pp. 99-102.

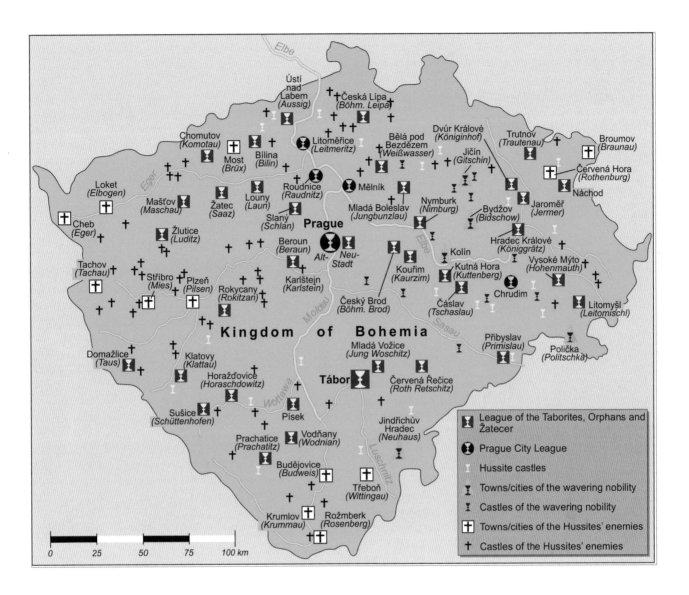

able above all to pose their demands on the new king. The Hussites even used the *Landtag* to demand that Sigismund grant them religious freedom. He should allow both forms of the Communion, forbid the denunciation of the Utraquists as heretics and strongly urge the Pope to allow lay people to use the chalice. In addition, there were a series of demands for changes to the country's administration that would have been to the advantage of the Bohemian ethnicities. Sigismund's response was carefully and cautiously formulated. He wanted to continue his reign in the tradition of his father, Charles V.[12]

Bohemia began to split. The Catholic Church quickly lost ground. Its last supporters were the still heavily German towns and cities in the north, on the slopes of the Erz Mountains, from Cheb (Eger) to Litoměřice (Leitmeritz). The mass of the Bohemian Hussites sought very moderate goals. The so-called "Calixtiners" (*Kelchbrüder* – Brothers of the Chalice) were completely ready to acknowledge Sigismund as king and also as the head of the Catholic Church. However, they demanded tolerance of the ideas of Jan Hus. The Calixtiners' center was Prague, and initially their most important representative was Čeněk von Wartenberg whom Sigismund had named as his representative. Directly after the Prague defenestration, a radical wing of the movement arose that rejected negotiations with the King because it was convinced of their futility.

---

12 PALACKÝ, *Der Hussitenkrieg 1419-1431*, pp. 52-54.

This group had its center in the Prague New Town (Czech *"Nové Město"*, German *"Prager Neustadt"*) and was led by Jan Želivský. His party wanted to only recognize the Bible in religious questions and thus rejected the authority of the Pope. This principle led to the radicals splintering into several groups as happened a hundred years later to the Protestants. The most important radical Hussite group would become the Taborites.[13]

Starting on 22 July 1419, the Taborites gathered on a mountain ridge about seventy kilometers southwest of Prague. Their name is derived from an episode in St. Mathew's Gospel (17,1-2) in which Jesus preached before a large congregation on a hill. The Bohemians believed that the hill was Mount Tabor. The idea of an approaching apocalypse quickly spread throughout the kingdom based on the sermon of the radical priests on that hill. The Taborite movement had great appeal above all to the broad rural population. [14]

Hussite groups armed themselves everywhere in the country. An army was raised in Pilsen (Czech: Plzeň), which had been the center of radical Hussitism since 1417, whose first leaders were the radical monk Václav Koranda and already battle-hardened Jan Žižka from Trocnov who was from the lower nobility. Žižka had been one of the ringleaders at the Prague defenestration. In the course of the autumn of 1419, he and Mikuláš of Hus turned to the scholars of the Prague University with the question of whether war was a legitimate means for the liberation of the word of God. The Magisters' answer was that it was legitimate to defend the faith with a weapon, but not to spread the Gospel with the sword. Žižka supposedly adhered to this demand throughout his life. In the meantime, however, the Regent and Čeněk von Wartenberg occupied and improved militarily important points in Prague, which especially annoyed the Taborites in the nearby New Town. On 25 October, a small band of Hussites around Žižka took the old Vyšehrad (*Burgberg* or "High Castle"). Consequently, at the beginning of November when the rural population wanted to gather for a meeting in Prague, they were repeatedly attacked by barons loyal to the King. Only the Hussites from the western part of the country, from Pilsen, were warned in advance and headed in the direction of the capital en mass. When they got to Nový Knín (Knien), a messenger arrived with a request for assistance from a group from the town of Ústí nad Orlicí (Austi). But even before the Pilsners could join with that detachment, they were wiped out by 1,300 knights under Peter von Sternberg. After the Pilsner group received reinforcements from Nový Knín, the knights did withdraw from the battlefield. As soon as news of the fighting at Nový Knín reached Prague, the out-

raged Bohemian burghers rallied around Mikuláš of Hus and Jan Žižka. Both of them decided to storm the *malá strana* district of Prague (*Prager Kleinseite*) and led their crowds across the Charles Bridge under fire from the royal cannon. After a long, bloody fight, they were able to take the entire Old City side including the castle. But the fighting continued for several more days. Only on November 13 could a five-month ceasefire be concluded. Because Žižka and some radicals were opposed to the compromises agreed between the Prazans and the King, he left Prague and went west and returned to Pilsen.[15]

Žižka had all of the Catholics expelled from Pilsen and attempted to make the city the first fortress and base for the movement. He persistently rejected the King's peace offerings. His little army was repeatedly engaged in fighting in the area around Pilsen. When an approximately 400 man strong Hussite army tried to return to the city in December, it was attacked by surprise about 17 kilometers to the northwest at Nekmíř by a 2,000 man Imperial cavalry army under Bohuslav von Schwanberg. However the rebels formed a *"Wagenburg"* - or "wagon castle" -*"vozová hradba"* - as the Bohemians called it, or laager from seven wagons they had along and took the mounted knights under fierce fire with heavy cannon. The Hussites were able to repel all the attacks. As the rebels moved further in the night, they were attacked again by three more royal garrisons before they reached Pilsen. The engagement at Nekmíř marked the beginning of Hussite warfare.[16]

These first Hussite successes did not seem to worry King Sigismund very much. Around Christmas 1419 he had returned to Moravian Brno (Brünn) from his not very successful Turkish campaign. The Utraquists of the Margrave's domain and from Prague rendered homage to him at Brno. Only western Bohemia seemed to be in any serious unrest.[17]

Yet south of Prague a new Hussite center was already developing. The old town of Ústí nad Orlicí (Austi), which was surrounded in part by a series of partially dilapidated castles, fell into Hussite hands on 21 February 1420. Within the shortest time, hundreds of peasants who adhered to the movement were streaming into the town. However, because it would be difficult to defend, they moved to the small nearby town of Hradiště. The Hussites founded a new religious center there that soon received reinforcements by some of Žižka's men from Pilsen. Pilsen's garrison was, however, so weakened that Žižka himself had to leave the city on 20 March. Pilsen was given back to the Catholics and in the following years became a bulwark against the Bohemian heresy. On

---

13 PALACKÝ, Der Hussitenkrieg 1419-1431, pp. 56-59; ŠMAHEL, Hussitische Revolution, pp. 1021-1040.

14 SEIBT, Tabor, pp. 175-178; PALACKÝ, Der Hussitenkrieg 1419-1431, pp. 61-64; ŠMAHEL, Hussitische Revolution, pp. 1037-1070.

15 PALACKÝ, Der Hussitenkrieg 1419-1431, pp. 65-73.

16 PALACKÝ, Der Hussitenkrieg 1419-1431, pp. 80-83; TURNBULL, Hussite Wars, pp. 24-33; TRESP, Söldner aus Böhmen, p. 24; DURDÍK, Hussitisches Heerwesen, p. 196-199.

17 PALACKÝ, Der Hussitenkrieg 1419-1431, p. 75-77.

Duke Friedrich of Saxony and Katharina
From *Das Sächsische Stammbuch*, sheet 80r,
appeared in 1546

Zikmund Lucemburskÿ (Sigismund of Luxembourg)
Son of Emperor Charles IV (Karl/Karol IV) and
stepbrother of Wenzel of Luxembourg
Drawing by Johannes Hartlieb

25 March at Sudoměř, while on the march to the south, Žižka, who only had about 400 men and twelve wagons, was attacked by a royal army of supposedly 5,000 knights. The skilled tactician Žižka formed his wagons into a temporary defense line between two fishponds. Additionally, the Hussites carried a few cannon with them. In this way, he was able to repulse the royal assault with heavy losses. The attacking forces tried to wade across a dried-up lake, even having to dismount, and were again beaten. On the next day, the Hussites continued on to Tabor. In the following months, Žižka tried to expand the area of influence of the "Taborites" - as the radical wing of the movement would soon be called – into the surrounding countryside[18]

18 PALACKÝ, Der Hussitenkrieg 1419-1431, p. 83-89;
    TURNBULL, Hussite Wars, p. 33;
    STÖLLER, Österreich im Kriege gegen die Hussiten, pp. 7-8.

THE HUSSITE MILITARY SYSTEM

The Pillars of the Army

The first Hussite armies were above all composed of levies from the towns and cities dominated by the heretics. Their contribution was made up of citizens' militias or also of mercenaries. Hussite-minded nobles and their subjects provided the cavalry and also recruited mercenaries. The Bohemian lower nobility also had experience in warfare because serving as mercenaries was the only possibility for employment for many of them during the reign of the House of Luxembourg. In this way, they got wartime experience in the minor feuds within the Empire, the major war between the Teutonic Order and Poland, or Hungarian King Sigismund's Turkish Crusades.[19]

The bulk of the volunteers, who crowded around this battle-tested or at least militarily trained nucleus, were certainly peasants and townsmen who possessed no experience in military service whatsoever. Each member of a commander's brotherhood had to hand over his personal property to the community when entering military service.[20]

With regard to social composition, the Hussite armies were possibly the most heterogeneous that medieval Europe had seen. Noblemen, peasants, mercenaries and volunteers fought side by side. They all pursued their own social and economic interests. To weld them into a disciplined army, a military system was needed, that endeavored, above all, to use religion as the greatest common motivating factor.[21]

Theological Justification

Although war and violence were omnipresent in the Middle Ages, the armed conflicts between Christians always posed a certain theological challenge. For the crusader armies within Europe itself this was hardly problematic because the Hussites, like the Albigensians, Catharists and Waldensians before them, were branded as heretics and the fight against them was even a *bellum sacrum* – holy war, as Pope Martin V made clear in 1421.[22]

Also, at the Prague University, the essence of "Just War" was heatedly debated. In this case, John Wycliffe's works also formed the theological foundation. Influenced by the Englishman's theses, the Magister Jan of Příbram authored *Bellandi materiaam*. That writing appeared in the autumn of 1419, when Čeněk von Wartenberg occupied the Prague Castle (Czech: *Hradčany*; German: *Hradschin*). However, Příbram's theses on Just War fit into a much older debate. Wycliffe actually drew his writing directly from Thomas Aquinas and his three reasons for a Just War, i.e., *auctoritas principis – causa justa* and *intencio recta*, i.e., the "legal authority", the "just cause" and the "right intent". But the Hussite movement was above all also directed against the rule of the Bohemian King. However, the Prague theologians derived the legal authority directly from God. When Pope Martin called for a crusade, the Prague Magister declared the war to defend the true belief to be not only for justice but also as a duty. With the appearance of the Taborite movement the fight against the anti-Hussite movement took on apocalyptic traits. The Taborite priests declared that it was a duty for the true believers to carry out God's laws and carry out his vengeance on Earth. From that arose a demand to kill all unbelievers, which, however, the Utraquist theologians strictly rejected. The priest Martin, named "Loquis" (i.e., powerfully eloquent), together with Johannes Jičín, Koranda and other priests wrote 19 articles. They believed Christ's return was immediately at hand, that this time was no time for mercy, but rather a time for vengeance. The chronicler Laurentius wrote of these articles:

"Five further: In this time of vengeance, all cities, villages and castles must be devastated, destroyed and burned down because neither the Lord God nor anyone else will enter them any more. Six further: [they said] that at this time of vengeance the Taborite brothers are the angels who were sent to show the faithful out of all the cities, villages and castles to the mountains like Lot from Sodom, and that the brothers and their followers are of one body to whom even the eagles will gather, no matter where they may be. They are namely the army sent by God over the entire world for removing all offenses from the empire of Christ, which is the quarrelsome Church, to drive out the evil ones from among the good ones and to carry out vengeance and the scourge on the nations of the enemies of the Christ's law and on their cities, villages and bulwarks".[23]

---

19   Kroener, Kriegswesen, pp. 9-10.

20   Berger, Kampfkraft der Hussiten, pp. 103-104; Tresp, Söldner aus Böhmen, pp. 24-25.

21   Kroener, Kriegswesen, p. 10.

22   Bleicher, Das Herzogtum Niederbayern, p. 84.

23   Cited in Laurentius-Chronik, pp. 137-138. *"5 Weiter: In dieser Zeit der Rache müssen alle Städte, Dörfer und Burgen verwüstet, zerstört und verbrannt werden, weil nicht mehr weder Gott der Herr noch sonst jemand in sie eintreten wird. 6 Weiter (sagten sie), daß die Taboritenbrüder in dieser Zeit der Rache die Engel sind, die geschickt wurden, um die Gläubigen aus allen Städten, Dörfern und Burgen auf die Berge hinauszuführen wie den Lot von Sodom und daß die Brüder mit ihren Anhängern jener Leib sind, bei dem sich, wo immer er auch sein wird, auch die Adler sammeln werden. Sie nämlich sind das von Gott über die ganze Welt geschickte Heer zur Beseitigung aller Ärgernisse vom Reich Christi, das die streitende Kirche ist, zur Vertreibung der Bösen aus der Mitte der Gerechten und zur Ausübung der Rache und der Plagen über die Nationen der Feinde des Gesetzes Christi und ihre Städte, Dörfer und Bollwerke".*

Eberhard Windecke (ca. 1380 – 1440/41), in the 1430s published a chronicle about the life of Emperor Sigismund.
The elaborate illustrations provide revealing information about weapons and equipment of armies in the time of the Hussites.

This question about Just War formed only one of many points of contention between moderate and radical Hussites. De facto their theological justification for conducting war was rooted in the theses of the very same Church theoreticians that the Crusaders invoked.[24]

Žižka's War Directives

Foundationally important for the cohesion of the Hussite armies was their high degree of discipline, which clearly distinguished them from any other armies of the High and Late Middle Ages. In 1420 the Taborites issued a first Chiliastic-based war directive.[25] After Jan Žižka changed over to the Orebites (Czech: *Orebité*; German: *Orebiten* – from the Bible's Mount Horeb) in 1423, he developed a separate moral and tactical directive. Žižka's War Directive is a direct further development of the Directive of 1420.[26]

The War Directive of 1423 consisted of two parts. The first contained a list of prohibitions. The soldiers of God should generally avoid any wrongdoing; in battle they should not allow themselves to be overcome by fear, but instead hold their positions in the order and they should/shall *"be wary of claiming enemy booty before they have concluded the fighting".*[27] As soon as the fighting has ended and the booty has been taken, it should, however, be made available to the common group and no one should keep anything for himself out of greed. A decisive factor contributing to the lack of discipline in knights' armies was individuals' lust for booty. The Hussites forbade this kind of self-aggrandizement under the threat of expulsion and hoped to thus maintain battlefield discipline. Booty found on the battlefield after the fighting was to be available to the community.[28]

The seventh article urges conscientious testing of fighters being accepted into the army and the eighth warns them to remove themselves from the battle line if they are only there for fame. The second half concerns the army's religious and moral constitution. The soldiers should be god-fearing and be obedient to their elected leader.[29]

Furthermore, the War Directive contained strict rules for behavior on the march, in battle and on sentry duty because they were seen as the foundation for military success. Thus on the march, the troops needed to maintain close order and they should remain together in their billeting. The march order that had to be maintained was described in detail.

"Quarreling, shouting and dissention"[30] were disapproved in the army and therefore it was additionally established that: "Also among us we do not want to tolerate such who are disloyal and disobedient, the liars, thieves, dice-players [gamblers], plunderers, drunkards and slanderers, lechers, and adulterers, as well as lewd and adulterous women and all apparent sinners".[31] Gambling, drunkenness and above all the women who were brought along with the army were thus considered as factors that threatened discipline. Desertion or personal enrichment by taking booty constituted especially serious offenses. The punishments were drastic and "so shall he who is caught, be he a prince, lord, knight, handworker, villain or any other person, be executed on his neck and his worldly possessions [confiscated], as is done to a dishonest scoundrel who in the eyes of God and the truthful brothers, steals away from the army wherever the army is located or lies".[32] Above all, the passage also illustrates the egalitarian principle that the members of the Orebite army had submitted to whether they were nobles, burghers or peasants. Furthermore, the War Directive also provided a religious code of conduct and precisely prescribed the form of prayers in the camp and Christian behavior in battle. Žižka linked both these elements. Whoever violated military discipline or actually deserted was considered as an apostate, a crime that should be punished by death.[33]

It is also interesting to consider Jan Hájek von Hodětín's War Instructions when looking at the question of how the War Directives of 1420 and 1423 were implemented in reality and also how they were further developed. The origin of Hodětín's War Instructions was controversial in Bohemian research for a long time. In the introductory portion of the directive, it is indicated that in 1413 King Wenzel tasked Hodětín with documenting his instructions. Some Czech researchers accept this;[34] others assert that they were first written after the time of the Hussites.[35] And others see, in the passed down sources, a War

---

24 SEIBT, Hussitica, pp. 16-53.

25 Translator's note: Chiliasm is the doctrine of Christ's expected return to reign on earth for 1000 years; millennialism.

26 DURDÍK, Hussitisches Heerwesen, p. 55-58; TRESP, Söldner aus Böhmen, p. 25.

27 DURDÍK, Hussitisches Heerwesen, p. 56. "… sich hüten, feindliche Beute zu fordern, bevor sie nicht den Kampf beendet haben".

28 TRESP, Söldner aus Böhmen, p. 26.

29 DURDÍK, Hussitisches Heerwesen, pp. 56-59; ŠMAHEL, Hussitische Revolution II, pp. 1297-1298

30 In modern German, *"Zank, Geschrei und Händel"* quoted from DURDÍK, Hussitisches Heerwesen, p. 64.

31 In modern German, *"Auch wollen wir unter uns nicht dulden solche, die ungetreu und ungehorsam sind, die Lügner, Diebe, Würfelspieler, Plünderer, Betrunkene und Schmähbuben, Unzüchtige und Ehebrecher, gleichwie unzüchtige und ehebrecherische Frauen und alle offenkundigen Sünder und Sünderinnen."* quoted from DURDÍK, Hussitisches Heerwesen, p. 64;

32 In modern German, *"… so soll er, wenn er ergriffen wird, er sei Fürst, Herr, Ritter, Knappe, Bürger, Handwerker, Fronsmann oder irgendein anderer Mensch, an seinem Halse und an seinem Hab und Gut gerichtet werden, so wie es einem ungetreuen Schurken geschieht, der sich von der Sache Gottes und der getreuen Brüder aus dem Heeres stiehlt, wo immer das Heer steht oder liegt".* Quoted from DURDÍK, Hussitisches Heerwesen, p. 65.

33 TRESP, Söldner aus Böhmen, pp. 25-26.

34 Among those accepting this are Tomek, Jan Žižka, and PALACKÝ, Der Hussitenkrieg 1419-1431, pp. 368.

35 These include TOMAN, Das hussitische Kriegswesen, pp. 421-429,

A Hussite handgunner
He is carrying a *"Stabbüchse"* (staff culverin)
as they were found with the Taborites.
He carries the ammunition in a pouch attached to his belt.

Lunyanov 2015

Directive that had its roots in 1413 but that was continuously developed further under the impressions from later experiences.

Hodětín's Instructions are the most comprehensive of their time. They include all seven articles that are concerned with the army's internal order, five about the marching order, and one each about sentry duty and obedience, and, as a novelty, with the function of the army's scribes. Interesting, and that makes dating the document difficult, are two articles about equipping the army wagons and maintenance of roads. Precisely the second issue, which deals with an infrastructure problem, points to a time when the war wagons were already used extensively. Apparently, deficient roads had often led to problems for the Hussite armies' movements, so the article possibly was recorded later.[36]

Another article about actions in enemy territory indicates that the Instructions possibly first were issued around 1430. In this context, there is also a very interesting article about behavior toward women. They were to be spared when possible and were protected from rape. That this article was recorded in a late Hussite War Directive is an indication that the leaders recognized a serious deficit in their soldiers' discipline in his matter.

In this context, the significance of popular songs cannot be underestimated. The piece, "Ktož jsú boží bojovníci" in Old Czech ("Die ihr Gottes Streiter seid" - "Ye Who are Warriors of God") perhaps contributed even more to anchor the ideals that Žižka's War Directives were seeking to put into the heads of the simple soldiers than the Articles themselves. In a catchy form, the song encompassed the essential tenets: fearlessness in the face of the enemy, piety, obedience, discipline and the prohibition against pillaging out of greed. The origin of the song is not clear. Many assert that it was written by Žižka himself.[37]

The Hussite War Wagon

A central element of Hussite warfare was the war wagon (Czech: bojový vůz or "tabor", German: Kriegswagen). The need to integrate a large number of simple peasants into their armies, who perhaps brought along scythes, threshing flails, and some crossbows and swords, led to the Hussite armies' very defense-oriented tactics. Otherwise they could not get the better of a well-armored mounted army of the Late Middle Ages.[38]

At the beginning of the war, the war wagon was a simple makeshift solution. Initially the Hussites used simple farm wagons for transporting weapons and provisions and when attacked they moved them together into a "wagon castle" or laager (German: Wagenburg). From there, the Hussites developed an improved type for military purposes. These wagons had a uniform length, wheel size and axel width and thus probably belonged to the first mass-produced military vehicles of the Middle Ages.[39]

The wagons' wheels were iron-rimmed. On one side there was a ramp that could be lowered to allow access to the wagon. In battle, soldiers with loaded weapons could get into the wagon via the ramp, because reloading of crossbows as well as handguns was a time-consuming affair. The sides of the war wagons were high enough that the shooters could comfortably rest their weapons on them. On the wagons' outsides (exteriors) an additional row of planks could be lowered as well. This double planking was to reduce the penetration of enemy missiles. Other depictions show wagons with a parapet in which were triangular firing ports for the shooters. There were also planks that could be folded down between the axels to prevent attacking soldiers from crawling under the wagons. Contemporary illustrations sometimes show these planks with triangular firing ports as well. So it is conceivable that shooters were also positioned there. Within the wagon there was a container for heavy fieldstone, the simplest throwing weapon for defending against attacking knights and footsoldiers. The wagon had an important psychological function for the Hussites: the mobile field fortification gave the poorly armed footsoldiers a feeling of security and protection from the crusaders' well-equipped, mounted forces.[40] See depictions on pp. 19, 22-23, 38, 53, 66, 67, 80-81, 96-97, 103 and 109.

A typical wagon crew consisted of two grooms, eight handgunners or crossbowmen, two soldiers with pavis shields who were to stand between the wagons, as well as eight men with pikes, scythes or war flails (called flail-men – Czech "cepníci", German "Flegler"). The heavy vehicles were drawn by only four horses.[41]

The handgunners were especially widely used in the wagon units. The first medieval handguns (culverins) were still very primitive weapons. They were so-called "Stangenbüchsen" in German, in English literally translated as a 'pole culverin.' A culverin found in 1898 at Tabor consisted only of a 42 cm (16 ½ inch) long steel barrel with a 17mm (3/4 inch) caliber. At the end of the barrel was a depression into which a simple round wooden staff could be fit-

---

DURDÍK, Hussitisches Heerwesen, pp. 73-74; also the German researcher Hans Delbrück adopted this variant. DELBRÜCK, Geschichte der Kriegskunst, pp. 562-563.

36 DURDÍK, Hussitisches Heerwesen, p. 72.

37 PALACKÝ, Der Hussitenkrieg 1419-1431, p. 363;
DURDÍK, Hussitisches Heerwesen, p. 61.

38 DURDÍK, Hussitisches Heerwesen, pp. 145-147;
TRESP, Söldner aus Böhmen, p. 27;
BERGER, Kampfkraft der Hussiten, pp. 105-107.

39 TRESP, Söldner aus Böhmen, p. 27;
DELBRÜCK, Geschichte der Kriegskunst, pp. 565-566;
BERGER, Kampfkraft der Hussiten, p. 107.

40 KROENER, Kriegswesen, p. 11;
TURNBULL, Hussite Wars, pp. 33-34;
DELBRÜCK, Geschichte der Kriegskunst, pp. 556-557.

41 TRESP, Söldner aus Böhmen, pp. 27-28;
DELBRÜCK, Geschichte der Kriegskunst, pp. 556-557.

ted as a shaft or stock. When firing, the shaft would be held in the armpit like a lance. There was no real aiming. The Bohemian (Old Czech) word for "Stangenbüchsen" was "pístala" (that actually means "pipe" and described the shape of the weapon), and "pístala" could possibly be the origin of our modern term of 'pistol.' In German it was also called a "Pfeifenbüchsen" or a 'pipe gun', or 'pipe culverin.'[42]

The handguns were produced with either a stave and hoop or a casting process (more about that in the chapter on artillery). A significant advantage was that the production process for guns was less expensive than for crossbows.[43]

Other versions consisted of a shorter barrel that was attached to a wooden shaft with several metal bands. An iron hook was forged below the mouth so the weapon could be placed on an edge of a wagon's side, on a parapet or on a pavis and that should help absorb the recoil. Thus, the gunner could also lay the shaft, or stock, on his shoulder and at least roughly aim at a target over the barrel. Contemporary depictions sometimes show the weapon being served by two men, one "aims" and the other holds the match to the touch-hole.[44]

The first handguns were fired with a red-hot iron rod, a so-called "Loseisen" and in some sources they are referred to very passably as "Pengeisen" – the German terms. These rods were bent at a right angle and shaped like a flattened spoon. To ignite the gunpowder the point of the iron had to be heated to at least 170°C (338°F). However, this means that the iron itself was a hindrance to the gunner when loading. Additionally, iron cools very quickly so that the gunner had to stand near a brazier filled with hot coals. Because an enormous plume of flames came out of the touch-hole when firing, the weapon also had to be kept away from the shooter's face.

In the 15th century, however, the 'match' was used increasingly. Handling it was simpler and less dangerous than the heated iron staff, and it could be used longer. The matches were soaked in potassium chlorate, so they only smoldered rather than burned.[45]

The projectile balls were already mostly being produced from lead in the Late Middle Ages and either cast or cut from a larger chunk of lead. Because the metal is very soft and in any case its shape is altered during loading and when fired, little attention was paid to making the projectiles uniform.[46]

The men carried the balls and the gunpowder in separate pouches. The man also carried the ramrod that was not yet attached to the weapon.[47]

Medieval pictographs show diverse possibilities for "aiming" these weapons. Most frequently, aiming is shown with the stock resting on the right shoulder. In those, the right arm holds the stock near the shoulder while the left is stretched out. That way both hands are grasping the weapon and the recoil can be better received. This firing method of holding the weapon allowed a relatively exact "aiming" (whereby the early culverins with poles with their short barrels were very inaccurate). In any case, a second man was needed to ignite the charge. It is however conceivable that in a Hussite wagon the left arm was free to apply the match because the gun was resting on the wagon's side or the firing port.

A different variant also shows the gun's stock resting on a shoulder; an extended arm holds the gun while the other arm ignites the charge. In this way one could also aim more precisely; however, the firing platform was not very stable and did not permit the recoil to be safely absorbed. In Kyeser's *Bellifortis* a man is also shown who rests a large *Stabbüchse* on a vertical pole and holds the stock with both hands while he is blowing in the touch-hole. This illustration is in itself not completely conclusive. Who is igniting the gun? Was it a second man? Or is it the shooter who has to take his hand from the stock to do so?[48]

Firing with the stock in the armpit seems to have been widely done. To do that, the bended right arm held the stock tightly against the torso and the left arm was extended to hold the gun with that hand. Thus the recoil was absorbed well, so the weapon could easily remain in place. However, it was still only possible to take rough aim at the target. And igniting the charge was not unproblematic because in order to light it with the match or the iron staff with the right hand the gun had to be held close because otherwise the weapon could not be secured in the armpit. A variation of this firing method was grabbing the gun with the right hand somewhat further forward so that the left hand was free for lighting the charge. But this again reduces the stability of the aim.

Another possibility for an unfettered firing required a second man to ignite the weapon. The man holding the gun could then grasp the stock with one hand very close to his hip and align it with an outstretched arm. Historical depictions occasionally show this variation when targets located higher are going to be engaged.

Firing with the stock or shaft pressed into the shoulder, as done with modern rifles, is not shown in contemporary illustrated sources. Because of the weapon's nature, it is also hardly possible. It is, however, conceivable that the guns, which were not attached to a staff or stock but

42 Lugs, Handfeuerwaffen I, p. 14;
    Turnbull, Hussite Wars, p. 35.

43 Schmidtchen, Kriegswesen, pp. 207-208.

44 Lugs, Handfeuerwaffen I, p. 14;
    Turnbull, Hussite Wars, pp. 35-36.

45 Dolínek/Durdík, Historische Waffen, p. 181;
    Lugs, Handfeuerwaffen I, pp. 14-15;
    Turnbull, Hussite Wars, p. 35; McLachlan, Medieval
    Handgonnes, p. 30.

46 Schmidtchen, Kriegswesen, p. 208.

47 Lugs, Handfeuerwaffen I, p. 15.

48 McLachlan, Medieval Handgonnes, pp. 29-33.

A Hussite wagon unit
In the background is a simple supply wagon. These were placed inside the laager (*Wagenburg*) during a battle. The war wagon in the foreground is unhitched. Both outermost planks were to reduce the impact of missiles. The crossbowman and the halberdier belong to the wagon crew. A peasant is just raising the flag bearing the chalice.

tied on a true shaft, would be handled by the wagon occupants in that they rested the weapon on the side of the wagon or the firing port, like when the later musket-fork was used to steady the weapon and the stock was held to the shoulder.

As already mentioned, there were two related possibilities for igniting the charge. Either the gunner himself applied the match or heated staff to the touch-hole or a helper did this. In Konrad Kyeser's "*Bellifortis*" there was already a *Stabbüchse* shown with a levered match. In the illustration a z-shaped rod passes through the wood shaft. One end of a rod, fork-shaped, holds the match over the touch-hole, the other end serves as a trigger. The principle is similar to the trigger of a crossbow. That way the weapon can be comfortably held tightly in the armpit and ignited without the danger of the gunner being burned by sparks leaping out of the touch-hole.

Modern attempts have shown that these early guns could definitely match bows and crossbows with regard to range. Depending on the quality of the gunpowder, they could fire balls from 600 to even 950 meters (660 to 1,040 yards). But the accuracy was very limited. At a distance of 25 meters (27 yards), eight out of ten shots could hit a man-high target. Also, with respect to penetration, the effective range was at the most to 50 meters (55 yards).[49] In any case, it is absurd to attribute the disappearance of armored knights to the introduction of firearms. Classical knighthood experienced its last heyday in the 15th century. Its simultaneous decline should above all be traced to what researchers today refer to as the so-called "infantry revolution".

The Infantry

Good portions of the Hussite armies were recruited from the urban levies or the peasantry, even when during the course of the war the portion made up of paid mercenaries continuously increased. It was above all the lower social classes – journeymen and impoverished farmers – who filled the ranks of the field armies. The armies' equipment improved constantly based on the extensive booty acquired by the field armies every year. Anyhow, the gambeson, the padded wams, supposedly was the most widespread piece of armor. It consisted of several layers of sewn linen filled with scraps of cloth, flax or raw cotton and it thus offered relatively good protection from blows from swords and blunt weapons

The simple clothing also changed significantly in the Gothic period. The broad linen shirt changed very little in the Middle Ages, but the "*Bruche*", the long pants-like undergarment became shorter and reached only to the knees. The leggings, which still consisted of two separate leg pieces, were laced up to the "*Bruche*" pants. In some cases, these could end in a foot, like modern tights. The woolen "*cotta*",[50] which could be pulled over the head and reached to the knees, found wide acceptance. Its body was somewhat wider and was made by the common people so that it had the least possible waste of cloth. On the other hand, the sleeves became narrower at the wrists and were provided with small slits that could be buttoned closed.

This detailed study from the Jena Codex shows a Hussite march column. The war flails are easily recognized.

49 SCHMIDTCHEN, Kriegswesen, p. 210.

50 The men's cotta of the 17th-18th centuries was a wide shirt made of wool or linen and was worn over the chemise.

Various depictions of handguns/culverins in Johannes Hartlieb's *Kriegsbuch*
Left: A handgun being fired with the classical method of a heated iron bar.
Right: Depiction of a *"Stabbüchse"* (staff culverin).

Depictions of handgunners in Windecke's Chronicle
In both illustrations the gunners hold their culverins with both hands.
It is therefore unclear how they ignited the gunpowder.

**Reconstruction of a war flail in the
Tabor Hussite Museum**
Husitské museum, Tábor

The normal footsoldiers, as well as the wagon crews used a large variety of polearms like halberds, pikes and morning stars. Glaives (German "*Glefe*") with their barbed hooks were of special importance to the wagon crews for pulling horsemen out of their saddles. Additionally, a larger number of threshing flails that the farmers brought with them were modified with spikes into "war flails" (Czech "*válečné cepy;*" German "*Kriegsflegeln*"). In the 15th century, this weapon was widely used thanks to the Hussites. Together with the war wagons, "flail units" (Czech "*cepníci*", German "*Fleger-Trupps*") were soon also formed in the Empire. An original "war flail" preserved in Prague consists only of a long shaft with four heavy chain links at the end whereby the last link is a big ring. This model is also called a "scorpion" ("*Skorpion*").[51] There were already many of these makeshift weapons before the time of the Hussites, like the war scythe ("*Kriegs-sense*"). They came in various models, either with a sharp curved blade, like on a hand-held sickle, or with an only slightly curved blade like a true scythe but that was directly mounted on a shaft. The glaive or "*Helmbarte*" is possibly a

further development of this improvised weapon.[52]Among the traditional polearms, the "awl pike" (German "*Ahl-spiess*") won special popularity with Bohemian mercenaries. This weapon had a long narrow thrusting blade with a square cross-section and a round plate ("*Brechscheibe*") that was to prevent a too deep penetration of the weapon into the enemy's body.[53]

The successful employment of large groups of footsoldiers who were in close formations and armed with pikes in the Late Middle Ages and gradually who won the upper hand over the High Middle Ages knights' armies, is called the "infantry revolution" today. Such developments could be observed in Scotland (Battle of Bannockburn, 1316), Flanders, Switzerland and even in Bohemia.[54] Different than with the West European foot troops, the Bohemians, however, used relatively short polearms with shaft lengths of 2 to 2.5 meters (6½ to 8 feet) at the longest. So the Bohemian infantry could not form hedgehog-like formations like the Swiss or the Scots. The infantry was instructed to protect the wagon castle (*Wagenburg/laager*) in the first phase of a battle. In this respect, the Hussite military system only minimally contributed to the infantry revolution.

The sword was also widely used by the infantry. Even the simple Bohemian peasants already had such weapons. A special Bohemian thrusting model was the "*Kord*", an early form of the dagger with a narrow blade.[55] The swords still followed traditional medieval cross-shape with a round pommel. The blades usually tapered from the tang (handle) to the point.[56]

Although the Hussites made wide use of handguns, the crossbow was still significantly more widely used by their shooters. For every handgun, there were three to four crossbows.

According to most of the depictions passed down, the Hussites mostly used simple crossbows. To arm them, the string was held in place by a hook on the man's waist belt and he placed his foot in a stirrup at the end of the bow and held it to the ground and by stretching upright with his legs he spanned the weapon. Another possibility consisted of using a "goat's foot" ("*Geißfuß*"), a two-piece lever, that was placed between the string and the bow's stave and then pressed through until the cord slipped over the pivoting nut. The fastening winches ("*Spannwinden*") that were being introduced at that time were already known but appear less frequently in contemporary depictions. The crossbow staves predominantly were made of wood, bone and animal sinews. In the early 15th century, the first steel bows appeared, but in Central and Eastern

51 Dolínek/Durdík, Historische Waffen, pp. 151-152;
    Durdík, Hussitisches Heerwesen, p. 112;
    Berger, Kampfkraft der Hussiten, p. 107; Demmin, Die
    Kriegswaffen, pp. 444-445.

52 Demmin, Die Kriegswaffen, pp. 447-451.

53 Boeheim, Waffenkunde, pp. 315-316;
    Dolínek/Durdík, Historische Waffen, pp. 135-138.

54 Nicholson, Medieval Warfare, p. 58.

55 Durdík, Hussitisches Heerwesen, p. 112.

56 Dolínek/Durdík, Historische Waffen, pp. 30-35.

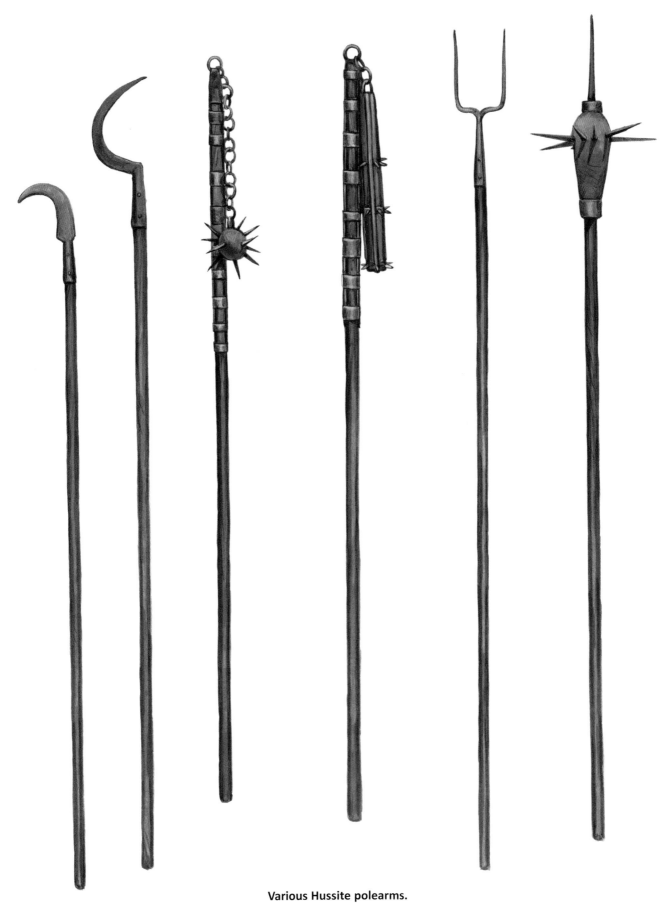

Various Hussite polearms.
On the far left are two simple war scythes for pulling horsemen out of their saddles, a chain morning star and a war flail for footsoldiers, along with a war fork, which was developed from a simple pitchfork, as well as a spiked club with a pike-head.

Europe people were very reserved about this innovation. Steel bows could break in cold weather while composite bows actually increased their capabilities at lower temperatures.[57] The bow, which the English were using with great success at the same time in the Hundred Years War, still played only a subordinate role as a weapon in the central German-speaking region as mentioned before. Its rate of fire was four times higher than the crossbow. While a practiced bowman could loose 12 arrows per minute, a strong crossbowman could manage only three.[58]

In any case, handling the bow took a lot of practice. In England there was a strong tradition of archery by the able-bodied population, but not on the Continent. Therefore, the relatively modest crossbow was used, like the handgun. Both weapons could also be handled efficiently within a short time by inexperienced shooters.

Crossbow bolts were very expensive compared to handgun munitions. Three bolts cost about the same as a pound of lead from which 24 balls could be made. The reason was the bolt's time-consuming production. A bolt consisted of three parts, the iron point usually with a rhomboid-shaped cross-section, the wood shaft, and the two wood or leather feather-like fletchings that were to give the missile its stability. The handgunner could, if needed, cast or cut his own handgun balls from a chunk of lead. But a professional group, the *"Pfeilsticker"* (fletchers), was needed for the production of bolts.[59]

Another antique weapon that the Hussites used, above all in the early phase of the wars, was the simple catapult. We see Hussite catapults in reports about the Battle of Sudoměř or the siege of the town of Prachatic.[60]

The Hussites likewise had a broad arsenal of protective equipment that was certainly considerably improved by the extensive booty they took over time. For helmets, the simple infantry preferred various forms of the war hat or iron kettle hat (German *Eisenhut* or French *chapel-de-fer*), which gave good protection from sword blows from above, or the simpler bascinet *"Barbe"* type that fit closely to the head. Based on its simple manufacture, the war hat was very popular with the infantry. It was supposedly adopted from the Byzantines during the Crusades. Its broad brim provided the footsoldiers protection from blows from above but also from the sun's rays.

A comparably simple type of helmet, which was popular with both the cavalry and the infantry, was the German bascinet that had evolved in the 14th century from the simple hemispherical helmet (German *"Hirnschale"* - "brain-pan"). The bascinet protected the skull, ears and nape, but left the face completely free.

Depictions of morning stars and clubs
in Eberhard Windeke's *"Geschichte Kaiser Sigismunds"*
(History of Emperor Sigismund).

---

57 DOLÍNEK/DURDÍK, Historische Waffen, pp. 173-174;
    DURDÍK, Hussitisches Heerwesen, pp. 110-11;
    TURNBULL, Hussite Wars, p. 23.

58 SCHMIDTCHEN, Kriegswesen, p. 176.

59 Harmuth, Armbrust, p. 172-174;
    BLEICHER, Das Herzogtum Niederbayern, pp. 236-245.

60 PALACKÝ, Der Hussitenkrieg 1419-1431, p. 171.

A simple Hussite peasant soldier ca. 1419.
For his protection, he only wears a gambeson.
He is armed with a war flail and a dagger.

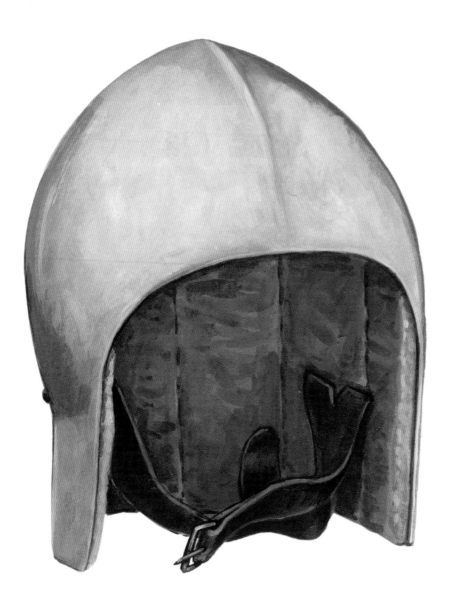

Helmets for footsoldiers
Left: A visor-less basinet that was also popular with horsemen.
Right: Two different types of war or iron kettle hats.

Contemporary depictions show a wide variety of helmet shapes. At the left a basinet, beside it three different types of "war hats" or "iron kettle hats."

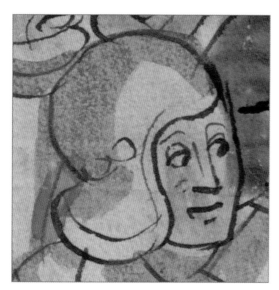

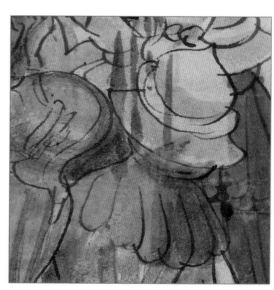

The so-called salet, salett, sallet or salad helmet (German "*Schaller*") was developed in the early 15th century from the war hat and the bascinet. This type of helmet fit more tightly on the head and ran in a streamlined manner to a point on the back of the neck. Preserved original salets from the mid-15th century have a visor or a slit for the eyes. In any case, manuscripts dated earlier like Kyeser's "*Bellifortis*", give evidence that this type of helmet was even in use before the Hussite period. The helmets were lined with multiple layers of linen for better comfort.

Popular kinds of shields were the large pavises, which were set on the ground, with which the gaps in the 'wagon castles' (laagers) could be closed, or the smaller handheld "Tartsche" shields. Both were made using a plywood-type technique with small wooden strips and then covered with leather. Finally, they were often very elaborately painted, and the paint was also intended to make them waterproof. The pavises had iron spikes on the bottom end with which it could be better anchored in the ground. In Bohemia the pavis was especially widely used even into the early 16th century, that is why later the term "Hussite pavis" also came into use. The Czechoslovakian Republic's national coat of arms intentionally referenced this tradition and adopted the pentagonal pavis shape.[61]

A preserved pavis from the Hussite era is located in Bilina. It has the biblical King David as the victor over Goliath painted on its surface. The chalice is emblazoned on David's shield. The Bohemians often made reference to this biblical story, seeing themselves as opposing a seemingly invincible superior force. Verses from a battle hymn by the preacher Jan Čapek are painted around the border of the shield.[62]

---

61 BOEHEIM, Waffenkunde, pp. 179-182;
    DURDÍK, Hussitisches Heerwesen, p. 114.

62 ROYT, Hussitisches Bildpropaganda, pp. 344-345.

Jan Žizka leads the Field Army
Jena-Codex, between 1490 and 1510.

A Hussite crossbowman
The tall pavis gives the crossbowman protection when arming his weapon. It is very simply painted with a chalice,
the movement's symbol. However, the painting could be significantly more elaborate.
On his belt he wears a hook needed for spanning the crossbow string.

A mounted handgunner.

It is not certain whether at the time of the Hussites there were already this kind of mounted gunners. The reconstruction is based on French depictions from the late 15th century. The horseman wears the armor of a knight from about 1400 with a basinet, chainmail shirt, gambeson, as well as arm and leg armor. He carries the handgun on a strap around his neck. He absorbs the recoil with his chest. The supporting fork for the weapon is attached to his saddle.

2015

The Cavalry

In the Hussite armies the infantry displaced the cavalry as the queen of battle. The Hussites' cavalry units only constituted a very small part of the total army strength. On average, for every horseman there were ten men on foot. Nonetheless, Žižka concerned himself with building up a separate cavalry in that he gathered men who knew how to ride and then provided them with horses and equipment captured from knights. A large number of the horsemen were armed with crossbows. It is also conceivable that a part of them were armed with handguns. There is evidence that this kind of armament was even first used in the French armies at the beginning of the 15th century. Illustrations from this period show them with long hand-cannon that rest on a fork whose end is attached to the end of the saddle's pommel. In turn, the end of the gun's shaft had a ring or a rope for carrying the gun around the neck. Getting a proper aim was even more difficult than for the footsoldiers, so the fork was to provide the needed stability to fire when mounted on an uneasy horse.[63] Furthermore, contemporary depictions also show Hussite horsemen with crossbows. Mounted archers and crossbowmen were present in many European armies at this time, but it can be concluded that lacking a heavy cavalry, the crossbowmen and handgunners formed a large part of the Hussite cavalry.

However, the Hussite cavalry did not have large numbers of heavily armored horsemen and that was for a good reason. A sizeable part of the wealthy Bohemian knights did indeed join the movement. Nonetheless, the Hussites were never in the position to put enough of the heavily armored - and therefore expensive - horsemen in the field to risk a battle with the powerful crusader armies. Hussite mounted forces consisted of a few, lightly armed and thus agile horsemen who also had other missions to perform than those of the German knights.

Despite that, the Hussite nobles' equipment would not have differed much from that of the crusaders. In the early 15th century, the pig-face bascinet or houndskull (*Hundsgugel*) came into use as the new type of helmet. It had finally replaced the heavy Great Helm (*Topfhelm*) that limited visibility. Most of the time it was not donned until immediately before the battle. In order to protect the head without a helmet, the knights strengthened their chainmail coifs with steel caps from which the bascinet developed. This ended in the back in a point in order to better deflect sword blows. And a kind of padding ("*Knautschone*") was developed between the helmet and the head for flexibility and protection. In the 14th century, this helmet was already supplemented with a visor that could be attached to the helmet in various ways. Originally a hinge was attached on the side of the helmet bowl so that the visor could simply be rotated upward. Then between 1330 and 1340 in Italy, an attachment using a

bolt on each side of the helmet appeared; it proved to be more stable and was generally introduced up until the early 15th century. This was made in such a way that the visor would be securely engaged when raised and, additionally, it could be removed without difficulty when necessary. In this period, especially in Italy and in the central German region, this visor took on a pointed shape that was not dissimilar to a dog's muzzle, which was why this helmet was called a "*Hundsgugeln*" (*Hund* is a dog and *Gugel* is actually a cloth hood, so a "dog's hood").[64]

Depiction of a war hammer,
that was used with the point.
(Eberhard Windeke's "*Geschichte Kaiser Sigismunds.*")

Because the knights in the European armies in the 14th and 15th centuries were protected by increasingly complex, better and heavier plate armor, massive clubbing weapons became more important. Among them were two weapons developed from the club: the mace and the morning star. The mace was a clubbing weapon with a striking head that could be used one-handed. The head could be either a massive ball or in the form of a series of thick blades arranged around the shaft. Fighting bishops liked to use the mace because they were forbidden to carry swords. Jan Žižka was also shown again and again in contemporary depictions with the mace.[65] This could however have been for purely iconographic reasons and simply symbolized a unity of military and religious leadership under Žižka that really did not exist as a mace. The second, simpler, further development was the

---

63 Delbrück, Geschichte der Kriegskunst, pp. 569.

64 Beaufort-Spontin, Hundsgugel, pp. 60-62.

65 Williams, The mace, pp. 34-35.

Ulrich von Rosenberg actually belonged to the Utraquists but fought for King Sigismund against the Hussites. The picture shows him in the typical armor of a central European knight about 1420. The helmet is a simple basinet without a visor. His torso is protected by a "coat-of-plates" (*Lentner*). It was made of several metal plates that were riveted to the inside of a cloth or leather wams. His shield is a typical Late Middle Ages horseman's "*tartsche*" with a notch for the lance.

The use of war hammers is often pictured in contemporary manuscripts like these detailed studies from the *"Geschichte Kaiser Sigismunds."* The war hammer is almost always used with the pointed end forward. In the picture on the right is it shown being used with the hammering side.

morning star, in which the striking head had a number of heavy spikes. The morning star was widely used by the Hussites as both a short-handled close combat weapon and as a polearm. Another clubbing weapon was the war hammer that originated in Eastern Europe and appeared there in the 11th century. The various names this weapon was given in German in the 15th century (*Rabenschnabel* – raven's beak, *Falkenschnabel* – falcon's beak or hawk's beak - *Habichtschnabel*, later also *Papageienschnabel* - parrot's beak) lead to the conclusion that the weapon above all was used with the pointed and not the blunt end. This makes sense since a strong blow with this weapon by a horseman could easily penetrate any armor. Naturally the battleax was still used as before as a weapon.[66]

In the course of the Middle Ages the shield decreased in importance as the horseman's protective device, which was evidenced by its getting smaller. Around 1400, it took on a rectangular, sometimes almost square shape, sometimes rounded. The frequently used horseman's tartsche shields, an easily carried form of pavis, had a deep notch in the upper right end in which the horseman could rest his lance.[67]

Despite its limited strength, this cavalry still performed important missions. On the march, the lightly armed riders would spread out and served as the army's eyes and ears. Sometimes they hurried several days' march ahead of the Hussite field armies. In battles, the well-rested mounted forces enabled a tenacious pursuit of the enemy. Even in this stage of the fighting the Hussite horsemen often inflicted heavy casualties.

Depiction of a war wagon (*Kriegswagen*) in Hans Talhofer's *"Alte Armatur und Ringkunst"* from 1459. The picture is a copy of a similar depiction in Konrad Kyeser's *"Bellifortis."*

---

66 Demmin, Die Kriegswaffen, pp. 455-463.

67 BOEHEIM, Waffenkunde, pp. 176-177, 181;
DURDÍK, Hussitisches Heerwesen, pp. 114-116.

In the early 15th century, the "*Hundsgugel*" (houndskull or pig-face basinet) became increasingly popular with knights.

Above left: A helmet with a flat arched visor like shown in many contemporary illustrations.

Below: A helmet with a pointed visor that was especially popular in the German-speaking regions.

These detailed studies from the *"Geschichte Kaiser Sigismunds"* show various heavy cannon at sieges. In both depictions they seem to deal with heavy versions of *"Tarasbüchsen"* (trestle cannon) as can be recognized by the wooden substructures. The third picture also shows a cannon on a wood *"terrasse,"* but a beam for

The Artillery

The Hussite armies were the first to use cannon on a grand scale as field artillery. The term "cannon" (German "Kanone") comes from the Italian *"canna"* (reed or pipe).[68]

Although primarily forged-iron cannon are found in museums today, the majority of Hussite artillery consisted of bronze cannon. However, because the material was very expensive for them, these were later often melted down and recast.[69]

In the early 14th century, along with the bronze casting process, cannon were produced above all using the hoop and stave process. For this, a number of iron bars (staves) were positioned as a ring and glowing iron bands (hoops) were added around them. As they cooled, the bands contracted and gave the cannon its solidity. The advantage of this production method was that nearly any trained blacksmith could use it as long as he had the necessary tools. The bronze casting method required special experience. In the casting method's favor, the hoop and stave cannon were not especially stable. Both these methods were nonetheless still used up into the 16th century. Also, in 1588 the majority of the Spanish Armada's cannon were manufactured with the hoop and stave process, while the English ships' cannon were of cast bronze.[70]

For the bronze casting process the first step was to produce a 1:1 scale model in which a wood pole was wrapped in ropes and clay. The surface was then smoothed and if desired adorned with decorations. After that the model was covered with tallow. Because the mouth was one of the cannon's weak spots, a longer "over-barrel" ("Überrohr") was attached that was later shortened. This way the thickness of the metal at the completed mouth could be increased. Finally, the actual casting mold was built around this model. This consisted of clay and was coated layer-by-layer while the model was turned over a fire so that the mass would dry out more quickly. The tallow melted and ran off and finally the shaft with the ropes was pulled out of the mold. This was strengthened with metal bands and later an "iron core" ("Kerneisen") in the size of the later caliber diameter was fitted into place. Only at the end of the process was the base piece added and the entire cast form buried. The molten metal was poured in and after it had cooled, the casing form could be broken up and the bore drilled out. The process took many days and was very expensive. Time and again the casting came out uneven or cracks appeared that the producer only noticed at the end of the lengthy process. Sometimes the cannon's surface was pristine and the producer did not see tiny cracks. A cannon produced in 1407 in Munich using this process exploded for that reason on its first test firing.[71]

68 TRESP, Söldner aus Böhmen, p. 28.

69 DURDÍK, Hussitisches Heerwesen, pp. 88-89.

70 SCHMIDTCHEN, Bombarden, Befestigungen, Büchsenmeister, p. 27.

71 SCHMIDTCHEN, Bombarden, Befestigungen, Büchsenmeister, p. 32;

absorbing the recoil is recognizable. Both cannon in the picture on the right deal clearly with "laying pieces" (*Legestücke*) or bombards. The bulge in the middle leads one to guess that both pieces are made up of two parts.

During the Hussite Wars, artillery grew in importance in such a way that the status of gun-makers ("*Büchsenmacher*") also increased. At the beginning of the 15th century, the production of cannon was very closely linked to the cities because they had not just the necessary financial means for their production, but also the corresponding skilled workers. This was no different in Bohemia from in the Empire. In 1419 in Prague, there were even six gun-makers at one time who lived off of orders from the Moldau metropolis, but also received orders from the smaller Bohemian cities and towns. But at this time cannon were also produced in towns like Jičín or like Stříbro, which had grown rich through silver mining. Then in the 1420s, the first evidence appears about gun-makers in Karlštejn (Karlstein), Prachatice, Most (Brüx), Kutná Hora (Kuttenberg) and Znojmo. In Bohemia gun-makers were well-paid artisans who were paid directly by the cities and towns. In Znojmo they received a regular salary and a supplemental weekly pay of 14 to 24 *Groschen*[72] for the production of certain cannon. For this reason, the urban alliances (*Städtebündnisse*) were of central importance for supplying the field armies above all with firearms. In 1421, at least 22 towns or cities belonged to the Prague City Alliance (Czech "*pražský městský svaz*", Ger-man *Prager Städtebund*), and in 1427, 33 belonged to the Alliance of the Taborites and Orphans (Czech "*táborský svaz a sirotčí svaz*" (also *sirotci*)", German *Städtebund der Taboriten und Waisen*).[73]

The most widely used cannon in the Hussite armies was the "terrace" or "trestle" cannon (Old Czech "*tarasnice*", German "*Tarasbüchse*"). This had an elongated barrel measuring from 21 to 29 times the caliber. As a rule, the caliber was from 40 to 50 mm (1½ to 2 inches) but could even reach 100 mm (4 inches). Initially these cannon fired only stone balls, but the Hussites began to forge them out of iron. Their effective range was about 250 to 300 meters (275 to 330 yards). The names "*tarasnice*" and "*Tarasbüchse*" derive from the stationary wood bed, the "*Tarasse*" or "*Terrasse*" on which they rested. Depictions from the 16th century show how the gunner braces against the rear of the frame when firing such a cannon in order to absorb the recoil. This technique was probably also used in the 15th century. Due to their light weight they were easy to handle and thus developed into a prototype of the modern field cannon. In any case the small caliber limited the *taranice*'s effectiveness.[74]

BLEICHER, Das Herzogtum Niederbayern, p. 211.

72 Translator's note: Groschen (from Latin grossus "thick", via Old Czech groš) was the (sometimes colloquial) name for a silver coin used in various states of the Holy Roman Empire.

73 DURDÍK, Hussitisches Heerwesen, pp. 86-88; BERGER, Kampfkraft der Hussiten, p. 102. The "Orphans" (Czech "sirotci", German "Waisen") was the name the Orebites adopted for their movement after Žižka's death.

74 DURDÍK, Hussitisches Heerwesen, pp. 95-97; TURNBULL, Hussite Wars, pp. 36-37;

The Hussite *houfnice* ballista was an important innovation. They were among the first representatives of cannon on mobile carriages. They first appear in written sources in the 1440s, but illustrations show them in the 1430s while late 15th century chroniclers claimed that these types of cannon were already used in the 1426 Battle of Ústí nad Labem (Aussig).[75] They had an essentially short barrel of three-and-one-half to four times the caliber measurement. No such cannon from the Hussite period remain today, but a near contemporary piece originating from Austria had a caliber of 160 mm (6¼ inches). The diameter of the powder chamber was, in contrast, significantly smaller. The barrel was secured to a wood base with iron bands and mounted on a two-wheeled carriage. At the end of the base there was an arc that permitted changing the elevation of the gun. The term "howitzer" comes from the Czech word "*houfnice*" ("*houf*" means "crowd", i.e., the weapon's target).[76] With their development of a mobile field cannon, the Hussites took an important step in the further advancement of the artillery branch.[77]

Beyond that, the Hussite armies had large cannon or bombards for sieges. These were heavy forged iron pieces that often could only be transported disassembled, only mounted on fixed platforms at the siege site. Therefore, they were also called "*Legestücke*" – "laying pieces". To absorb the enormous recoil, abutments were built and the barrels were chocked with wood wedges. Their range was very limited due not in the least to their very short barrels (about triple the caliber). They could reach a maximum range of over 1,000 meters (1,100 yards), but they were effective up to no more than 500 meters (550 yards) at the most.[78]

At these great ranges the bombards' effect was drastically reduced. The heavy stone balls bounced off the walls without effect. The still inefficient gunpowder also contributed to this weakness. The ideal stoichiometric ratio of 6.4 parts saltpeter, 1.2 parts coal and one part sulfur was first discovered in 1597.[79] The *Feuerwerksbuch* of 1420 gives three different mixture ratios, all with too little saltpeter and too much sulfur. For "common" powder, i.e., the type used most frequently, the ratio was 2 to 0.5 to 1; for the better powder it was 2.5 to 0.5 to 1 and for the strong powder it was 3 to 0.5. to 1. At least it was known at that time that the saltpeter was decisive in enhancing effectiveness.[80]

BERGER, Kampfkraft der Hussiten, p. 107.

75 Translator's note: The name of Ústí nad Labem is formed from the Old Czech "*ustie*" ("river mouth") and "*Labe*" (the River Elbe). It thus literally means "Mouth-upon-the-Elbe", in reference to its location at the Bilina's confluence with the Elbe. The old German name was Aussig.

76 DURDÍK, Hussitisches Heerwesen, pp. 98-100;
TURNBULL, Hussite Wars, p. 37;
BERGER, Kampfkraft der Hussiten, p. 107.

77 A contention that Hans Delbrück refutes.
See DELBRÜCK, Geschichte der Kriegskunst, p. 568.

78 DURDÍK, Hussitisches Heerwesen, pp. 100-106.

79 SCHMIDTCHEN, Bombarden, p. 115.

80 HASSENSTEIN, Feuerwerkbuch, p. 25.

Various depictions of howitzers in Johann Hartlieb's *"Kriegsbuch"*
In all the pictures the arc for changing the elevation of the barrel is easy to see. In the picture above left the master gunner (*Büchsenmeister*) is firing a kind of grapeshot.

If the master gunners tried to increase the amount of gunpowder, it increased the risk that the cannon would burst, which due to the still immature casting process was already happening too quickly. In the early 15th century, the powder-to-projectile weight ratio was only 1:13. Only at the end of the century did it rise to 1:2. Until then the guns' effectiveness and lifespans were very limited. During the siege of the Karlštejn (Karlstein) Castle in 1423, the large Prague bombard *"Prazka"* burst after only six shots, the *"Jaromirka"* after seven, while the *"Rychlice"* fired 30 times before it burst. The walls suffered the most damage from the conventional ballista instead.[81]

The Bohemian cities and towns apparently were not the only ones producing powder for the cannon. Merchants from the Imperial city of Nuremberg made many trips with whole wagonloads to the Hussite towns and cities. King Sigismund as well as the other Imperial princes complained about it. There are some existing letters in which the city council defends against the accusations that Nuremberg merchants had sold gunpowder to the Hussites. The frequency of these letters gives reasonable suspicion that the trade often took place because even the Pope proscribed these commercial activities.[82] In 1424, the merchants of the city of Regensburg were warned by Sigismund "that no one shall give the heretics in Bohemia and elsewhere any assistance, help or council with words or with other works,

neither with any food, drink nor other relief, be it with wine, bread, grain, salt, merchandise, foodstuffs, spices, armor, guns, powder or no other things which might be named, whereby you shall not do any other things, whatever you call them, while on your way.[83]

Despite their highly developed artillery system, the Hussites still relied on trebuchet-catapults for sieges. In 1420 the Prazans and Taborites shot at the Hradschin Castle with large catapults. In 1422 the Karlstein Castle was subjugated with five ballistae. These counterbalance catapults reached considerable sizes and had great ranges. The platform for a trebuchet that was used in the 1428-29 siege of the Lichnice Castle is still visible today. It measures 36 by 25 meters (39.4 by 27.3 yards) and is 470 meters (514 yards) from the castle. A similar platform is located 300 meters (328 yards) from the Sion Castle, which one of Sigismund's armies attacked and destroyed in 1437. It is in the shape of a rectangle with a measurement of 20 by 26 meters (22 by 28.4 yards).[84]

---

81 PALACKÝ, Der Hussitenkrieg 1419-1431, p. 321;
     TURNBULL, Hussite Wars, p. 37.

82 POLÍVKA, Handelsbeziehungen, pp. 164- 166;
     PALACKÝ, Urkundliche Beiträge I, Nr. 152, pp. 163-164 and Nr. 176, p. 189-190; Nr. 385, p. 432.

83 In Middle High German (MHG), *"daz nyemand den keczern zu Behem vnd anderswo kain fürdrung, hilff vnd rate mit wortten noch mit werken tun, noch in keinerlay speise, tranck, noch oder ander nötdürfft raichen solle, es sey mit wein, brot, getrayd, salcz, kauffmannschafft, speczereyen, würczen, harnüsch, püchsen, puluer, oder chainen andern sachen, wie die mochten benennet sein, woran daz were, tun solle in dheinen weg".*
     Cf. PALACKÝ, Urkundliche Beiträge I, Nr. 294, p. 339; and Nr. 295, pp. 340-341 is almost a word-for-word appeal to the six cities (*Sechsstädte*).

84 DURDÍK, Hussitisches Heerwesen, pp. 110-111;
     BERGER, Kampfkraft der Hussiten, p. 102. Translator's note: Sion is a small castle ruin in the Czech Republic, near Kutná Hora. It was founded between 1426 and 1427 by Hussite Jan Roháč of Dubá.

Depiction of a light battering ram in the so-called *"Feuerwerksbuch"* from the second half ot the 15th century.

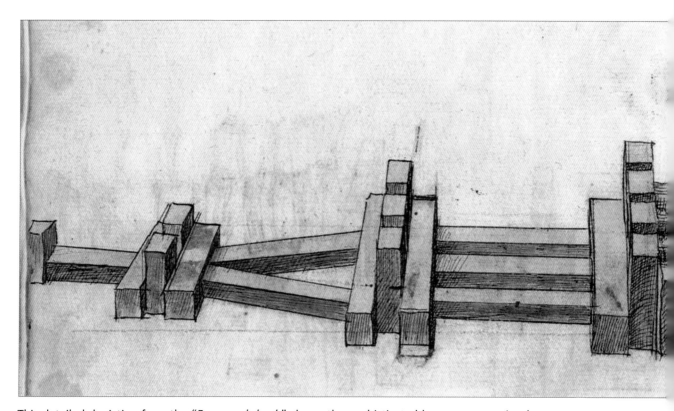

This detailed depiction from the *"Feuerwerksbuch"* shows the sophisticated beam constructionthat was necessary to

The massive wooden mantlet was supposed to protect the cannon's crew from enemy projectiles while they were loading the gun. The massive beam structure behind the bombard was to absorb the weapon's recoil (picture from the *Feuerwerksbuch*)

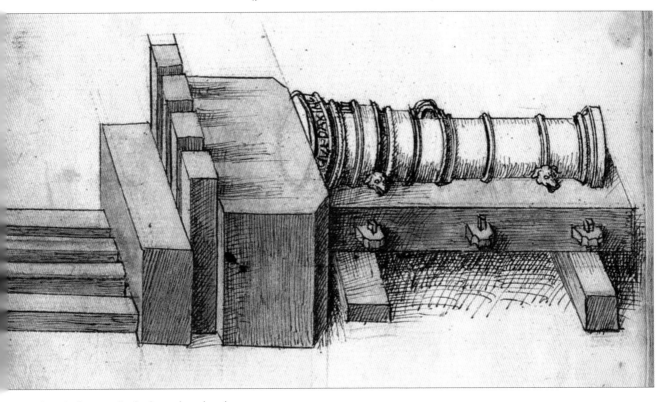

absorb the recoil of a large bombard.

All pictures show *"Taborbüchsen"* - "Tabor hanguns"
The so-called *"Taborbüchse"* or "Tabor handgun" or "Tabor culverin" consisted of a simple iron pipe with a thickened mouth and a touch-hole. A wood staff, which served as a stock, was placed in the socket. This form of the handgun was widely used in the early 15th century.

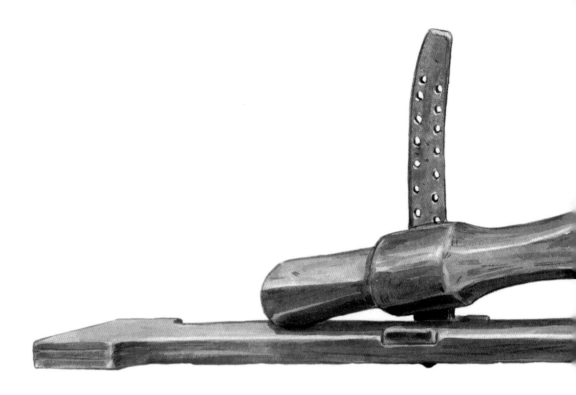

"*Tarasbüchse*" ("Trestle" or "Terrace Cannon" on a wagon with drawbar / "*Tarasbüchse*" on a wagon)
At the time of the Hussites, the field artillery, except for howitzers, were not yet mobile but rested on fixed platforms.
Only at the beginning of the 15th century did cannon on wheeled carriages gain significance in Europe.
Two colored pen drawings by Ulrich Bessnitzer in the "*Zeughausinventar von Landshut*"
(Arsenal Inventory of Landshut) from 1485.
Universitätsbibliothek Heidelberg: HeidICON. Die Heidelberger Bildatenbank
<http://HeidICON.uni-hd.de> Universitätsbibliothek Heidelberg

Most "*Tarasbüchsen*" had a small caliber and could be served by two men. While they were initially employed as stationary cannon in fortifications, the Hussites also used them in the field.

Matches for cannon.
Above: an igniting staff or match with a rope wick.
Below: Three iron rods heated to a glow for igniting the powder charge.

FLAGS

It is difficult to establish a complete heraldry for the Hussite forces because many Bohemian nobles joined the army who brought along their own coats-of-arms and banners.

On the other hand, the field armies had only two widely used symbols. The most broadly used was the chalice as the basic symbol of their religious demands (the 'communion in both kinds'). The chalice's implementation took very different forms including simply as a silhouette, but also as ostentatious as a sculpted version.[85]

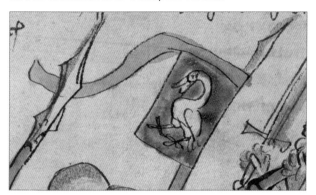

In both of these studies from the *"Geschichte Kaiser Sigismunds,"* the goose is recognizable on the Hussites' flags.

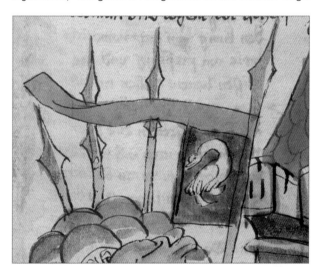

Along with the chalice, the goose was a popular symbol. The goose was a symbolic translation of the name "Hus" (*"husa"* is Czech for goose). Sometimes both symbols were combined. Thus, there are contemporary depictions that show flags with a goose drinking out of the chalice.

Red seems to have been the most popular basic color, while the chalices were most often shown in yellow or black. See pages 32, 77 and 81.[86]

ARMY STRUCTURE

Research on the Hussite army's organization does not yet provide definitve details about structure and manpower. However, it is certain that the field army was better organized and more integrated than other European field armies of this era.

The Czech historian Jan Durdik suspects that all four branches of the Hussite army - wagons, infantry, cavalry and artillery - possessed their own captains or commanders.[87] In the sources, only a commander for the wagons and one for the cavalry are indicated. The existence of a captain or commander for the infantry and one for the guns does appear sensible, but it would be difficult organizationally because both of those branches were also part of the war wagon forces. Even though knights and lower nobility dominated as leaders, based on their military training, there were definitely also captains with peasant backgrounds or from the artisans' guilds. The stonemason Mares Krsnak was the captain with the Taborites. He died at the Battle of Lipany. On the other hand, two brothers from Padarov were simple farmers before the war. Velek Koudelnik, a captain for the Orphans had worked before as an artisan in the *Prager Neustadt*; his successor, Cert, was a board-cutter, while it is assumed that Pesek Zahradnik came from the ranks of the horticulturists (*zahradnik* = gardener).

Along with the army's tactical divisions, there also existed a social division in the communities. Levies from individual cities and towns or rural areas always remained together and bore the names of the most important city or town of their region. The levies were again led by their own captains.[88] But the social division was a unique characteristic of the Orebite army that Jan Žižka created with his 1423 War Directive. On the other hand, the Taborite army appears to have been more regionally structured because in the source texts the names of the elders are always shown with the city or town names. For example, in one text it reads *"Wir... Hauptleute, Herren, Ritter, Edelknechte, Priester Prokop und andere Älteste der Gemeinen von Tabor im Feld und zuhause, von Klattau, Pisek, Schüttenhofen, Prachatitz, Taus..."* - "We captains, lords, knights, squires, the Priest Procopius and other elders from the community of Tabor, in the field and at home, from [the towns of] Klatovy, Pisek, Sušice, Prachatice, Domažlice..."[89]

In contrast, in a comparable source about the Orebite army, it reads: *"Wir Jan Bruder Žižka vom Kelch ... und alle Gemeinden der Herren, Ritter, Edelknechte, Städte..."* – "We, Jan the brother Žižka of the Chalice ... and all the communities of lords, knights, squires, towns ..."[90]

After a successful four-month siege the castle was conquered and burned by Emperor Sigismund's allies in 1437. Nowadays only scattered parts of the basement stone walls with some arches and stairs remain of the original castle. Source: Wikipedia.

85   TURNBULL, Hussite Wars, p. 23.

86   Ibid., p. 47.

87   DURDÍK, Hussitisches Heerwesen, pp. 150-151;
     BERGER, Kampfkraft der Hussiten, p. 103.

88   BERGER, Kampfkraft der Hussiten, p. 103.

89   SEIBT, Hussitica, p. 163.

90   Ibid., p. 162.

In this basic issue about equality regardless of class origin, one can find a possible reason for the blind commander's [Žižka's] break with the Taborites. In any case, the Taborites' regional structure had a marked advantage for the army's mobilization. The Orebite army may have had significantly greater difficulties in gathering personnel from its communities that were located multi-regionally and were socially segregated. In Žižka's army there were communities of lords, knights and burghers, of artisans, of villeins and peasants. These communities above all made up the basic organizational units. Disciplinary authority rested within them, e.g., addressing offenses while on sentry duty. Additionally, the community representatives were involved in the distribution of booty. It cannot be said with certainly, but it is very likely, that the community representatives and captains were often, maybe always, the same persons, because the community representatives also belonged to the Council of the "Oldests" (Czech *"rada starších"*, German *"Rat der Ältesten"*).

Žižka's War Directive established this structure in writing. The War Directive of 1423 named the blind commander, Žižka, as the first captain, i.e., the most senior commander. He was assisted by a council of the oldest captains (often simply call the "Oldest" – *"Ältesten"*) who supposedly were the leaders of the individual branches. Questions regarding guard duty and march orders, but also about military operations, were to be resolved collaboratively by this council.

The composition of an individual war wagon unit has already been presented. Ten war wagons were subordinate to a *"desátník"* (German *"Zehnerschaftsführer"* - leader of ten) whose job was above all to ensure that the marching order was maintained. He also organized the wagons' positioning during the set up of a *Wagenburg* (Czech *vozová hradba* or laager). The *desátník* was subordinate to the captain of the wagon column (*Hauptmann der Wagenreihe*), who commanded the complete march column. The commander of war wagons (Czech *"hejtman nad vozy"*, German *"Hauptmann der Kriegswagen"*) was the head of the wagon branch.[91]

The cavalry was divided into various groups that were primarily important when the army was on the march. In the lead of each army movement was a vanguard (*honci*) with a "lost group" (*Stracenci*, German *Verlorenen Haufen*), the actual reconnaissance unit as well as a reserve (*posilci*). The march columns' flanks were secured by skirmishers (*stranci*). The captain of the cavalry commanded all the mounted troops.[92]

Supposedly only those soldiers who were not assigned to the war wagons were subordinate to the captain of the infantry. Their smallest tactical formation was the *"rota"* (German *"Rotte"*), which was probably separated into pikemen and flail-men and shooters (crossbowmen, archers and handgunners) according their kind of armament. It is possible that the *rota* also formed the tent and cooking group. They were subordinate to a *"rotný"* (German *"Rottmeister"*). However, in battle larger groups were under a *"setník"* (German *"Hundertschaftsführer"* – a centurion) who was of greater importance.[93]

Primarily for organizational reasons it was certainly sensible to put the guns under a gun captain (*"Hauptmann der Büchsen"*). However, there were no tactical groupings in the form of batteries under him. In battle the cannon operated independently under an artillery captain (Czech *"střelmistr"*, German *"Büchsenmeister"*).[94]

The Taborites divided their army into a "Homeland Army" (Czech *"zemská hotovost"*, German *"Heimatheer"*), the so-called "Old Tabor" (*"Alte Tabor"*) and the actual field army, the "New Tabor" (*"Neues Tabor"*). The field army was employed for the offensive campaigns while the Home Army represented an early form of home guard (German *"Landwehr"*) that should only be mobilized for defensive situations and emergencies.[95]

The army organization established by Žižka was probably retained by the Orebites, later Orphans, after his death, but also adopted partially by other Hussite armies. However, over the course of the war, the religious element gained in importance when an "administrator of spiritual affairs" (*"Verwalter der geistlichen Angelegenheiten"*) was established at the head of the Council of the Oldests (Czech *"rada starších"*, German *"Ältestenrat"*). Thus, Procopius the Bald (*Prokop Holý* or *Prokop Veliký*) became the leader of the Taborite field army after Žižka's death. Procopius' position apparently was even more domineering than that of the blind commander. Although he had no military experience, within a short time he became both the religious, political as well as the military leader of the army. The priest Prokupec (in German also called *Prokop der Kleine* - the Small) earned a comparable - but also not quite as dominant - role in the Orphans' army.

The Homeland Armies (German *"Heimatheere"*) had completely independent organizations. They had their own captains who commanded the forces in case of an operation and who were only subordinate to the senior captain. How the Homeland Army's mobilization went differently can be seen from Žižka's letter of 11 September 1422 to the citizens of Domažlice: "And therefore, my dear brothers, I inform you that we are gathering the people from all sides against this enemy and spoiler of the Bohemian land; so your priests can say you should urge the people to fight against this Antichrist, you may yourselves even shout it out in the marketplaces that all who can, whether old or young, should be ready at any hour".[96]

---

91 DURDÍK, Hussitisches Heerwesen, pp. 145-148.

92 Ibid., pp. 148-150.

93 Ibid., p. 146.

94 Ibid, pp. 144-146.

95 BERGER, Kampfkraft der Hussiten, p. 103.

96 In modern German, *"Und deshalb, meine lieben Brüder, gebe ich euch kund, daß wir das Volk an allen Seiten sammeln gegen diese Feinde und Verderber des böhmischen Landes; so möget auch*

Characteristics of the Prague Levy

Prague as the Hussite movement's most important center had its own army, which was certainly established based on directives other than those for the Taborite and Orebite field armies. A statute concerning military service obligations for the Prague citizenry was issued in 1371, before the movement began. It divided the city into four "quarters" (Czech "čtvrť") that were to share responsibilities for the levies outside the city. Irrespective of financial circumstances, each citizen was obligated to equip himself and when needed to go to the field. The participants in military operations were therefore relieved from any payments for the following two tax days (German "Steuertage").[97] The people remaining in the city's quarter had to take over these payments. Two captains were in charge of the quarter. The community appointed one captain and the city council appointed the other. Because army duty was very unpopular, by the 14th century the Prazans had already begun to hire mercenaries as replacements who as a result represented the professional core of the Prague levies.[98]

During the Hussite Wars, Prague retained this not unusual structure, which was essentially unchanged in the larger cities of central Europe. Additionally, they hired mercenaries extensively, using money extracted from Church holdings. They were supported by more poorly equipped groups from the city's poor. An edict from 1422 instructed the innkeepers and homeowners to produce a register of those living in their quarter so they could be identified and recruited if needed.[99]

The Prague City Levy was more similar to the Taborite and Orebitie Homeland armies than the field armies. The city's citizenry resisted the creation of a standing army and relied on this militia system throughout the entire war. Additionally, an established senior commander was never chosen. During the First Crusade (1420) the City Council selected Hynek Krusina von Lichtenburk as the commander-in-chief; in 1421 Jan Želivský took over the religious, political and military leadership of the City Levy and included a similar role to that held later by Procopius the Bald with the Taborites. However, in military affairs, he relied heavily on his captain, Jan Hvezda, who later was supposed to become one of Žižka's successors with the Taborites. After Želivský's disempowerment and execution, the senior captain's position was no longer filled.[100]

On the March

On the march, the war wagons always moved in several rows or columns. Ideally, there were four such columns: two inner (Czech "placni"), consisting of the transport wagons and two outer (Czech "krajni"). The outer columns were longer so that those overlapping, located in the front and back, could close into a Wagenburg without difficulty while those wagons to the side only had to completely maintain their order. The overlapping vanguards were called "okridji" in Czech.[101]

If an average field army had more than 300 wagons and one assumes that the length of the placni was only two thirds of that of the krajni, then the outer wagon column would consist of 90 wagons and the inner of 60. Wulf calculates the length of a wagon drawn by four horses (including the interval to the one in front) to be about 12 meters (40 feet). With that, the outer column would have been about 1,100 meters (1,200 yards) long on the march.[102]

This maneuver was ordered and controlled using signal flags where every first and last wagon of a column had such signal flags. To rapidly close into a Wagenburg required intensive training.[103] However, there are no reports about army maneuvers to be found in the sources.

What Late Middle Ages armies of this period were supplied with can be deduced from the diverse requirements (German "Anschlägen") of the crusader armies. For example, the Lusatian League (Lausitzer Sechsstädte literally the Six Cities of Lausitz),[104] whose rural and urban levies came closest to those of the Hussites structurally in 1421, said they must have: "money, wine, beer, meat, bacon, sausages, lard, fish, butter, Bohemian cheese, small cheese, satz, tyschlag, hand towels, cauldrons, tripods, spices, utensils, waxed staves, skewers, exsse, grave shovels, haulkin, pots, shovels, mallets, wagon tarps (?), arrows, rope (?), rope for tying cattle feed, tents with poles and their tools, feedbags, oats and ein moss for them, wooden pails, copper drinking vessels, Lithuanian shields, pans, tringtoppen, braziers, milk cans, schutzemeister, barbers,

---

Ihr Euren Priestern sagen, sie sollen in ihren Predigten das Volk zum Kampf auffordern gegen diesen Antichrist, selbst aber möget Ihr es auf den Märkten ausrufen, daß alle, die da können, ob alt oder jung, bereit seien zu jeder Stund". Quoted from DURDÍK, Hussitisches Heerwesen, pp. 45-46.

97   "Steuertage" were those days when taxes were due, however, that did not always happen on a regular basis.

98   DURDÍK, Hussitisches Heerwesen, pp. 46-47.

99   BERGER, Kampfkraft der Hussiten, p. 102.

100   DURDÍK, Hussitisches Heerwesen, pp. 47-49.

101   PALACKÝ, Der Hussitenkrieg 1419-1431, p. 368;
      TURNBULL, Hussite Wars, p. 38;
      DELBRÜCK, Geschichte der Kriegskunst, pp. 555-556.

102   WULF, Wagenburg, p. 38.

103   TURNBULL, Hussite Wars, p. 38.

104   Translator's note: The Lusatian League, or literally the Six Cites of Lausitz (Lausitzer Sechsstädte) or Upper Lausitz Six City Union (Oberlausitzer Sechsstädtebund) in the German lands was an alliance created on 21 August 1346, by the cities of Görlitz (Gorlicz – part now in Poland), Lauban (Luban - Poland), Sythaw (Zittau), Bautzen (Budissin), Lubow (Löbau) und Kamenz. It functioned as a defensive and offensive treaty for the protection of trade routes and to increase their political power against the nobles who were increasing becoming robber knights. Source: https://www.oberlausitz.de/die-oberlausitz/sechs-staedte-bund/

carpenters, gunsmiths, guns, powder, rerebraces [biceps armor], cowls (?), sabatons [foot armor], iron flails, peas (?), [and] vegetables".[105]

**Depiction of a war wagon (*Kriegswagen*)
in Kyeser's "*Bellifortis*."**

Army Manpower

The Taborites' and Orebites' field armies or "field brotherhoods" (Czech "*polní obce*", German "*Feldbruderschaften*") were the first standing armies of their time. They could be strengthened immediately before the campaigns with volunteers, but they also remained in existence as military forces in peacetime. In 1424 after Jan Žižka's death, his army, whose members now called themselves "the Orphans" (Czech "*sirotci*", German "*die Waisen*") consisted of 4,000 men with 300 war wagons. At the same time the Taborite army included about 6,000 fighters.[106] If one sets the crew of a war wagon at 2 handgunners as well as one howitzer (Czech "*houfnice*") or *tarasnice* in five wagons, and a larger cannon in 20 wagons, then such an army would have available more than about 600 handgunners, 60 smaller and 15 larger cannon. Whether the number increased, especially of heavy guns on the "beautiful rides" (Old Czech *spanile jizdy*, German *Herrliche Heerfahrten*) of the late 1420s when the Hussite army took along 2,000 and more wagons, must be doubted.

All of the Hussite armies seldom united for a battle or a campaign. At Ušti in 1426 and Kladsko (Glatz) in 1428, three such armies joined forces; supposedly all the Hussite forces united for the 1429-1430 "beautiful ride" as well as to defend against the Fifth Crusade in 1431. On these occasions it appears that the Hussites – like the crusader armies as well, had significant problems supplying armies of 10,000 men or more for longer periods. In 1426, 1428 and 1431 they only joined their forces for a short time in direct expectation of battles. During the movement through the Empire in 1429-30, the army already divided itself into five columns out of logistical necessity and marched through the country with a 50-kilometer (31-mile) wide front.[107]

The baggage train with merchants, women and possibly children took on significant size, also in operations outside Bohemia. For example, in December 1429, the city of Görlitz received word about the strength of Procopius' the Great's Hussite army: "Their total strength consisted of 30,000, of which half should be fighting men. They have no large pieces [heavy weapons], no cannon, if then 4 stone-firing cannon that each fires a *Zehntner*".[108]

---

106 Tresp, Söldner aus Böhmen, p. 28;
     Delbrück, Geschichte der Kriegskunst, p. 570.

107 Delbrück, Geschichte der Kriegskunst, pp. 571-572.

108 In MHG, "*Alle ire redlichste macht nicht wol uf 30.000 sein werde, do nicht wol die helffte streitbar volck soll sein. Haben noch kein grossen gezeug, weder Büchsen, wenn allein 4 steinbüchsen, der yede nahent einen Centner swer scheuchst*". See: Palacký, Urkundliche Beiträge II., p. 85.
     Translator's note: A "*Zehntner*", from Latin "*centenarius*", derived from "*centum*" meaning "hundred", is an obsolete name for a unit of weight which was used predominantly in Germany, Austria, and Switzerland, and some other regions. Like the notion of hundredweight, the zentner is the weight of 100 units, where the value of the unit depends on the time and location. Traditionally the unit was one hundred pounds (German Pfund), or roughly

---

105 In the MHG, "*Gelt, wein, byr, fleisch, speck, seitenfleisch, schmaltz, fysche, putter, behemische kese, cleine kese, satz, tyschlag, hant tücher, kessel, dreifuss, würze, vnsletlichte, wichsinne stöckel, spisse, exsse, grabescheit, haulkin, muldin, schauffeln, schlegel, kriptücher, pfele, strenge, futterstricke, gezelt mit stangen vnd sinem gerethe, futtersecke, hobir vnd ein moss dorzu, hulzyne kannen, kopperinne tringgefese, lythische schilde, pfannen, tringtoppen, roste, brantreithe, schutzemeister, balbirer, czymmerleuthe, bochsenmeister, bochsen, pulver, poffeysen, kawlin, fusseysen, eiserne flegel, erbis, zugemüse*". Quoted in Palacký, Urkundliche Beiträge I, Nr. 140, p. 151.

This picture shows the **employment of a war wagon loaded with stones against infantry**, a tactic used by Jan Žižka in the Battle of Malešov (German: Maleschau).

Use of a storming ladder with hooks, for securing it to the capstones of a castle wall.

The pictures come from a copy of Kyeser's *Bellifortis* by Hans Talhoffer from 1459.

According to that, the strength of Procopius' army was about 15,000 combatants, which corresponds to the estimates of modern researchers like Krocker.[109] The same number of women and children might accompany the body.

Castles and Field Fortifications

The use of *Wagenburgen* (laagers) with greater numbers of cannon already shows how much the Hussites depended on defensive positions. Hence they also developed some innovations in the construction of field fortifications and castles.

During the 1420 siege of Prague, Jan Žižka had temporary field fortifications constructed on the Vitkova (Veitsberg) ridge. The narrow ridge in the east of the city was of strategic significance because the two castles on the Hradschin and the Vyšehrad were occupied by Royal forces. Žižka ordered building of two wooden towers in the form of blockhouses. A wall with a ditch in front of it was constructed. Varying information indicates that this ditch was interrupted by a series of small bastions of heavy timbers so that the defenders could take the attackers under flanking fire.[110]

One of the most important Hussite fortification complexes is the religious center at Tabor. The city was already well protected in the north and south by the Luznice River and the Tismeciner stream. The old Hradiste Castle was located to the west of the city. It was located on an elevated spit of land that was surrounded on three sides by valleys and rivers. The focus of the new fortification complex, which the Hussites starting building there in 1420, lay to the east. A double city wall with tall defensive towers, which were capable of housing a number of cannon, was constructed there. The inner ring had many half-round towers, which were open on the back, from which

---

50,000 grams – the precise value being context-dependent – making one zentner equal to about 50 kilograms or 110 pounds. Source: https://en.wikipedia.org/wiki/Zentner.

109 KROCKER, Sachsen und die Hussitenkriege, p. 32-33.

110 PURTON, Late Medieval Siege, p. 237;
DURDÍK, Hussitisches Heerwesen, p. 187.

**Depiction of a battering ram in
Johann Hartlieb's *"Kriegsbuch"***
The roof was supposed to provide protection from
enemy missiles and was often covered with wet animal
hides to hinder setting it on fire.

**Interesting depiction of a catapult in
Johann Hartlieb's *"Kriegsbuch"***
The torsion catapult got its elasticity from the twisted
ropes on its throwing arm.

handgunners could bring flanking fire on anyone trying to climb the walls with ladders. At first sight, the towers were at irregular intervals, but this apparent chaos followed a system because there were no blind spots between them. Most of the towers have five loopholes (two in the third story and three in the fourth story) for *tarasnice* guns. These were located high enough that they could shoot over the first wall. The outer wall had a row of bastions that projected far outside the fortress and enabled them to direct flanking fire at the enemy. So, Tabor is one of the first polygonal fortresses in Europe. Furthermore, one of the cannon towers constructed in the Hradiste Castle is one of oldest of its kind in Central Europe. The land in front of Tabor's walls sloped steeply and could be effectively covered by cannon, handguns and crossbows to a distance of up to 300 meters (ca. 330 yards).[111]

The access to the city was through a cleverly devised triple gate system that was protected by a barbican, a fortification with a deep moat.

While loopholes for black powder cannon were already in use in England and France in the 14th century, Tabor was probably the first central European fortification complex with such devices, which were probably also developed independent of any western examples.

The "Tabor" system of double wall fortifications was also used by the Hussites in other Bohemian towns and for the strengthening of castles in which a shield wall, supplied with the low bastions and round towers, protected older fortifications. The use of towers that were open in the rear had several advantages. First, should an attacking enemy capture a tower, they could not protect themselves from counterattacks from the direction of the city. Additionally, the dense smoke created by firing the guns could be better vented.[112]

111 Purton, Late Medieval Siege, p. 237;
     Durdík, Hussitisches Heerwesen, pp. 181-183;
     Palacký, Der Hussitenkrieg 1419-1431, p. 85.

112 Purton, Late Medieval Siege, p. 236.

Siege Warfare

Due to the complex networks of relations and loyalties in Bohemia, the Hussite Wars were also marked by lengthy sieges. This was most evident in the capital, Prague, where the two mountain castles remained in the Royalists' hands in 1420 while the rest of the city had for the most part joined the Hussite movement. During the city's siege by the crusader army in the summer, the fighting was mostly limited to visible psychological demonstrations. Both the Prazans and the crusaders erected pyres for burning people at the stake in order to make the threatening fate clear to the enemy. Over time, the besieged even composed written appeals in which they tried to convince the crusaders of the essence of the Four Prague Articles.[113]

The Hussites also used such psychological means of pressure in 1421 in the siege of the city of Most (Brüx) in northern Bohemia. Shortly before that, they were able to capture the brother of the Most's castle commander, the knight Ramphold Gorentz, in nearby Belina (Belin). Then they tied him onto a battering ram and tried to force the defenders to surrender. According to legend, Ramphold did call to his brother that his life counted less than the overall issue. With a heavy heart, the commander ordered his gunners to kill his brother. The shot succeeded and the garrison withstood the siege.[114]

After their victory at the Veitsberg, the Prazans invested the Vyšehrad. The Hussites constructed a ditch with a wall at the foot of the castle hill, on one hand in order to shut in the garrison, but on the other hand to protect the New City side from sorties by the garrison. South of the castle, the Botic stream was tied into the ditch system, which was strengthened so well that the field sentries could camp there in safety. In the following weeks the fighting around the Vyšehrad was limited to an inconclusive artillery duel between the city and the castle on the hill. On 15 September the Royalist garrison finally had a minor morale success as the chronicler Laurentius reported: "On the other side, namely the city side, they [the Prazans, author's note] placed two machines, so-call *praky* [catapults] behind the church of the [Blessed] Virgin on the Botic, that the prudent *Vyšehrad* artillery captain fired from the circular chapel of the Saint Margaret [church] and destroyed the [Prazans'] Botic [position]".[115] But the Prazans also held out against them: "But with a great cannon, which they had emplaced after breaking through the wall of the little *"Auf der Wiese"* (in *Viridi* – on the Meadow) Church, they caused much damage to the [royalist] *Vyšehradern*".

However, soon the food shortage became noticeable within the garrison that was loyal to the king. Even though Sigismund promised his soldiers quick help, many weeks passed. In October the horses in the castle were slaughtered because the garrison ran out of meat. Actually, at the end of October, Sigismund requisitioned a number of boats in Leitmeritz because he planned to relieve the castle from the Moldau side. When the Hussites learned about the plans, they blocked the river with thick chains and large posts. On 28 October, Sigismund moved from Karlštejn Castle toward Prague and set fire to many villages along the way to signal the hard-pressed garrison that help was on the way. The king actually reached the city, supplied the Hradschin with provisions and then moved on to Kutná Hora (Kuttenberg) where he intended to raise a new army. In the hope of being relieved by the king soon, the Vyšehrad garrison decided to take up negotiations with the Hussites. If they were not relieved by 31 October, they would hand over the castle with all of their guns on 1 November.[116]

The royal army did actually appear before the gates of Prague on 31 October and Sigismund planned to attack the Vyšehrad's besiegers on the following day, and the garrison would make a sortie at the same time. However, the deadline established between the garrison and the Hussites had already passed, so the Prague forces occupied the Vyšehrad's gates. The relief army eschewed attacking the Prazans' entrenchments because they were arranged so that they could repel not only an attack by the garrison but also an attack from the outside. Despite that, Sigismund ordered the Moravians and Hungarians to attack in two different places, and it was successful initially. They pushed the Hussites at St. Pankraz into a group, but then suddenly the situation changed and Sigismund's knights retreated from the captured entrenchments pursued by the Prazans. Among the 500 dead were some prominent Bohemian and Moravian nobles. After the battle the royalist garrison evacuated the castle on the hill.[117]

As a rule, however, the Hussites tried to avoid longer sieges and attempted to take cities and towns first with surprise attacks. In November 1420, they appeared before the southern Bohemian town of Prachatic. After the town had rejected the demand to surrender, Jan Žižka ordered an attack. The Hussites brought up storming ladders to the walls. The towns' garrison could hardly put up a defense because they were being so suppressed by a concentrated

---

113 ŠMAHEL, Hussitische Revolution II, p. 1093.

114 In the Nazi period, a Fascist Sudeten-German armed industrial militia group (*Kampfgruppe*) formed with the name "*Rampold Gorenz*", with reference to this story.

115 In MHG, "*Auf der anderen Seite, nämlich der Stadtseite, stellten sie [die Prager, Anm. d. A.] hinter dem Chor der (seligen) Jungfrau am Botic zwei Maschinen, sogenannte praky (Schleudern), auf, die aber dennoch der umsichtige Vyšehrader Büchsenmeister von der Rundkapelle der heiligen Margarete aus mit Pfeilschüssen gegen den Botic zerstörte*". See: Laurentius-Chronik, p. 160.

116 PURTON, Late Medieval Siege, pp. 235-236; PALACKÝ, Der Hussitenkrieg 1419-1431, pp. 155-159.

117 PALACKÝ, Der Hussitenkrieg 1419-1431, pp. 160-162.

Depictions of military equipment in the so-called "*Feuerwerksbuch*" from the second half of the 15th century.
Above is a heavy pavis with several iron spikes to securely anchor it to the ground and two loopholes for shooters. The covered wagon below was used to safely approach an enemy castle's walls.

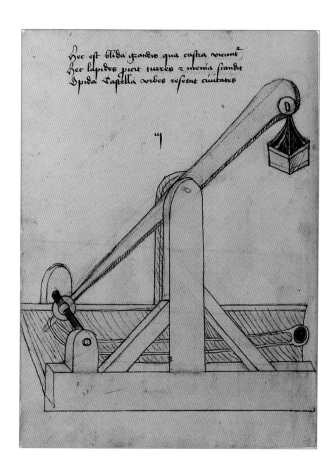

Depiction of a simple counterbalance catapult (trebuchet or German *Blide*) in Kyesers "*Bellifortis.*" A long rope is attached on the left end of the throwing arm on which a basket is hung with the material to be hurled.

hail of fire from Hussite handguns, crossbows and catapults that they barely dared to come out from behind the crenellations. The attack was a success.[118]

Other sieges were carried out with enormously great effort, like that of Švihov (Schwihau) in 1425. A thousand horsemen and 8,000 footsoldiers besieged the castle, belonging to a minor Bohemian noble. The Hussites employed three catapults and heavy cannon. However, what was decisive was that they cut off the water to the besieged so that the garrison stacked arms after two weeks.[119]

The Hussites also used undermining of walls, e.g., in November 1425 at the siege of the Austrian town of Retz.[120] In 1433 in Prussia, the Hussites attempted to dig a tunnel under the walls of the Konitz castle. But the tunnel caved in and buried most of those working on it. The Teutonic Knights were only able to save four of the men.[121]

The Hussite's siege artillery was composed of modern heavy bombards as well as conventional catapults. For example, on 10 December 1424, Electoral Prince Friedrich I of Saxony informed the Council of the city "that the heretics have gathered together, and namely have four armies and fourteen trebuchets and cannon, and lots of other equipment. And they have camped directly before [the town of] Aussig (Ústi nad Labem) and mean to force and take it".[122]

---

118 Ibid., pp. 171-173.

119 ŠMAHEL, Hussitische Revolution II, p. 1352.

120 STÖLLER, Österreich im Kriege gegen die Hussiten, p. 35.

121 In MHG, *"daz die keczcer in großer sampnunge syn unde nemlich vir grosse her habin und haben virczen blyden unde buchsen unde andern geczug mehir, denne sie y gehabt habin, - unde habin sich gereite vor Außk gelagert und meynen, daz zcu notigen unde zcu gewinnen"*. See: ŠMAHEL, Hussitische Revolution III, pp. 1580-1581.

122 CDS I B 4, Nr. 386, Nr. 251.

This depiction from the *"Feuerwerksbuch"* shows a bombard's position in front of the actual siege lines. The path to this main line is protected by a wooden fence.

Inside Bohemia the Hussites conducted sieges very successfully in that they could employ a massive amount of artillery. In the last December days of 1420, for example, they besieged the fortified Kunratice manor that blocked the most important trade route just outside of Prague. The Hussites occupied a nearby hill where they placed several heavy bombards and three large trebuchets. They opened with such an effective fire that all the roofs were destroyed. On 25 January 1421, after a four-week siege, the commandant, Ritter von (Knight of) Fulstein agreed to capitulate. The castle was subsequently burned to the ground and never rebuilt.[123]

The following year, the Hussites besieged Karlštejn Castle with even more effort. They erected four "battery positions" (German *"Batteriestellungen"*) for trebuchets and cannon and bombarded the fortress from all sides so that they were all heavily damaged. The Hussites' five catapults were said to have hurled a total of 9,032 stones,

1,822 barrels of "refuse" (German *"Unratfässer"*) and 22 earthen vessels filled with fire into the castle. The cadavers of horses, cows, donkeys and sheep were also counted in the barrels of refuse that the besiegers hurled over the castle's walls in the hope that a plague would break out among the garrison. Yet the garrison of the fortress on the steep rocky promontory withstood the siege and was able to negotiate a ceasefire.[124]

Generally, whether the siege would be conducted from all sides or focused on just one point depended on the size of the besieged object and the geographic characteristics. As a rule, a heavily fortified headquarters would be erected on a location that dominated the objective. The castle or the accessible area was cut off from the outside world by a ditch. To protect against sorties the spoil was piled up to form a wall in which the Hussites often emplaced wooden bastions. Sometimes these bastions were made of prefabricated pieces that were brought

123 Purton, Late Medieval Siege, p. 236;
     Palacký, Der Hussitenkrieg 1419-1431, pp. 199-200.

124 Purton, Late Medieval Siege, pp. 236-237; Palacký, Der
     Hussitenkrieg 1419-1431, p. 321.

A heavy bombard during a siege.
The cannon is loaded and the soldier raises the heavy protective mantlet for firing. For sieges the Hussites often constructed very extensive earthwork systems to cut off the castle from the outside world.

along for the siege. The catapults and cannon were consolidated in one or more rectangular, round or polygonal battery positions. At the siege of the Lichnice Castle in 1428, a single siege fortification with five bastions was erected. During the siege of Grabstein a similar fort was erected 250 meters (275 yards) from the castle on a point that was built up five meters (16.4 feet) higher. These forts could be defended on all sides in case of an attempt to relieve the object.[125]

It is striking that the Hussites set to work for long periods at sieges in Bohemia; however, those often failed against the German cities and towns. The large medieval German towns were well fortified. Many had modern cannon and well-filled armories for equipping their citizenry. The Hussites avoided drawn out sieges of those towns. Their operations outside Bohemia were to obtain food not for extended occupation of territory. If a town resisted the first Hussite assault, it had a good chance that the siege would be abandoned and they would move on. The siege of Bautzen in 1429 only lasted three days and was ended when the Hussites' commander was killed during an unsuccessful attempt to storm the city's walls. Görlitz on the Neisse River was never really besieged by the Hussites. Their armies appeared more than a half dozen times before the city's gates. Several times the suburbs were burned, but the Hussites did not dare undertake a siege of the fortified city. The same was true for the fortified border city of Zittau. When the Hussites appeared before Schweidnitz (Świdnica, Poland) in January 1429, they found the town well prepared for an attack: "They now say there that they were, by the grace of God, well prepared and that they fired very well [intensively] with cannon, handguns etc., so they [the Hussites] went and burned the suburbs extensively".[126] Also the cities and town in Silesia and the Lausitz had extensively expanded their arsenals with modern cannon and handguns at this time. The Hussites broke off their siege of Konitz in Prussia in 1433 after six weeks because their provisions ran out.[127]

Another detailed **depiction of a "trebuchet"** in the Talhofer versoion of the *Bellifortis* of 1459.
http://www.kb.dk/da/nb/materialer/haandskrifter/HA/e-mss/thalhofer/thott-2_290.html

125 PURTON, Late Medieval Siege, pp. 237-238.

126 In MHG, *"Da sy nu sogin, das dy weren von Gotis Gnaden alle wol bestalt worden, vnd das man vndir rechte sere schos mit Büchsen, pischaln ec da gingen sie abe und branten des dy fürstat recht sehre"*. Modern German: *"Da sie nun sagen, das sie von Gottes Gnaden alle wohl gestellt wären, und das man von hier recht sehr (=intensiv) mit Büchsen, Pischaln (=Handbüchsen) e.t.c schoß, da gingen sie aber und brannten die Vorstadt recht sehr"*. Quoted from PALACKÝ, Urkundliche Beiträge II, Nr. 567, p. 13.

127 ŠMAHEL, Hussitische Revolution III, pp. 1580-1581.

SPIES AND ASSASSINS

In 1426 in Saxony, the Council of Rochlitz reported to the Leipzigers that they had heard "how two students want to set fire to the towns and have asked the heretics for money in return".[128] The fear of Hussite supporters was especially strong in lands like the Margraveship of Meissen. The University of Leipzig was the gathering place for theologians who wrote anti-Hussite tracts, and thus became a potential target for attacks. The city fathers saw the greatest danger in the students who traveled through the country. Accompanying the warning cited above was a detailed description of the potential assassins. "One wore a gray patched coat that is lined below the throat with blue cloth and has a black robe of Barchent [a woolen cloth] and a grey hood, while the other had a gray coat with tight sleeves and a black cap and has black hair".[129]

In the Lausitz and in Silesia there was great fear of assassins setting fires inside the city walls. In December 1429, the council of Görlitz received an anonymous warning: "I have recently verbally informed our mayor, with what sneaky cleverness our enemies the heretics surreptitiously creep through these towns and deceive everyone here in the land or in Silesia with their deceitful looks".[130]

There was also significant fear of spies. In the summer of 1430, the Duke von Saxony informed the Council of Dresden, that "A messenger to Saaz who should appear today and go out into our land for scouting".[131] The spy wore a blue cowl, black and white pants and a jacket into which he had hidden his letters. In a time when most people had only one set of clothing, the description in this letter was more thorough than the physiognomic details.

However, the "spies" very often had a missionary function. Their main focus was to spread the Hussites' beliefs. Also, within the German cities, especially at the universities and Church schools, there were educated, mostly young men who argued about the ideas of Wycliffe and Hus. They were seen in the communities as being a threat not just to religious peace but also to their own security. So, for example, in 1426, a burgher in Dresden, suspected of being a heretic and spy, was "sacked", i.e., stuck in a sack and thrown into the Elbe River.[132]

In contrast in Franconia in the 14th century, small Waldensian communities had developed that theologically were very close to the Hussites. They also offered wandering Hussite preachers lodging who traveled from there throughout the south of the Empire. At the same time, the imperial city of Nuremberg developed into the most important center of anti-Hussite journalism.[133] And yet Nuremberg merchants were not only repeatedly supplying Hussite towns with gunpowder and weapons, but also with important information.[134] This weighed even more heavily because Nuremberg was also one of the Empire's political centers where the princes met and made plans for the upcoming crusades. So it can be assumed that city's merchants informed the Hussites about these plans in a timely manner.

---

128 MHG, *"wy das czwene studenten dy stete an legen wollen vnde von den ketczern geld darvmme genomen haben".* Quoted in CDS II 8, Nr. 158, p. 102.

129 MHG, *"Der eyne hat eynen grauwen geflickten mantel an, der ist vnden vmme den hals mit blauwen tuche gefutert vnde hat eyne swarcze vndiroppe an von parchan vnde eyne grauwe kogel uff, so hat der ander eynen grauwen rock an mit angeczogen ermeln vnd eyne swarcze muetcze uffe, vnd hat swarcz har".* Quoted in CDS II 8, Nr. 158, p. 102; Krzenck, Hussitenkriege, pp. 61-63.

130 In MHG, *"Ich habe nest uwern Bürgermeister müntlichen wol awszgerichtet, mit welcher hinderlistiger gescheydikeit vnser fynde dy Ketzer durch jren Reysigen gezewg betrigelichem mynen erschleichen dese Stete alhy im Lande, ader dy in der Slesia".* Quoted in Palacký, Urkundliche Beiträge II, Nr. 624, p. 82.

131 In modern German *"Ein Bote zu Saaz sei, der sich heute erheben und heraus in unsere Lande nach Kundschaft gehen solle".* In MHG, *"eyn bote zcu Sacz sy, der sich hute irhebin und heruß in unsire lande noch kuntschaft gehin solle".* Quoted in MHG in Richter, Hussitischer Spion, p. 145.

132 Meinhard, Dresden und die Ketzerbewegung, p. 110.

133 Machilek, Hussiten in Franken, pp. 23-27.

134 Polívka, Handelsbeziehungen, pp. 165-166.

TACTICS

For fifteen years, the Hussites decided their battles more or less with a "standard program" that developed out of their experiences in the battles at Nekmíř and Sudoměř. To complete the operations, the *Wagenburg* finally was added in the 1426 Battle of Ústi (Aussig).

The concept of the *Wagenburg* was, however, not completely new. The south German military theorist Konrad (or Conradis) Kyeser (1366-1405) showed examples of war wagons and also the *Wagenburg* in his treatise "*Bellifortis*". Kyeser had acquired extensive military experience in Italy and also King Sigismund's campaigns against the Ottomans. The "*Bellifortis*" originated at the Bohemian Žebrák Castle in response to the devastating defeat that Sigismund's crusader army suffered against the Turks at Nikopolis in 1396. It is therefore not unlikely that the work, finished in 1405 shortly before Kyeser's death, was known to Bohemian nobles serving with the Hussites, and possibly to Žižka himself. However, an edition was dedicated to King Wenzel, and Žižka was the captain of his bodyguard for a time.[135]

The disciplined cooperation of all the available branches – infantry, cavalry, artillery and *Wagenburg* - was decisive for the success of the Hussites. At the end of the 1420s, the crusaders attempted to copy Hussite weapon systems, like the *Wagenburg*, but failed in a grandiose manner at the battles of Tachov and Domažlice. These defeats made it clear that the Bohemians' success was not tied to a single tactical or technical innovation, but on the functioning of the complex interplay of the individual branches.

The Hussite war wagons could already move from the march into a formation that could rapidly form a *Wagenburg* when needed. When they did that, the wagons were arranged such that the front right wheel overlapped with the left rear wheel of the adjacent wagon. These wheels were secured to one another with chains so the wagons could not be separated. A contemporary depiction also shows that the outside wheels were chained in a manner they could no longer move (see page 81).

The horses were unharnessed and moved to safety by the supply wagons, somewhat away from the battle line. The wagon drawbars were placed in a vertical position or removed. The *Wagenburg* was usually rectangular, less frequently arranged in an oval.[136]

If a more permanent camp was established, the Hussites also began to dig ditches and to cover the wheels with the spoil. Openings were left at certain intervals between the wagons to give the cannon fields of fire. Soldiers with pavises blocked these gaps with their shields as needed.[137]

Fifteen to twenty men occupied a wagon. That included crossbowmen and handgunners, simple soldiers who threw stones at attacking enemies, but also flail-men and pikemen who attempted to push or pull enemy knights from their saddles. A group of footsoldiers were gathered inside the camp and waited for the right moment to counterattack.[138]

It was not unusual for tried and tested fighters to be dubbed as knights shortly before the battle in order to bolster their motivation and to spur their comrades. For example, this happened shortly before the Battle of Kutná Hora (Kuttenberg) in December 1421.[139]

Ideally, the Hussites set up their *Wagenburg*s on the counter slope of a hill, i.e., just below the hilltop. This had the advantage that the camp itself would be protected from enemy artillery fire while their own howitzers could still effectively take the enemy under fire. Additionally, an uphill attack very quickly tired out the horses of an enemy knight's army. Some of the hills that the Hussites chose as positions were so steep that their opponents had to dismount and attack on foot, like at the Battle of Horic in 1423. In this case, the weight of the armor exhausted the knights even faster. It was said about one of Žižka's engagements in Hungary that same year: "But when they [the Hungarians, author's comment] undertook to attack [Žižka], in that the horsemen dismounted and attacked him on foot, they were cut down by him, then the horsemen's fighting skill is different than the footsoldiers' because it is an unaccustomed thing for them".[140] The *Wagenburg*s finally presented insurmountable obstacles for Late Middle Ages cavalry and infantry. Granted it was possible to overturn a wagon with ropes, but the chained together wagons formed an almost impenetrable wall. At a short distance, the knights' armies came up against a deadly hail of crossbow bolts and gunshots. Also, the larger cannon more seldom fired cannon balls, but more often a load of lead, stone or clay balls similar to later grapeshot. At that time, the gunfire caused an enormous noise that was perhaps more important than the fired

---

135 FELDHAUS, Kyeser, pp. 768-769;
 POPPOLOW, Militärtechnische Bildkataloge, pp. 259-260.

136 TURNBULL, Hussite Wars, p. 34;
 BERGER, Kampfkraft der Hussiten, p. 107;
 KROENER, Kriegswesen, p. 11;
 DELBRÜCK, Geschichte der Kriegskunst, pp. 566-567.

137 TURNBULL, Hussite Wars, p. 34-35;
 DELBRÜCK, Geschichte der Kriegskunst, p. 566.

138 TURNBULL, Hussite Wars, p. 34;
 DURDÍK, Hussitisches Heerwesen, pp. 172-174;
 DELBRÜCK, Geschichte der Kriegskunst, p. 567.

139 PALACKÝ, Der Hussitenkrieg 1419-1431, p. 269;
 DURDÍK, Geschichte der Kriegskunst, pp. 172-174.

140 "Als aber sie ihn anzugreifen unternahmen, indem die Reiter absaßen und zu Fuß gegen ihn stürmten, so wurden sie von ihm niedergeschlagen; denn anders ist die Geschicklichkeit der Reiter zum Kampf, anders des Fußvolks, weil es jenen eine ungewohnte Sache". Quoted from DELBRÜCK, Geschichte der Kriegskunst, p. 569.

projectiles because the most widely used kind of gun, the *taranice*, could not be elevated which made aiming impossible. The enormous thunderclap greatly exceeded the effects of rounds. This was because the warhorses of the early 15th century were hardly used to this kind of battlefield noise yet. They reacted with fright, tried to break away and as a result caused significant disruptions in their own attacking ranks. The Hussites tried to increase this effect by having their guns fire in one simultaneous salvo, like they did at Ústi (Aussig). Since loading was very time-consuming and this salvo was unleashed at a short distance, it must be assumed that the black powder weapons were as a rule only fired one time and then the infantry took up the fight.[141]

If the enemy attack lost its momentum or the opposing force showed the first signs of panic, the Hussites started a counterattack. The infantry streamed out of the *Wagenburg*, initially on the sides, in order to hit the enemy attacking from the front in their flanks. Sometimes the Hussites created an opportunity for their enemies to sink their teeth into the *Wagenburg*, like at Ústi, where the Saxons could break partway into the ring of wagons. Thus tied up in the front, the flanks and rear of the crusader army was especially vulnerable to rapid powerful counterattacks. Because the horsemen had lost their most important advantage – the attack's shock effect, the infantry could use their greatest advantage, numerical superiority. The Hussite pikemen and flail-men, in greater numbers, pulled the knights out of their saddles and put an end to them.[142]

In this last phase of the combat, the knights fighting on the Hussite side and their mounted soldiers also attacked. With their fresh horses, they took up the pursuit of the defeated opponents.[143] If medieval battles were often limited to the mere collision armies on the battlefield, then it was not unusual that the Hussites would pursue their enemies for several miles and thus turn simple defeats into military catastrophes. Some campaigns were decided by a single large battle and only in this manner was the Hussite movement able to prevent armies invading from all directions from uniting forces. Thanks to the disciplined collaboration of the wagons, cannon, infantry and cavalry, whose employment followed a strictly sequential and agreed upon plan, one can talk about "combined arms operations" in the context of Hussite tactics.

Jan Žižka only once deviated significantly from this defensive process - in 1424 at Malešov (Maleschau). However, even here he also exploited an advantageous ele-vated position. Because the backs of the hills over which his enemies could attack were very narrow, the front on which they could attack was limited to just a few yards, he had wagons loaded with stones rolled down the hill. So he passed up the defensive action and instead stopped the enemy's attack with an immediate powerful counter-thrust.[144]

The Hussite *Wagenburg* tactic was especially synchronized against the weaknesses of their opponents' armies. Although the crusader armies increasingly brought along artillery, they seldom employed it in a battle. The infantry was only used as an auxiliary for the cavalry. It lacked the cohesion and the aggressiveness of the early Swiss *Landsknechte*. The artillery and infantry would have been fully capable to effectively attack the defensive Hussite *Wagenburg*s. But the crusader armies also had a very simple capability that they did not recognize. Since the Hussites gave up any initiative at the beginning of a battle, it is conceivable they could have not attacked but rather surrounded the *Wagenburg*, starved it out and forced it to move out so the formation would have to open up. The idea that the war wagons could be used offensively, like how the chariots of antiquity surrounded the enemy at high speed, was disproven long ago by research. The wagons were too heavy and the draft horses too weak for such a daring maneuver. Hussite war wagons reached a walking pace at best. Additionally, in such a maneuver the horses were far too susceptible to enemy fire. Just the death of a single draft horse could ruin the plan to encircle an opponent.[145]

Only on one occasion were the Hussites forced to disperse a *Wagenburg*. It occurred in 1431 in Hungary, where an Orphans' army was surrounded by a large number of light cavalrymen and forced into battle. The Hussites tried to withdraw in good order and immediately closed ranks in case of a threatening attack. Only the Hungarians' uncoordinated actions saved the field army from total destruction. Despite that, the campaign ended with a defeat. This time the heretics who were used to being victorious did not take home any booty.

The German armies lacked light cavalry, even if it was a fraction of the strength that the chroniclers attribute to it, yet it must have been possible for cavalry to effectively surround a Hussite *Wagenburg*.

On open ground, outside the protection of the *Wagenburg*, the Hussites proved to be very vulnerable. In 1421, one of their armies was defeated by an army from Meissen under Friedrich the Warlike (*Friedrich der Streitbar*) at Most (Brüx). The Hussites had left their *Wagenburg* to carry out a surprise attack on the Meissners, were

141 TURNBULL, Hussite Wars, pp. 37-39;
   DURDÍK, Hussitisches Heerwesen, p. 174;
   BERGER, Kampfkraft der Hussiten, p. 107;
   DELBRÜCK, p Geschichte der Kriegskunst,. 568.

142 TURNBULL, Hussite Wars, pp. 38-39;
   DURDÍK, Hussitisches Heerwesen, pp. 174-175.

143 TURNBULL, Hussite Wars, p. 39;
   DURDÍK, Hussitisches Heerwesen, pp. 174-175.

144 DURDÍK, Hussitisches Heerwesen, pp. 175, 214-221.

145 ROGERS, Tactics, p. 216; WULF, pp. 11-23;
   NICHOLSON, Medieval Warfare, p. 58;
   DELBRÜCK, Geschichte der Kriegskunst, pp. 571-573; though the most recent Žižka biographer describes such manoevers, see:
   VERNEY, Warrior of God, pp. 27-29.

A mid 15th century depiction of a War Wagon.
The arquebuse of the man standing on the right of the wagon is too modern for the Hussite period and
Hussite War wagons also used no sickles. Bows were not unknown, but uncommon compared to crossbows
Apart from that, the details in equipment are very interesting.

defeated on the open battlefield and fled so that their enemies were also able to storm the *Wagenburg*. In 1428, another Hussite army, which was on its way back from a pillaging operation, was badly defeated by a Lausitzer levy at Chrastava (Kratzau). The Lausitzers approached near the Hussites unhindered and attacked them before they could close up their *Wagenburg*. In 1433, a Palatine (*Pfälzer*) levy also scored a spectacular victory in a similar manner at Hiltersried in Upper Bavaria.[146] If the Hussites themselves had been on the offensive, or had they failed to take up their complete defensive position, they were completely vulnerable.

The Hussites won battles so often by simply employing their "standard program" that it eventually reached a point at which an experienced enemy commander was able to use the Hussite tactics against them. Diviš Bořek z Miletínka had originally fought at the side of Jan Žižka, but later switched to the camp of the more moderate Calixtiners. He worked his way up to not only be a key political leader but also based on his military experience became the commander in chief of a joint Hussite-Catholic army, which decisively defeated the Taborites and Orphans at the Battle of Lipany on 30 May 1434. Miletínka carried out an attack with his numerically superior army against his opponent's *Wagenburg*. After a short artillery duel,

he feigned a retreat that prompted the Taborites and Orphans to take up the pursuit. After he had lured his enemy out of their secure *Wagenburg* that way, Miletínka succeeded in exploiting his numerical superiority and achieved a decisive victory. His army overran the radicals' *Wagenburg*, and Procopius the Great was killed.[147]

The Silesians succeeded in defeating the Orphans in a similar manner near Náchod on 9 August 1427. Initially they were clobbered by the Hussites and forced to flee. When their escape route was blocked, however, they took courage out of desperation and counterattacked and beat back the Hussites. But it is not known whether they had established a *Wagenburg* before the battle.[148]

The Hussite armies were by no means invincible. But apparently the crusaders' successes were more coincidental or due to the Hussites' individual mistakes, so that they were unable to draw any tactical lessons from those instances. From that Miletínka's actions at Lipany can only be seen as intentional exploitation of the tactical weaknesses of the *Wagenburg*. He was the one who not only defeated the Taborites' and Orphans' army, but also positively destroyed the tactical nimbus that went along with the *Wagenburg*.

146 WINKLER, Hiltersried.

147 DURDÍK, Hussitisches Heerwesen, pp. 242-247.

148 WULF, Wagenburg, p. 18-20;
   PALACKÝ, Der Hussitenkrieg 1419-1431, p. 451.

19th century depiction of the battle of Lipan.
Historical art of this period presents peasant armies in a romanticised fashion with no defensive armor and improvised weapons, while Hussite forces in this battle would have been well equiped with both.

THE HUSSITE WARS

The Unlucky King

Just after the Prague Defenestration as the first Hussite armies were coming together, King Sigismund arrived in the Moravian city of Brno (Brünn) on 15 December 1419. Sigismund, as the son of Charles IV (Karl IV) and Wenzel's half-brother, was the new head of the house of Luxembourg, but the most recent unrest already showed that it was going to be difficult for him to carry through on his claims for Wenzel's crown. Sigismund summoned the Bohemian nobles to Brno. Furthermore, he notified the Imperial Princes, the Knights of the Teutonic Order and King Wladislaw of Poland that he was considering holding a court day in the beginning of 1420 in Silesian Breslau (now Wrocław, Poland). After he had returned to his Hungarian kingdom for a few weeks, he received the most influential Bohemian nobles in Brno. His sister-in-law, Sofia, the sister of the late King Wenzel, let him know that she was in no condition to continue handling affairs of state. Therefore, Sigismund put these duties in the hands of a respected nobleman, Čeněk von Wartenberg, who took his seat in the Hradschin Castle. At the same time he tried to calm the Bohemian nobles by promising not to oppose the "Communion in Both Kinds," i.e., to allow them to practice religion however they wished.

However, shortly thereafter he changed this position in Breslau where he met with important representatives of German princes. Although his Bohemian advisors recommended to deal tactfully to with his rebellious subjects and not to bring any foreign armies into the kingdom, Sigismund decided against their counsel. On 5 January 1420, he published an announcement according to which all Bohemian cities were subordinated to him and the Roman Church. And Sigismund went even further. A well-known Prague merchant, Jan Krasá was arrested in Breslau because he had spoken critically about the burning of Jan Hus. The authorities tried to force him under torture to condemn the "Communion in Both Kinds" as a heresy, but refused. Krasá was tied to horses and dragged through the city and finally on 15 March 1420 he was burned at the stake. At the same time Sigismund declared heresy a capital crime and threatened anyone who could be convicted with the confiscation of their personal property. Now it was clear to his Bohemian subjects what kind of rule they could expect.

The First Hussite Crusade

The Hussite Rebellion was quickly recognized as a potent threat to West European Christianity. Thereupon, on 1 March 1420 in Florence, Pope Martin V – at King Sigismund's urging – called for all of Europe's armies to go on a crusade. The King raised an army to move on Prague.[149]

While the Catholic armies were still gathering at Świdnica (then German "Schweidnitz," now in Poland) a small Hussite army under Mikuláš of Hus (Czech: Mikuláš z Husi, German: Nikolaus von Hus) carried out a campaign against the Rosenberg lords in South Bohemia who stood closely on Sigismund's side. During the campaign, Mikuláš captured a number of castles and towns. In the spring of 1420, Žižka also started a campaign that however soon stalled at a siege of the Rabi Castle. Rabí, in the country's southwest, was Bohemia's largest and strongest fortification because just a few years earlier it had been extensively expanded and modernized during the nobles' conflicts with King Wenzel. Despite that, Žižka succeeded in storming this bulwark within a very short time. He did spare the garrison, but apparently burned some monks and a handful of Church jewels. The Hussites greatest problem at this time was that they were numerically too weak to occupy captured locations on a lasting basis.[150]

In the meantime, King Sigismund's army had arrived "with many princes, knights and men-at-arms and also other pious people"[151] at Kutná Hora (Kuttenberg). On 31 May the King sent a letter to Ulrich von Rosenberg,[152] who should assemble an army and destroy the new Hussite fortress at Tabor. If his forces were not sufficient to do so, then the King wanted Rosenberg to come to him in Prague.[153]

In Prague the moderate Utraquists´ attempt to come to a settlement with the royal garrison in the Hradschin Castle failed. In fact, in the meantime the Prazans had occupied the hilltop castle, then it was handed back over by the commandant Čeněk von Wartenberg to mercenaries loyal to the King. When the Utraquists learned of the call for a crusade, they feared Sigismund's revenge and called to the Taborites under Jan Žižka for help. He took

149 PALACKÝ, Der Hussitenkrieg 1419-1431, pp. 90-92; ŠMAHEL, Hussitische Revolution II, pp. 1071-1073; KROCKER, Sachsen und die Hussitenkriege, p. 2.

150 PALACKÝ, Der Hussitenkrieg 1419-1431, pp. 100-101; ŠMAHEL, Hussitische Revolution II, pp. 1069-1070.

151 Quoted in PALACKÝ, Urkundliche Beiträge I, Nr. 23, p. 29 in Middle High German (MHG), "mit wil fursten Rittern vnd Knechten vnd auch andern fromen lewten…"

152 Ulrich II. von Rosenberg (Czech: Oldřich II. z Rožmberka; 13 Jan. 1403 - 28 Apr. 1462 in Český Krumlov/ Krumau) was the commander of Bohemia and from 1438 to 1444 its governor as well as regent of the House of Rosenberg/Rožmberka. Source: https://de.wikipedia.org/wiki/Ulrich_II._von_Rosenberg

153 PALACKÝ, Urkundliche Beiträge I, Nr. 25, p. 30.

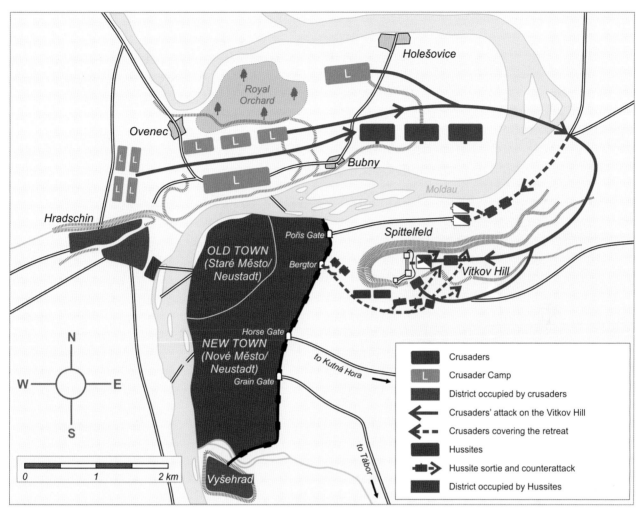

Siege of Prague and the Battle on the Vitkov Hill (Veitsberg)

action immediately and was able to badly defeat two smaller Catholic armies in Benešov (Beneschau) and Poříčí nad Sázavou (Porschitz an der Sasau). As he had already done at Sudoměř (Sudomer), Žižka formed his war wagons into a *Wagenburg*. After the Royalists' first attack was repulsed, they withdrew from the battlefield discouraged. On 20 May 1420, the Hussites concentrated their forces in Prague. Žižka and his victorious troops entered the city triumphantly but soon differences arose between the rich burghers of Prague and the Taborites. The Taborites strictly followed a version of Christianity oriented on poverty and they reacted with distress to the Prazans in their colorful, fur-lined clothing. They found the burghers' expensively groomed beards especially repulsive. Some Taborites reacted so angrily that they stopped Prazans on the street and wanted to shave them while threatening them with weapons. Žižka had some difficulty restoring order. It came to the most significant confrontation when the Taborite wives who had come along burned down the wealthy St. Catherine Cloister and attacked the

nuns. The differences in the Prazans' pragmatic ideals and the Taborites' desire for profound social changes clearly became evident.[154]

The King's forces, however, controlled not only the Hradschin but also the old Vyšehrad (*Königsberg* – King's Mountain). The Hussites had nonetheless cut it off from the New City (*Neustadt*) with ditches. In order to keep open the city's last streets capable for sorties, Žižka erected temporary fortifications in the form of blockhouse-like towers, ditches and walls on the Vitkov Hill (Veitsberg) east of the city. Additionally, almost 2,500 Prague citizens, above all the Germans, were expelled.[155]

To stop the acts of violence in the city, the Elders met in individual groups. They decided to fight the "Hungarian" King Sigismund and anyone who opposed distributing the chalice "in Both Kinds." Additionally, priests should return

---

154 VERNEY, Warrior of God, pp. 70-73.

155 PALACKÝ, Der Hussitenkrieg 1419-1431, pp. 92- 103, 112-113;
     ŠMAHEL, Hussitische Revolution II, pp. 1074-1089.
     DURDÍK, Hussitisches Heerwesen, pp. 200-201.

An Infantry melee during the Hussite Wars
(from Eberhard Windecke's
"Geschichte Kaiser Sigismunds")

to the apostolic life, i.e., refrain from greed and luxuries as well as simony. They also appealed the common people for piety, e.g., in that they forbid excessive drinking in inns and on holidays, wearing of expensive and fanciful clothing. These decisions formed the foundation for the Four Articles of Prague that were issued shortly thereafter, on 3 July. They demanded free sermons, recognition of the Communion with the chalice, the abolition of Church rule and freedom from unjust worldly rule.[156]

On 12 June, the crusader army appeared before Prague and established its camp in the *Tiergarten* hunting preserve. Contemporary chroniclers give the number in the Crusader army as between 100,000 and 200,000 men; actually the strength would have only slightly exceeded 50,000 men. Nevertheless, the crusader army was so large that some Bohemian cities and towns submitted to the King without any resistance. Only the people of Prague, Tabor, Žatec (Saaz), Louny (Laun), Slaný (Schlan), Pisek, Klatovy (Klatauer), as well as a part of the nobles and the peasantry were willing to defend Prague. Sigismund again hesitated to employ his heavy artillery against that city that his father had cultivated to be one of Europe's most shimmering metropolises. The longer the Hussites could

hold the capital, the more the size of the crusader army became a burden, because such a powerful army was only very difficult to support for a longer duration.[157]

A letter from the city of Nuremberg (Nürnberg) informed the councilmen of the city of Ulm that the King *"had camped with great forces before Prague, here this side by the Tiergarten, and those of the Hussites captured by the army, his Grace had burned and the Duke of Austria and von Rosenberg should lie with a great force before Tabor. So our lord the King prepared guns and wants to storm the court of the Duke of Saxony and desires also to settle folk in the town."*[158]

In the meantime, Ulrich von Rosenberg's forces besieged Tabor. He also received levies from Leopold von Krayg and Heinrich von Puchberg. Puchberg was personally asked by King Sigismund *"to ride to the noble Ulrich von Rosenberg, our dear loyal one and help him win and destroy Tabor on the Hradyssczko."*[159] Interestingly the "dear loyal one" (*"liebe Getreue"*) Ulrich von Rosenberg himself was an Utraquist Hussite.

Meanwhile, Duke Albrecht assembled another 4,000 knights and men-at-arms in Austrian Freistadt who were to join the besieging army in July. However, Albrecht moved with the bulk of his army directly to Prague. When Žižka, in Prague, learned of the situation threating Tabor, he sent out 350 horsemen under Mikuláš of Hus, possibly the Hussites' entire mounted forces in Prague, who should come to the aid on the besieged. Mikuláš of Hus departed on 25 June, broke through the siege ring and appeared at Tabor on the 30th. A messenger snuck through to the besieged. When Mikuláš of Hus attacked the crusaders' camp, the town's garrison started a sortie and scored a complete victory over Rosenberg's forces. Mikuláš of Hus' forces and the captured military equipment considerably strengthened Tabor's garrison.[160]

156 PALACKÝ, Der Hussitenkrieg 1419-1431, pp. 115-116, 134-138; PALACKÝ, Urkundliche Beiträge I, Nr. 33, p. 33.

157 PALACKÝ, Der Hussitenkrieg 1419-1431, pp. 109-111; ŠMAHEL, Hussitische Revolution II, p. 1092 ŠMAHEL Šmahel estimates the crusader army's strength at only 30,000 men; SEIBT, Vom Vítkov bis zum Vyšehrad, pp. 188-190.

158 Quoted from PALACKÝ, Urkundliche Beiträge I, Nr. 36, p. 38, in MHG, *"mit grosser macht für Prag hie disseit beym tyergarten gelegert hab, vnd was der Hussen in das her gefangen werden, die lass sein Gnade alle prennen, vnd der Herre von Österreich wer dennoch nicht komen, doch were man sein im her wartend, sunder der Herre von Österreich vnd der von Rosenberg mit Im sullen mit grosser macht liegen vor eim thabor bei awsk. So lass unser Herre die Kunig die puchsen zubereyten, und well des Herczogen von Sachsen hof stürmen, vnd well auch volk in die kleinen stat legen."*

159 Quoted from PALACKÝ, Urkundliche Beiträge I, Nr. 30, p. 32, in MHG, *"zu dem Edeln Vlrichen von Rozemberg, vnsern lieben getrüen reiten vnd Im den Thabor auf dem Hradyssczko zu gewinnen vnd zu stören helffen."*

160 STÖLLER, Österreich im Kriege gegen die Hussiten, pp. 8-9; PALACKÝ, Der Hussitenkrieg 1419-1431, pp. 118-120; ŠMAHEL, Hussitische Revolution II, pp. 1089-1091; DURDÍK, Hussitisches Heerwesen, pp. 171-173.

Emperor Sigismund besieges a Bohemian Town.
This is one of the few depictions in the *"Geschichte Kaiser Sigismunds,"*
(Kaiser Sigismund's History) that shows the use of a trebuchet-catapult.

On the same day, Sigismund received another serious blow. In eastern Bohemia, Alesch Wrzesstiowsky von Riesenburg had called a popular assembly. After a large crowd of peasants had come together and participated in a Hussite priest's sermon, this group succeeded in capturing the town of Hradec Králové (Königgrätz) that same evening. When Sigismund learned about it in Prague, he immediately dispatched a large contingent from the crusader army to the town but which immediately turned around when they saw its strong and well-manned walls.[161]

Meanwhile, the King was forced to hurry more and more. A large army like his could not be kept together very long. On 12 June, he had a reasonable success when he was able to get reinforcements and fresh provisions to the Hradschin's hard-pressed garrison.[162]

The attempt to reach a peaceful solution failed again because the Papal Legate Ferdinand of Lucca refused to hear the Hussite demands. Therefore, on 13 July the crusaders crossed over to the eastern bank of the Moldau and prepared for their attack on the Vitkov Hill (Veitsberg). They feigned an attack on the *Spitalsfeld* or *Spittelfeld (field of the hospital)*. When the Prague defenders let themselves be provoked into a counterattack, they suffered heavy losses on the open field. The crusaders subsequently withdrew from the battlefield in good order.[163]

On 14 July, the Meissen and Silesian heavy cavalry began their attack, allegedly under the personal command of Friedrich von Meissen. The fortifications on Vítkov Hill were only lightly defended (although some sources spoke of only 30 to 60 men and women, which is probably too low). Initially the Meisseners were able to capture the southern wooden tower. However, the attempt to storm the wall made of sod failed. The Meisseners were could not bring their superior numbers to bear on the Vitkov Hill's narrow ridge. Žižka personally led the defense.[164]

Finally, a counterattack launched from the city was decisive. Several hundred Hussites, led by a priest, stormed out of the *Bergtor* (Mountain Gate) and attacked the flank of the already exhausted Meisseners. Panic broke out among the knights. They streamed back and some of them were driven back to the steep cliff of the Vitkov Hill by the pursuing Prazans and plummeted. The chronicler Laurentius reported: "*And when the enemy had seen the Sacrament and heard the tolling of the small bell as well as the loud shouts of the people, they turned around overpowered by rising fear, in that they hurried away from there, and tried to pass one another in their fleeing. Because they ran in such haste, they could not stop and many fell from the high cliff and broke their necks, and many were killed by the pursuers.*"[165] The battle was also decided because the Hussites repulsed the attack by the crusaders from the Hradschin and the Vyšehrad to relieve the Vítkov Hill castle. Then numbers of the crusaders' losses vary as well. Some sources talk about 500 men; Laurentius speaks of 300, other of 144 or just seventy. Considering the very small number of defenders, the estimates seem legitimate. The bulk of the knights probably died during their disorganized flight. The number of dead was ultimately very small when considering the crusaders' great strength, but the defeat appeared to have broken their morale. After these setbacks, the crusaders withdrew from Prague and the army just dissolved.[166]

However Sigismund did not want to wait to be crowned King of Bohemia. On 28 July, the act was done festively in the Hradschin castle. Shortly thereafter, on 2 August, the Luxembourgoise king left the rebellious city. As the crusaders departed the city, they took King Wenzel's treasure and much of the Church's gold and silver with them. Sigismund had important works of art melted down in order to pay his troops, but was forced to dismiss the bulk of his mercenaries a little later.[167]

The Hussites, unified and inspired by their victory, agreed on the adoption of the Four Articles of Prague. Sigismund for the time being withdrew his forces to Kutná Hora. Žižka also marched to the south with his army. He joined with Oldřich II. z Hradce (German: *Ulrich von Neuhaus*), a South Bohemian nobleman. They captured the fortified town of Lomnice (*Lomnitz*) and then marched to Nová Bystřice (*Neubistritz*) that belonged to Oldřich's neighbor Leopold von Krayg. It is possible that during this action, the first Hussite forces also marched into Lower Austria.[168]

161 PALACKÝ, Der Hussitenkrieg 1419-1431, pp. 120-121. Palacký estimates the strength of the army that Sigismund sent to Hradec Králové (Königgrätz) at 10,000 men, but cites no documentary sources.

162 PALACKÝ, Der Hussitenkrieg 1419-1431, pp. 122-123; VERNEY, Warrior of God, pp. 71-72.

163 PALACKÝ, Der Hussitenkrieg 1419-1431, pp. 127-129; ŠMAHEL, Hussitische Revolution II, pp. 1093-1094; DURDÍK, Hussitisches Heerwesen, p. 201.

164 DURDÍK, Hussitisches Heerwesen, p p. 201-203; ŠMAHEL, Hussitische Revolution II, p. 1094; VERNEY, Warrior of God, pp. 76-78; SEIBT, Vom Vítkov bis zum Vyšehrad, pp. 185-187.

165 Quoted in Laurentius-Chronik, p. 105, in modern German, *"Und als die Feinde das Sakrament erblickt und den Klang des Glöckchens sowie das laute Geschrei des Volkes gehört hatten, machten sie, von aufkommender Angst überwältigt, kehrt, indem sie schnell davoneilten und einer den anderen im Lauf zu überholen suchte. Da sie in solchem Sturmlauf sich nicht halten konnten, stürzten viele vom hohen Felsen herab und brachen sich das Genick, und sehr viele wurden durch die Verfolger getötet."*

166 PALACKÝ, Der Hussitenkrieg 1419-1431, pp. 131-133; ŠMAHEL, Hussitische Revolution II,, p. 1094; DURDÍK, Hussitisches Heerwesen, pp. 205-206; VERNEY, Warrior of God, pp. 79-81; SEIBT, pp. 187-196.

167 PALACKÝ, Der Hussitenkrieg 1419-1431, pp. 142-148; ŠMAHEL, Hussitische Revolution II, pp. 1094-1102; STÖLLER, Österreich im Kriege gegen die Hussiten, pp. 9-10; BLEICHER, Das Herzogtum Niederbayern, p. 94.

168 PALACKÝ, Der Hussitenkrieg 1419-1431, pp. 148-149; STÖLLER, Österreich im Kriege gegen die Hussiten, p. 10.

Sigismund besieges Prague. Depiction from the *"Geschichte Kaiser Sigismunds"*.

Afterwards, Žižka turned his attention to Ulrich von Rosenberg. In October, the Hussites besieged the Klein Bor Castle and in the end set it ablaze. But when a relief force of various South Bohemian nobles approached, Žižka's forces had to retreat. Hard pressed, they lost a few hundred men. Yet when the army had returned to České Budějovice (Budweis), Žižka invaded the Rosenberg's territories again. Rosenberg went to and pleaded with King Sigismund, who however could not provide him any help at the time. In November the Taborites appeared before the fortified town of Prachatice. Žižka's demand that the town surrender was rejected so he had the town stormed. The Hussites carried out a real bloodbath on the population. A little later, the strategically important castles of Pribenice and Divis fell into the Hussites' hands. As a result, Rosenberg had to agree to a ceasefire that was supposed to last until 4 February 1421.[169]

Then Žižka's Taborites rejoined the Prague levies and moved to West Bohemia, where Sigismund wanted to have his army support Pilsen, a city which the Hussites would fiercely oppose in the coming years. Yet in the face of the Hussites' unified strength, the King began to withdraw to Znojmo (Znaim) from where he hoped to strengthen his alliance with the Duke of Austria.[170]

The Hussite movement had also spread to the Margraveship of Moravia. The picture was like in Bohemia. The Church, the towns and parts of the nobility remained true to the king; the peasants, the artisans and other parts of the nobility supported the movement. Following with example of Tábor, the Hussites founded a fortified camp on a marshy island in the Bečva River before the Hungarian town of Ostra.[171]

From there they devastated the surrounding countryside. After they destroyed the Welehrad Monastery and burned its precious library, the Bishop of Olomouc (Olmütz) and some local barons asked the Duke of Austria for military assistance. In the spring, the first attempt to capture the island failed with heavy losses.[172]

In contrast, the situation on the Vyšehrad worsened appreciably. After the king's garrison had carried out a few successful sorties against the Prazans, Sigismund assumed that they could hold out for a while without his help. The beginning of October, a delegation of noblemen from the Hradec Králové region arrived and offered to take up negotiations with the Prazans on his behalf. Sigismund wanted to make this contingent upon them giving up the siege whereupon the Prazans offered to entrust the castle to the noble from Hradec Králové during the negotiations. Incensed, Sigismund is said to have yelled: "*I would rather shit on their noses than leave the Vyšehrad. I would rather these peasant louts disappear from Hradec Králové that they deceitfully brought [this situation] upon themselves!*"[173] Indeed because the garrison's supplies were exhausted and the hoped-for relief by the King did not occur, the castle capitulated on 1 November 1420 at 8 o'clock in the morning.

Shortly thereafter the King's relief army appeared before the city's gates. Sigismund, who was on a nearby hill, gave the signal to the shut-in garrison to make a sortie to take the besiegers in a pincer movement. Some of the German mercenaries did want to obey the order, but their officers thought their honor had been attacked and so they felt obligated to keep their word. When the attack did not happen, the Bohemian and Moravian nobles tried to convince Sigismund of the senselessness of an attack and to withdraw his forces. Additionally, an attack on the Hussite positions with their moats and strong walls had little chance of success. Sigismund was furious and showered his retainers with insults and that way provoked them to attack. The Hungarian and German units were supposed to make a frontal attack on the enemy camp while the Bohemians and Moravians were to advance through a swampy low-lying area on the left flank. His cavalry actually was able to break into the enemy camp. But the skilled Hussite commander, Hynek Kušina, brought up the Orebitie units as reinforcements. The Prazans also took part in the counterattack with renewed courage and pushed the royalists out of their camp. When the King saw that the Germans and Hungarians were beginning to give ground, he gave the order to retreat. A simultaneous attack to relieve the Hradschin's garrison was also repulsed.[174]

The Spread of the Hussites in Bohemia

After the Vyšehrad's capture, Prague temporarily developed into the movement's center. In those weeks, the Taborites initially passed up claiming its leadership role. On 5 November 1420, the Prague Hussites composed an aggressive letter to the country in which they threatened war and destruction on anyone who opposed the Prague cause.[175]

Although the Prague Hussitism was a completely unique, difficult to grasp form of the confession in which the Bohemian metropol's cultural and social characteristics played an important role, the city was very friendly toward Taboritism at that time. From that perspective,

169 PALACKÝ, Urkundliche Beiträge I, Nr. 48, p. 50;
   PALACKÝ, Der Hussitenkrieg 1419-1431, pp. 166-174;
   ŠMAHEL, Hussitische Revolution II, pp. 1127-1131;
   STÖLLER, Österreich im Kriege gegen die Hussiten, pp. 10-11;
   VERNEY, Warrior of God, pp. 91-95.

170 STÖLLER, Österreich im Kriege gegen die Hussiten, p. 12.

171 PALACKÝ, Der Hussitenkrieg 1419-1431, pp. 212-213;
   STÖLLER, Österreich im Kriege gegen die Hussiten, p. 12

172 PALACKÝ, Der Hussitenkrieg 1419-1431, pp. 213-214;
   STÖLLER, Österreich im Kriege gegen die Hussiten, p. 12.

173 "*Ich scheiße ihnen eher auf die Schnauze, als daß ich vom Vyšehrad weiche. Diese Bauernlümmel sollen mit lieber aus Königgrätz verschwinden, das sie arglistig an sich gebracht haben!*" quoted from ŠMAHEL, Hussitische Revolution II, p. 1118.

174 Ibid., pp. 1120-1121.

175 PALACKÝ, Der Hussitenkrieg 1419-1431, pp. 175-180.

it's hardly a wonder that the former Premonstratensian[176] monk Jan Želivský took over a new religious-political leadership position. Throughout his lifetime, Jan Želivský was always able to find a compromise in the tense relations between the Utraquists and the Taborites. Only through him could all the parties in Prague see it not just as the country's capital but as the movement's center.[177]

But even Želivský could not prevent the tensions between the Utraquists and Taborites from escalating violently. As a result, in November 1420 the Prazans initially forced Mikuláš z Husi and eventually all the Taborite minded priests out of the council assembly. The first armed clashes between the two groups resulted in Žižka cutting short his campaign in southern Bohemia and returning to Prague where a ceasefire between the quarrelling parties was worked out on 10 December. During a council session, which was supposed to resolve the theological differences for good, Procopius of Plzeň (Pilsen), the University's rector posed new charges against the Taborites. They had in the meantime adopted an increasingly radical position, not only on religious but also on political issues. They demanded Bohemia be a republic, the abolition of any class differences, the abolition of "special" (private) property, the destruction of all churches that were dedicated to the honor of saints and not God, and the abolition of the belief in purgatory. These demands seemed so radical that some of the moderate Utraquist Hussites actually branded them as heretical. No agreement about the dispute could be reached during the first council meeting. Mikuláš z Husi, who had left the city in a fit of anger, fell from his horse just before the city's gates. He was brought back to Prague, where he died before the end of the year.[178]

The Prague Hussites reaped an important religious-political success as a result of his death. On 21 April 1421 the Archbishop of Prague, Conrad of Vechta (Czech: Konrád z Vechty; German: Konrad von Vechta) declared his belief in Hussitism, accepted the Four Articles of Prague, and declared that he would not acknowledge Sigismund as the legitimate Bohemian king. Konrad was the highest ranking Church official so far to take this step.[179]

It was possibly due to Conrad's change of mind that on 27 May 1421, Sigismund was moved to declare that he was ready to negotiate about the Four Articles of Prague so long as Hussites did not question his being king.[180]

In the first months of 1421, the Hussites gained a series of small but important successes in the east and north of Bohemia. During those weeks, Sigismund was remaining in Litoměřice (Leitmeritz) and Most (Brüx) in order to prepare for a new campaign along with the Electoral Prince of Brandenburg and the Margraves of Meissen. Over the turn of the year 1420-1421, the Prague levy was able to capture the fortified Kunratic palace. At the same time, Jan Žižka was operating in Plzeň's lands. There the Taborites occupied the Chotisov (Chotesau) Monastery, the town of Kladruby (Kladrau), the Švamberk (Schwamberg) Castle and finally besieged the town of Tachov (Tachau), all in a rapid succession.[181]

Sigismund hurried to Plzeň to relieve the city and raised a new army for which he had to request massive support from the southern German princes. In the meanwhile, fire had broken out in the suburbs of Tachov in which not only dozens of Hussite war wagons were destroyed, but also many horses died. Because Žižka now felt too weak to attempt an attack, he withdrew from the town. He placed a part of his army in the occupied cities, castles and monasteries, took the bulk of his forces back to Tabor in order to strengthen the Taborite field army, and to ask the Prazans for help. Meanwhile Sigismund tried to take back the town of Stříbro (Mies) and the Kladruby Monastery but was unsuccessful.[182]

The Prazans responded to Žižka's request for help and sent him a 7,000 man strong army with 320 wagons that joined with the Taborites in mid-February at Dobříč (Dobritsch). As both armies were uniting, King Sigismund left the Plzeň area and moved to Litoměřice from whence at the end of February he moved further to Hungary. The Hussite army got busy with besieging Plzeň. After their cannon had heavily damaged the city walls in many places, the Pilseners agreed to negotiations that led to a ceasefire valid until 1422. In the agreement, the city council committed to ask the King to accept the Prague Articles. During the ceasefire the citizens repaired the city walls and strengthened them appreciably.[183] The West Bohemian nobles' resistance against the Hussites in the so-called "*Pilsener Landfrieden*" ("General Peace of Plzeň") ensured above all the Empire's Franconian and Bavarian areas had better protection from Hussite encroachments.[184]

---

176 The Order of Canons Regular of Prémontré, also known as the Premonstratensians, the Norbertines and, in Britain and Ireland, as the White Canons (from the colour of their habit), are a religious order of Canons regular of the Catholic Church founded in Prémontré near Laon in 1120 by Norbert of Xanten, who later became Archbishop of Magdeburg. Source: https://en.wikipedia.org/wiki/Premonstratensians.

177 PALACKÝ, Der Hussitenkrieg 1419-1431, pp. 183-185.

178 PALACKÝ, Der Hussitenkrieg 1419-1431, pp. 189-197; VERNEY, Warrior of God, pp. 102-106.

179 PALACKÝ, Urkundliche Beiträge I, Nr. 78, pp. 78-81, Nr. 80, pp. 83-84; SEIBT, Konrad von Vechta, pp. 246-249.

---

180 PALACKÝ, Urkundliche Beiträge I, Nr. 107, p. 105.

181 PALACKÝ, Der Hussitenkrieg 1419-1431, pp. 199-202; ŠMAHEL, Hussitische Revolution II, pp. 1159-1165; VERNEY, Warrior of God, pp. 107-109.

182 PALACKÝ, Der Hussitenkrieg 1419-1431, p. 202; VERNEY, Warrior of God, pp. 109-110.

183 PALACKÝ, Der Hussitenkrieg 1419-1431, pp. 203-204.

184 BLEICHER, Das Herzogtum Niederbayern, p. 196.

The Hussites advanced further into the Žatec (Saaz) area and hemmed in the still heavily German influenced town of Chomutov (Komotau). The town was stormed and fell after two days on 16 March 1421. The Hussites, who had been insulted before by the defenders, carried out a veritable bloodbath and were said to have only spared a few women and children as well as 30 men. Fifteen hundred to 2,500 people were murdered and then the town was put to the torch.[185]

Chomutov's fate had such a frightening effect on the region's population that afterward the people voluntarily opened their gates to the Hussites. Louny and Žatec offered them no resistance. Jan Žižka returned to Tabor in March, and the united armies continued to operate in the north of Bohemia.[186]

In the east of the country, the Hradec Králové Hussites suffered a serious defeat on 22 March. They had advanced with a levy against the Opatowiec Monastery. During their movement they were attacked by a royalist cavalry army at Podolschan and badly beaten losing 300 prisoners alone. This defeat led the united army, operating in the north, to march to the east to support the forces from Hradec Králové. On their march they captured Tussen on the Elbe (Lázně Toušeň) and Český Brod (Böhmisch-Brod). The few German mercenaries defending the town fled into a church that was then set ablaze by the attackers. The capture of Český Brod had the same horrifying effects as that of Chomutov a few weeks earlier. In a rapid succession, Kolín (Kolin), Nymburk (Nimburg), Kozlov (Koslau) and the Opatowiec Monastery as well as some castles and the Teutonic Order's Commandery (Deutschordenskommende) at Dobrowic opened their gates to the Hussites. Voluntarily surrendering did not always protect them from the Hussites' rage. The Opatowiec Monastery, which the Hussites hated, was burned down after surrendering. Of the East Bohemian towns, only Jaroměř (Jermer) remained in the King's possession.[187]

After the ceasefire expired in South Bohemia, the Hussites undertook to again capture České Budějovice. They became increasingly active in Moravia and threatened Znojmo whose burghers sent an urgent letter to Sigismund requesting military assistance. The Hussites even pushed into Lower Austria and destroyed the little town of Dobersberg.[188]

In Moravia the Taborites' and Prazans' combined army encircled the town of Jaroměř, which like Kutná Hora in Bohemia, was an important base loyal to the king. During the first attempt to storm the town on 13 May, the Hussites succeeded in occupying the moats around the town, so the defenders asked for safe conduct. They were guaranteed it, but two days later, as residents were leaving the Taborites fell upon many of Jaroměř's burghers, stabbed them to death or drowned them in the Elbe River. All the priests who did not recognize the Prague Articles were burned at the stake. Jaroměř subsequently remained a Hussite stronghold until the time of the Counterreformation.[189]

On 29 May when the town of Litoměřice and on 7 June when the garrison of the Hradschin in Prague surrendered to the Hussites, the movement had gained control over almost all of Bohemia except for a few towns and castles on its periphery.[190]

However, in 1421, the Taborites were having major problems with internal conflicts. Their most important military leaders, like Žižka, increasingly distanced themselves from their spiritual leader Martin Húska. He had laid out more and more radical beliefs and tried to introduce a classless community with common ownership of property in Tabor. As a result in April 1421 he was forced to leave Tabor with his followers. When he was called back to the town a little later, it only happened because they wanted to force him to denounce his theses. Húska refused. They took him prisoner, but he did not retract his teachings even under torture. On 21 August 1421, he was burned at the stake in Roudnice.[191]

The priest was accused of, among other things, being close to the Picards. This was a new faction of the Taborites, who rejected the chalice and the host and instead simply distributed common bread to the community at Mass. Besides other theological differences, it was above all this practice that contravened one of the Hussite basic principles and even got the Taborites to oppose this sect. The Picards were therefore persecuted by all the other Hussites and wiped out in the course of 1421. This most drastically impacted another sub-group, the Adamites. This group described themselves as the direct descendants of Adam and Eve and rejected all church-related forms of Christianity. Supposedly they went around their community mostly naked and celebrated sexual orgies outdoors. The rather puritanical Taborites even more violently disliked this promiscuity. Žižka sent out one of his captains, Borek Klatovsky, against the Adamite stronghold in the Nežárka River Valley. But the Taborites' first attacked was repulsed and Borek was killed. Finally Žižka himself had to go to the Nežárka Valley. Under his leadership the Taborites stormed the castle, which was located on an island in the river. Most of the Adamites died in the battle. Forty prisoners were later burned at the stake.[192]

185 PALACKÝ, Der Hussitenkrieg 1419-1431, pp. 205-206; BLEICHER, Das Herzogtum Niederbayern, p. 110; VERNEY, Warrior of God, pp. 111-112.

186 PALACKÝ, Der Hussitenkrieg 1419-1431, p. 206; VERNEY, Warrior of God, pp. 112-113.

187 PALACKÝ, Der Hussitenkrieg 1419-1431, pp. 207-209; ŠMAHEL, Hussitische Revolution II, pp. 1163-1165.

188 STÖLLER, Österreich im Kriege gegen die Hussiten, pp. 13-14.

189 PALACKÝ, Der Hussitenkrieg 1419-1431, pp. 215-216; ŠMAHEL, Hussitische Revolution II, pp. 1166-1167.

190 PALACKÝ, Der Hussitenkrieg 1419-1431, pp. 220-221.

191 PALACKÝ, Der Hussitenkrieg 1419-1431, pp. 211-240; ŠMAHEL, Hussitische Revolution II, pp. 1131-1158

192 VERNEY, Warrior of God, pp. 116-118.

This depiction from the *Jenaer Kodex* shows a classic cavalry battle between Hussites (left) and crusaders (right). A mounted crossbowman is among the Hussite horsemen. Noteworthy in the depiction is a crusader who has impaled a child on his lance.

Depiction of a War Wagon in Konrad Kyeser's "*Bellifortis*." The good equipment of the two footsoldiers riding along in almost full armor, including *Hundsgugel* helmets is interesting. The soldier on the right appears to carry a sort of war flail, the one on the left a war scythe. Note that Hussite war wagons did not use scythes on their sides, nor does this one correspond to their normal construction.

The Second Hussite Crusade

At the end of February 1421, a new Imperial Assembly (*Reichstag*) met in Nuremberg. The four Rhenish (Rhine region) electors, the Archbishops of Mainz, Trier and Cologne as well as the Count of the Palatine (*Pfalzgraf*) Ludwig, agreed with the King to also join him in the future in the fight against the Bohemian heretics. To do this, Ludwig and Konrad von Mainz even temporarily set aside their own territorial differences. Also the remaining high officials of the Empire who arrived in Nuremberg a little later, the Margraves of Meissen and Baden, the Landgrave (*Landgraf*) of Hessen and the Bishops of Wurzburg and Speyer voiced their support. On 13 April the new papal legate, Cardinal Branda de Castiglione appeared before the Princes' College (*Fürstenkolleg*). He had Pope Martin V's authority to grant absolution to all participants in the crusade. He vehemently called on the Electors to support the impending war.

In the summer of 1421 the Empire's forces assembled around Cheb (Eger). Some contemporaries estimated the force's strength at 100,000 horsemen; others spoke of 200,000 men, both horsemen and footsoldiers. The Empire was indeed theoretically fully capable of standing up such an army, yet these estimates seem doubtful. But so many princes never had been so unified, that they could really allow their military capabilities to be completely exhausted.[193] There is also the question of whether Sigismund would have been able to supply such a large army in a relatively thinly populated land like Bohemia. Consider that Friedrich II ran up against the limits of being able to supply considerably smaller armies in the Second Silesian War or in the War of Bavarian Succession.

In a letter written on 22 September 1421, a German who took part in the war, wrote, *"I also know that the heralds estimate that among the knights, we have about four thousand knights and squires."*[194] If one calculates the footsoldiers, based on the *"Nürnberger Anschlag"* of 1422,[195] at five to six men per horseman, then it would reduce the size of the levy for the Second Crusade to a more realistic 30,000 men,[196] still a quite imposing army. This army consisted primarily of contingents from the four Rhenish Electors of Cologne, Mainz, Trier and the

Kurpfalz. In addition there was another army that Sigismund himself wanted to lead from Hungary, as well as Duke Albrecht of Austria's levy.[197]

On 5 August, Frederick the Warlike (Friedrich der Streitbare), Margrave of Meissen, was already able to bring a small Hussite army to battle near Most (Brüx). A Prague detachment under the radical Jan Želivský had erected a *Wagenburg* there at the village of Saras from where they launched actions that ravaged the surrounding countryside and attacked the castle at Most. But the town was well fortified and had modern cannon for its defense, the powder for which Frederick the Warlike had loaned them *"in our great hardships and needs against the Taborites, Wycleffists and Hussites, our most profound enemies, who are camped before our town and who want to conquer us with force."*[198] The arrival of the army from Meissen initially surprised the Hussites. When the Meisseners approached the town from the north on 5 August, the Prazans however moved confidently against them along the flank of a ridge. In what appeared to be a favorable moment, they attacked the knights on an open field. This proved to be a grave mistake. The Meisseners were fresh and rested and held their formation, so that the Hussite attack petered out. When the Most Castle's garrison also risked a sortie and hit the Prazans in their flank, their ranks began to waver. The Hussites fell back, with the Meisseners in close pursuit. Then the knights came under fire from the Hussite guns, but it did not have the desired effect this time. The Meisseners pushed further forward, which unleashed panic among the Prazans. They abandoned their cannon and the *Wagenburg* and fled up along the Elbe. For Želivský, this defeat was not only a military setback, but it also undermined his political position.[199]

On 28 August the Rhenish forces moved down the Cheb Valley (Egertal) reaping destruction. Amazingly even the German sources reported the merciless actions of the army's commanders: *"So we inform Your Excellency that a good friend has passed the message and written, and according to his opinion, that our gracious lords, ... the Electors, planned to move on next Whitsuntide [28 Aug.] to Eger [Cheb] and they intended to come together next Sunday [31 Aug.] on the other side of the forest to confer there and to take care of the matter. Additionally our lords, the Electors, have publicly announced in Eger's market square that one should kill anyone in Bohemia, except*

193 PALACKÝ, Der Hussitenkrieg 1419-1431, pp. 241-244, 251-252; Sachsen und die Hussitenkriege, p. 3.

194 In Middle High German (MHG), *"wisse ouch, das die herolt uberslagent habend, daz wir von ritterschaft bi den viertausend ritteren und knechten habent."* Quoted in KROCKER, Sachsen und die Hussitenkriege, pp. 3-4.

195 The *"Nürnberger Anschlag von 1422,"* literally the "Nuremberg Posting of 1422," was one of two such documents issued by the Empire to the Electors, which in this case laid out requirments for personnel and equipment for the military levies, among other instructions. Source: LIPOWSKY, Felix Josef, Uebersicht der deutschen Geschichte: zweite Band (vol. 2) (MUNICH: Joseph Lentner, 1794), p. 122.

196 KROCKER, Sachsen und die Hussitenkriege, p. 4.

197 STÖLLER, Österreich im Kriege gegen die Hussiten, p. 14.

198 In MHG, *"in unsern groszen beswerungen und noten wider dy Thyborn, Wicleffen und Hussen, unsere swere finde, die vor uns und unser stat gelegen sint und uns mit machte haben wollen uberhoupt gewinnen."* Quoted in CDS 1 B 4, Nr. 177, p. .

199 PALACKÝ, Der Hussitenkrieg 1419-1431, pp. 246-249, 279-288; ŠMAHEL, Hussitische Revolution II, pp. 1200-1203; MEINHARDT, Im Dienste des Königs, p. 117; KROCKER, Sachsen und die Hussitenkriege, p. 5; PURTON, Late Medieval Siege, p. 236.

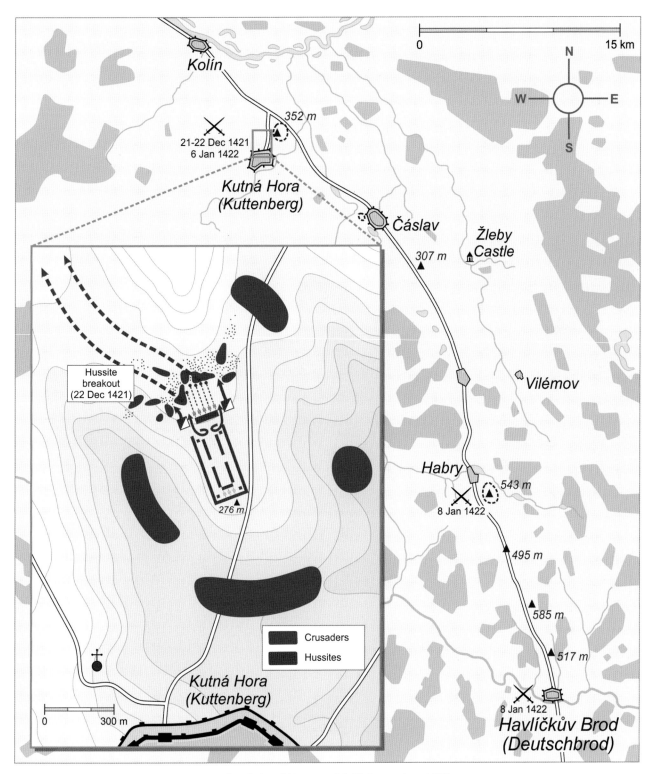

Battle of Kutná Hora on 21-22 December 1421

Next double page:

This picture from the *"Kriegsbuch" by* Johannes Hartlieb is one of the most detailed depictions of a battle during the Hussite Wars. A *Wagenburg* is shown on the right side. The wagon wheels are chained to one another so the wagons cannot be pulled apart. Between the wheels' axils are large wooden planks so that no one can crawl under the wagons. The wagon's crew consists of crossbowmen and hand-gunners as well as flail-men. The man in center of the right front wagon is throwing a stone. The footsoldiers in the left front wagon show a lot of details, e.g., one spanning a crossbow with his foot as well as many types of helmets. The frequent depiction of chainmail shirts is also noteworthy. The infantry unit on the hill is gathered around a large bombard. Among the horsemen in the background are also some armed with crossbows. The typical Hussite symbols are recognizable on the flag and tent: the goose and the chalice.

Auß geleſen hervolk mag ſich in wol geriſten wagen alſo
we ſlieſſen vnd vergraben vnd groſ vortſaul haben vor allem
gewalt

for children, who do not have their reason [sense, i.e., the right religious belief] and that one also should not bring along any women in the army." [200]

At the same time the forces of Meissen marched over the Erz Mountains and captured Chomutov (Komotau) and Kadaň (Kaden). Chomutov's Hussite garrison set fire to the city and retreated to Žatec (Saatz). They awaited support from more forces from Silesia and the Lusatian League (German: *Lausitzer Sechsstädten*, literally *Lausitz Six Cities*) in the northeast, as well as from Sigismund in the south. [201]

At the beginning of September the army from the Rhine region captured the village of Mašťov (Maschau), where the troops committed terrible excesses, as the Nuremberger observer mentioned above reported: *"The captain of the castle and eight with him remained alive and were the princes' prisoners; the others were despicably clubbed to death and burned, eighty-four were hung with rope; later they found a pastor and three in the house whom they threw over the wall and they were also burned. Furthermore the common people who ran out, who can (sic) (could) not speak German or appeared to be Bohemian, was captured, killed and burned."* [202]

After that success, the army advanced to the fortified town of Žatec where the advance came to a halt. The citizens of the town withstood six assault attempts. Eyewitnesses reported that every day 100 to 150 of the crusader army's soldiers died from the town's cannon's fire. The number may be exaggerated, but it illustrates the impression that the employment of Hussite artillery left. The supply situation for both sides worsened rapidly because raiding parties preferred to burn grain stores to prevent them falling into enemy hands rather then securing them for their own supporters. [203]

After the capture of Kadaň, the Meisseners under the personal leadership of the Margrave had proceeded in the direction of the Elbe and attempted to capture the castle of Bílina (Bilin) and the town of Litoměřice. On 13 September, two army elements from Prague consisting of mercenaries and rapidly raised rural levies appeared before Bílina. Thereupon the Meisseners quit the siege and withdrew to join the main army at Žatec. [204]

At this point the Taborite army under Jan Žižka besieged the mighty Castle Rabí for a second time. The old commander personally participated in storming the walls and during the action he was struck in his healthy eye by an arrow. Despite all the efforts of the best doctors in Prague, Žižka now became completely blind. [205]

Žižka, who had somewhat recovered from his wound and worried about the advance of the Meisseners, stood up against the crusader army, which was still tied up with the siege of Žatec. However there, the princely leaders were arguing. Frederick the Warlike was pressing to quit the town, which was putting up stiff resistance, and to move on to Prague, which the Elector of the Palatine however could not reconcile with his idea of honor. But the residents of Žatec were not considering surrendering the town. The crusaders' losses increased so much that the commanders finally decided to simply starve out the town and to pillage the surrounding countryside. The army was crumbling; more knights and men-at-arms were going home every day. Finally it was so weakened that when news of Jan Žižka's advance was received, the Palatine forces also pleaded for an immediate withdrawal. When the crusader army burned its camp, Žatec's garrison made a sortie. The Hussites were able to capture many guns, crossbows and other war materiel as well as several hundred prisoners. [206]

On the other hand, in the south, Sigismund and Duke Albrecht were now just marching out with their armies. The King first advanced to Olomouc and by November had brought the most part of Moravia under his control again. Yet Duke Albrecht did not push into Moravia with a powerful army until 20 October. He then relieved the threatened town of Znojmo and captured the town of Jaspitz that lay to its north. Subsequently he took the castle belonging to Sezima of Kunštát, the Hussite nobleman who had

---

200 In MHG *"Also lassen wir ewr weisheit wissen, daz vns ein vnser guter frewnde botschaft getan vnd verschriben hat auf sölich meynung, daz vnser gnedig herren … die Kurfürsten haben sich am nehstuergangen pfintztag (28 Aug.) zu Eger erhaben zu ziehen vnd sie meynten als am nehstuergangen sunntag (31 Aug.) yenseit walds zu einander zu komen, sich da zu vnterreden vnd all sache für hand zu nehmen. Item vnser Herren .. die kurfürsten haben einen offen markt zu Eger rüffen lassen, vnd daz man im lant zu Beheim meniklich tot stahen sülle awszgenomen kinder, die ir vernunft nit haben, vnd daz man auch kein frawn in dem her mitfüren noch ziehen lasen solle."* Quoted in PALACKÝ, Urkundliche Beiträge I, Nr. 134, p. 144.

201 The Lusatian League (German: *Oberlausitzer Sechsstädtebund*; Czech: *Šestiměstí*; Polish: *Związek Sześciu Miast*) was a historical alliance of six towns in the Bohemian (1346–1635), later Saxon (1635–1815) region of Upper Lusatia (German: Ober-Lausitz), that existed from 1346 until 1815. The member towns were Bautzen, Görlitz (Zhorjelc), Kamenz (Kamjenc), Lauban (Lubań), Löbau (Lubij) and Zittau (Žitawa). Five of the towns are located in present-day Germany, while former Lauban today belongs to Poland and is known as Lubań. Source: Wikipedia.

202 In MHG, *"Der hawbtman auf dem sloss vnd VIII mit Im beliben bey leben vnd seyn der fürsten gefangen, die andern wurden yemerlich zu tod geslagen vnd verprant, der weren an einem sail LXXXIIII; ein pfaff vnd drey fund man dernach im haws, die wurff man vber die mawr awsz vnd wurden auch verprant. Item das fussvolk, daz da awszlawfft, was niht dewtsch kann oder einem Beheim gleich ist, das werde gefangen, zu tod geslagen vnd verprant."* Quoted in PALACKÝ, Urkundliche Beiträge I, Nr. 135, pp. 145-146.

---

203 KROCKER, Sachsen und die Hussitenkriege, p. 4; BLEICHER, Das Herzogtum Niederbayern, pp. 110-111..

204 PALACKÝ, Der Hussitenkrieg 1419-1431, p. 252.

205 PALACKÝ, Der Hussitenkrieg 1419-1431, p. 249; ŠMAHEL, Hussitische Revolution II, p. 1173.

206 PALACKÝ, Der Hussitenkrieg 1419-1431, pp. 249-254; KROCKER, Sachsen und die Hussitenkriege, p. 5; BLEICHER, Das Herzogtum Niederbayern, pp. 111-112.

led an attack on Lower Austria in the summer. Indeed, in November Albrecht had already returned with his army, and Sigismund stood with his army alone in Bohemia.[207]

Žižka and the Prazans decided to simply not let the crusaders advance to the capital but to halt them at Kutná Hora. The city had become an important supply base for Sigismund the previous year. It was the second largest city in Bohemia and its predominantly German population had not joined the Hussite movement. Additionally Kutná Hora had achieved a considerable degree of prosperity through silver mining. Also in the summer, Kutná Hora had conducted an unsuccessful campaign against Kolín. After the joint Prazan and Taborite army had begun its victorious operations through north and east Bohemia, the city did request it be spared and in April 1421 it surrendered to the Hussites. Peter Zrmzlik was named the city's senior provost, but died in August, whereupon Kutná Hora again escaped Prague's control. The Hussites occupied the city in mid-December. Because the city did not lend itself to defense, Žižka decided to deploy his forces on the close by Sukberg (Suk Mountain) after the arrival of the crusader army. The Hussites left the city amidst small skirmishes. Sigismund's army then surrounded the mountain on which the Hussites had formed a *Wagenburg*. The Hussites were afraid of the crusaders' large numbers - they may have even been 10,000 men and consisted of contingents from Hungary, Austria, Moravia and Olomouc.[208]

On 20 December the crusaders attempted their first attack on the enemy *Wagenburg*. But rather than sacrificing his cavalry in an attack on the *Wagenburg*, Sigismund drove a large cattle herd at the Hussites. While the field army's attention was focused on that for a time, the King's troops forced their way into the city. The Kutná Hora miners opened the city gates too willingly. Immediately after capturing Kutná Hora, a hunt began for those among the populace who were Hussite supporters that ended in another slaughter.[209]

The following night, Žižka decided to break out of the encirclement. He positioned several cannon on the narrow side of his camp, covered by infantry and flanked by the cavalry. In the early morning hours the cannon fired a near simultaneous salvo that caused great confusion among the sleeping crusaders. Immediately after that, the Hussite cavalry charged into the enemy camp and the chaos increased. Žižka exploited this event. He had his *Wagenburg* separate and drive down through the enemy camp during which the shooters kept up a constant fire. The breakthrough succeeded and the crusaders did not pursue their enemies further.[210]

Žižka retreated toward Kolín where he assembled more men. Sigismund on the other hand decided to put his forces into winter quarters south of Kutná Hora. His Italian commander, Pippo Spano, recommended that he withdraw from Bohemia because their mercenaries' morale had noticeably sunk after the defeat. Indeed Sigismund did not fear any further attacks by the Hussites.

Because there had been no pursuit, Žižka decided a little later to return and to attack Sigismund. On 6 January he attacked the king's forces that were scattered in camps at Kutná Hora and shattered them. The crusaders withdrew to Havlíčkův Brod (Deutschbrod). The Hussites went after them doggedly and attacked them again on 8 January. The Hungarians were badly defeated and streamed back over the Sazava River. Because those fleeing stalled at a narrow bridge, some knights tried to cross the frozen river. But due to the weight of the heavily armored knights, the ice broke in many places. The current was quickly filled with wagons, horses and men struggling for their lives. Many crusaders drowned or froze to death. In the following days the corpses of 548 knights were supposedly pulled from the icy river. The Hussites captured large amounts of war materiel, among other things, wagons and cannon.[211]

The Hussites immediately began besieging Havlíčkův Brod. The bombardment of the walls caused such heavy damage that the garrison wanted to surrender the day after the battle. At this point in time some of the Hussites had already gotten inside the town, which they pillaged and completely destroyed. The Hussites had a big celebration of their victory in this winter campaign. Many men were knighted outside Havlíčkův Brod. And Sigismund was so shocked at this renewed defeat that he did not set foot in Bohemia for many years and is said to have handed over the leadership of his armies to others.[212]

While Sigismund was fleeing from Žižka's victorious bands, Duke Albrecht had already assembled a new army in Eggenberg in early January. But because of the king's catastrophic defeat, at first he did not dare any further advances into Moravian territory. The Hussites finally advanced to Jamnitz on 10 March, which they besieged in vain. When a small Austrian relief army arrived to help its

207 PALACKÝ, Der Hussitenkrieg 1419-1431, pp. 263-164;
STÖLLER, Österreich im Kriege gegen die Hussiten, pp. 15-17.

208 VERNEY, Warrior of God, pp. 148-150.

209 PALACKÝ, Der Hussitenkrieg 1419-1431, pp. 265-269;
ŠMAHEL, Hussitische Revolution II, pp. 1229-1231;
DURDÍK, Hussitisches Heerwesen, pp. 206-207;
VERNEY, Warrior of God, p. 150.

210 PALACKÝ, Der Hussitenkrieg 1419-1431, pp. 269-271;
ŠMAHEL, Hussitische Revolution II, p. 1231;
DURDÍK, Hussitisches Heerwesen, pp. 207-209;
VERNEY, Warrior of God, p. 152.

211 PALACKÝ, Der Hussitenkrieg 1419-1431, pp. 271-273;
ŠMAHEL, Hussitische Revolution II, pp. 1231-1232;
DURDÍK, Hussitisches Heerwesen, pp. 211-212;
VERNEY, Warrior of God, pp. 153-155.

212 PALACKÝ, Der Hussitenkrieg 1419-1431, pp. 273-274;
ŠMAHEL, Hussitische Revolution II, pp. 11232-1233;
DURDÍK, Hussitisches Heerwesen, p. 212;
VERNEY, Warrior of God, pp. 156-157.

citizens, Žižka's troops even fled. Nonetheless, they were able to strengthen their position in Moravia again in the early part of 1422.[213]

In the meantime, decisive political changes were occurring in Prague. A growing opposition to Jan Želivský was developing centered around the charismatic priest Jakoubek ze Stříbra (German: Jakobellus von Mies) whose writings had created a theological foundation for the Hussites' armed struggle. On 7 March 1422 Jakoubek accused Želivský of a violent act and two days later had him executed in the Prague market square. However, the priest's beheading led to an uproar in the city. Želivský still had a strong following as before especially among the New Town's poor. His supporters moved through the city killing and looting and captured several councilmen. The Jewish Quarter was especially badly damaged although the Sons of Abraham had nothing to do with Želivský's death. During the subsequent new council elections, Želivský's supporters occupied most of the positions. But the party lacked a political leader. It was soon evident that it was Želivský who could get the moderate Prazans, the New Town's poor, as well as the Taborites and Orebites to cooperate. After his execution, the internal differences developed into open splits.

The Third Hussite Crusade

Due to the tense situation in southern Bohemia, King Sigismund saw himself as forced to make greater concessions to the Duke of Austria in order to retain him as an ally. Albrecht was named governor of Moravia and received expanded authorities over Brno and a number of other cities. The Duke received subsidies from the King's and the Pope's treasuries and additionally Sigismund had to keep 1,000 *Spieße* on Moravian soil. In early 1422, the Duke was actually able to achieve some successes in South Bohemia.[214]

At the same time, further signs of a split in the Hussite movement were beginning to appear in Bohemia. Because the Hussites had declared Sigismund's coronation as invalid, they sought rival candidates. The candidates should if possible also bring about international recognition of the movement, i.e., they should come from abroad. A first attempt to convince the Polish King Wladislaw Jagiello to accept the crown failed. Instead Wladislaw's brother, Vytautas (German: Witold), the Grand Prince of Lithuania sent his nephew Sigismund Korybut (Lithuanian: Žygimantas Kaributaitis) with an army to Prague in April. He was ready to accept Wenzel's crown. Korybut was supposed to function as the land's governor. He was able to initially unite the various quarreling movements. Even Žižka accepted his leadership. Wladislaw Jagiello had agreed to Korybut being sent there. He saw above all a

means to put pressure on Emperor Sigismund to cease his support for the Teutonic Order in Prussia. Vytautas did not go himself to Bohemia primarily because he feared a Papal ban. By sending a representative, he could deflect the political responsibility at any time.[215]

Yet Jan Žižka increasingly took an independent stance from a religious perspective. After Jan Želivskýs execution, Žižka distanced himself from both the Prazans and the Taborite priests. He took a position between the two parties, based on the religious-political motivated ideas that the East Bohemian Orebites supposedly supported. After Žižka's death, his supporters formed a separate religious party that differed from the Taborites, in among other things, that they venerated the saints as before, observed Lent, believed in the Transsubstantiation[216] and performed services in regalia. To do this, Žižka also rejected the difference in the classes. Despite this, the split between his followers and the Taborites became so marked in the course of 1422, that both religious groups then raised their own armies, and Žižka no longer commanded the Taborites himself.[217]

At first Korybut was able to hold these new groups together. That unity allowed the Hussites to become active again in South Bohemia and Moravia. They took back many towns and pushed forward as far as Austria where a number of border towns went up in flames.[218]

The Third Crusade that began in 1422 already had more the character of a relief action than a campaign of subjugation. The army assembled for it was supposed to relieve the royal castle of Karlštejn (Karlstein) north of Prague. King Sigismund tasked Friedrich I of Brandenburg with the command of an army that numbered about 4,000 knights and 30,000 footsoldiers.[219]

The efforts to raise this relief army however only progressed very slowly. For example, the Bishop of Wurzburg reported on 29 September 1422, *"that our lords, the Margraves of Meissen were not able to acquire many people, so we understand very well that they will not be strong*

---

213 STÖLLER, Österreich im Kriege gegen die Hussiten, pp. 18-19.

214 Ibid., p. 19. A *Spiess* or *Spieß*, meaning „spear was a tactical unit with approximately four members one of whom was a mounted knight or man-at-arms.

215 PALACKÝ, Urkundliche Beiträge I, Nr. 193, p. 210;
PALACKÝ, Der Hussitenkrieg 1419-1431, pp. 152-155, 185, 254-260, 301-312;
ŠMAHEL, Hussitische Revolution II, pp. 1234-1256;
STÖLLER, Österreich im Kriege gegen die Hussiten, pp. 19-20;
BEZOLD, Sigismund und die Reichskriege, pp. 65-67.

216 Transsubstantiation is (especially in the Roman Catholic Church) the conversion of the substance of the Eucharistic elements into the body and blood of Christ at consecration, only the appearances of bread and wine still remaining.

217 PALACKÝ, Der Hussitenkrieg 1419-1431, pp. 290-296.

218 PALACKÝ, Der Hussitenkrieg 1419-1431, pp. 300-320;
STÖLLER, Österreich im Kriege gegen die Hussiten, p. 20.

219 PALACKÝ, Der Hussitenkrieg 1419-1431, pp. 312-316; Sachsen und die Hussitenkriege,, p. 5. However, according to the "Nürnberger Anschlag" it numbered 5,910 horsemen and 37,400 fotsoldiers. Per STÖLLER, Österreich im Kriege gegen die Hussiten, pp. 20-21, Duke Albrecht of Austria also assembled a levy that however did not see action; BLEICHER, Das Herzogtum Niederbayern, pp. 123-127.

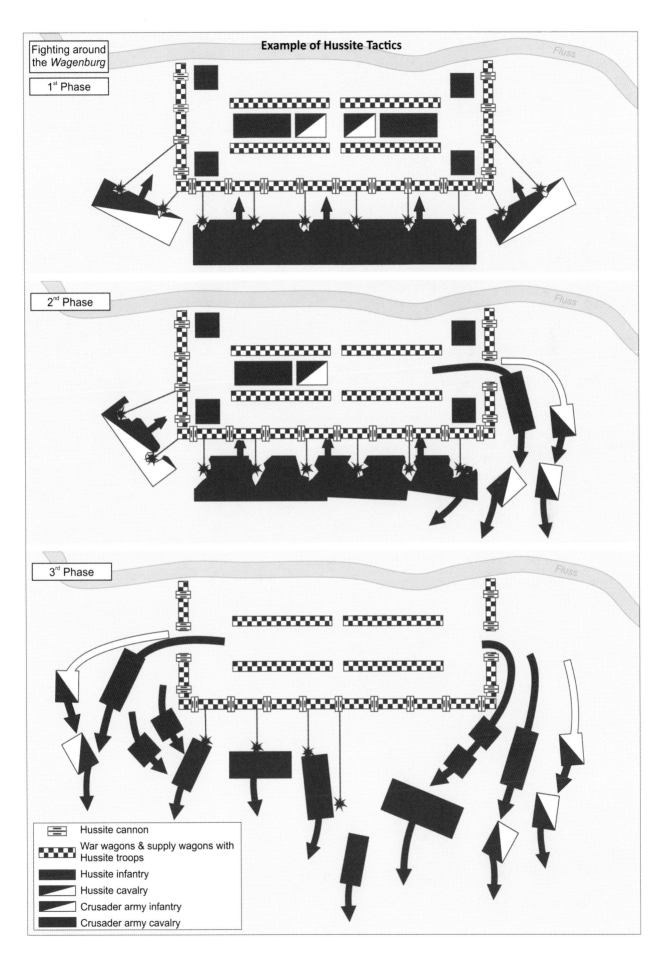

Example of Hussite Tactics

Fighting around the *Wagenburg*

1st Phase

2nd Phase

3rd Phase

Fluss

Legend:

Hussite cannon
War wagons & supply wagons with Hussite troops
Hussite infantry
Hussite cavalry
Crusader army infantry
Crusader army cavalry

in mounted men-at-arms, because they recruited no one this side of the forest, even though many of them would have happily ridden to them."[220] And on October second, the Bishop announced *"So they understand and saw in Nuremberg that this action will not go forward felicitously, that it would be better to turn around than to go in there."*[221] Friedrich notified the Margrave of Meissen, who was gathering his army in the Erz Mountains that he only had assembled about 1,700 horsemen at the beginning of October. The Margrave, a Wettiner,[222] responded, *"that our brother, our cousin and we will have three hundred Glefen and three hundred handgunners and what pertains to them, indeed three thousand horses. Also Hans von Polenz wrote to us that Hans von Biberstein should come along to the Lausitz with a hundred pikemen."*[223] A little later Friedrich the Warlike determined with great concern that he was just going to have to rely on himself alone. For example, in a letter of 9 October, Wilhelm II reported to Friedrich I of Brandenburg that the country could raise hardly more than forty armored men to go to the Lausitz.[224] It looked better with the Silesian princes and the Six City League (*Sechsstädtebund*). *"Also the Polish princes and the princes of Silesia and the Six Cities have not one and one half hundred armored men, but also wagons and foot [soldiers], one with the other, that it comes to four thousand men."*[225]

On 14 October, Friedrich von Brandenburg's army, which was considerably weaker than hoped for, marched into Bohemia. A day later he sent a messenger to the Karlštjen Castle's garrison to inform them *"We so want to spare neither bodies nor blood and sincerely come to your rescue with all our ability."*[226] But Friedrich knew his army was far too weak and a little later asked the Margrave of Meissen to hurry to his aid. The Brandenburger himself hurried to North Bohemia in order to confer with the Margrave [Wettiner] at Most on 20 October. Subsequently he went back toward Tachov to ask the West Bohemian nobles for support. Friedrich von Meissen remained in place with his forces, while Friedrich von Brandenburg marched eastward. Quarrelling seems to have broken out within the army, since the Bishops of Wurzburg and Bamberg went home with their vassals, the levy from Cheb had to be kept in place with force, while the Margrave of Meissen did not want to depart from Most. A serious plague had broken out in the Silesian and Lausitzer levies, which forced both of them to return home.[227]

In the meantime, the Hussites' efforts to bring about the fall of the Karlštejn Castle were endangered by internal disputes. While the Prazans' army of about 4-5,000 men and 200 horsemen was camped before the fortress, the Taborites' levy tried to capture the Hradschin. The surprise attack was however repulsed by the burghers. The unrest in the capital forced Sigismund Korybut to frequently leave the besieging troops at the Karlštejn order to shore up his shaky rule. He did not risk asking Žižka and the Taborites for military support. Korybut feared that by doing so he would become militarily dependent that would quickly also become a political dependency.[228]

The unsuccessful surprise attack however deepened the rift between the Prazans and the Taborites even further. They became even more radical under the leadership of Václav Koranda. While the Taborite army remained in the field, a series of synods took place in the southern Bohemian fortress in the course of 1422 that theologically distanced the brothers even further from the Utraquists. This radicalization eventually also alienated Jan Žižka, the Taborites' most important commander.[229]

While the crusader army was falling apart and many units had already marched out of Bohemia, the Karlštejn garrison and the Hussites came to an agreement on

---

220 In MHG, *"wie unsere heere die Marggraue von Missen nicht fil Volks gewynne, so versten wir auch sust wol, dasz sie von Reysigen zewge nicht seer stark werden, als sie dann hie disseyd waldes nymand geworben haben, wiewohl derselben viel gerne mit jn geritten weren."* Quoted from PALACKÝ, Urkundliche Beiträge I, Nr. 213, p. 239.

221 In MHG, *"So man vmb Nuremberg verstunde und sehe, dasz dis Zugk nit trefflich furgehen wurde, dasz dann besser were, man kerte in der Zyt hie awssen umb, denn dortynnen."* Quoted from PALACKÝ, Urkundliche Beiträge I, Nr. 214, p. 241.

222 „The House of Wettin (German: Haus Wettin) is a dynasty of German counts, dukes, prince-electors and kings that once ruled territories in the present-day German states of Saxony, Saxony-Anhalt and Thuringia. The dynasty is one of the oldest in Europe, and its origins can be traced back to the town of Wettin, Saxony-Anhalt. The Wettins gradually rose to power within the Holy Roman Empire. Members of the family became the rulers of several medieval states, starting with the Saxon Eastern March in 1030. Other states they gained were Meissen in 1089, Thuringia in 1263, and Saxony in 1423." Source: https://en.wikipedia.org/wiki/House_of_Wettin.

223 In MHG, *"dasz vnser bruder, vnser vetter vnd wir dryhundert mit glefningen vnd dryen hundert schutzzen und mit dem, dasz dartzu gehoret wol dry Tusend Pferde haben werden. Auch hat vns Hans von Polentzk geschriben, dasz Er hans von Biberstein mit hundert spissen zu dem Lande zcu Lusitz kommen solle."* Quoted from PALACKÝ, Urkundliche Beiträge I, Nr. 218, p. 244.

224 The Lausitz, also called Lucatia, is a region of central Europe in eastern Germany and southwest Poland between the Elbe and Oder Rivers.

225 In MHG, *"Ouch habin die Polnischen fursten und die fursten zu der Slesien und zu den sechssteten nicht danne anderthalb hundert gewopente, sundern uf waynen und zcu fusse eyns mit dem andern, das es louffet wol uf vier tusent man."* Quoted from CDS 1 B 4, Nr. 212, p. 129.

226 In MHG, *"So wollen wir weder leib noch blut sparen vnd euch getrewlich zu rettung und zu hülffe komen nach allem vnseren vermügen."* Quoted from PALACKÝ, Urkundliche Beiträge I, Nr. 225, p. 252.

227 PALACKÝ, Urkundliche Beiträge I, pp. 240-261; BLEICHER, Das Herzogtum Niederbayern, pp. 128-129.

228 PALACKÝ, Der Hussitenkrieg 1419-1431, pp. 317-318; BEZOLD, Sigismund und die Reichskriege, pp. 70-73.

229 VERNEY, Warrior of God, pp. 173-175.

8 November 1422. A one-year ceasefire was concluded that also included the castles of Valdek (German: Waldeck) and Hořic.[230]

However, Sigismund had to pay back the most important Electors for their respective efforts. Margrave Friedrich I of Meissen especially profited from his campaigns. In 1422 he was given several castles in the *Vogtland*[231] and when the last of the Ascanian[232] Electors of Saxony died in November of that year, the Margrave got raised to the next level in the nobility. An extended conflict broke out over the Ascanian succession between the Wettiners and the Hohenzollerns who had also established themselves in Brandenburg, temporarily tying up the forces of both dynasties and relieving the pressure on the Hussites in the north. On 15 April 1423, Sigismund also liened the Margrave the Bohemian towns of Most and Ústi, which Friedrich had defended the previous year.[233] But these territorial gains would prove to have serious consequences for the Wettiners.

Internal Ruptures

In the meanwhile the political conditions in Prague had changed again. The Prague burgers tried to conclude an alliance with the Hussite nobleman in order to end the war. Sigismund Korybut, who up until then had been able to hold the parties together with great effort, was called away from Prague by Vytautas again in November 1422, after Poland was able to accomplish its territorial interests against the Teutonic Order. Vytautas cleverly got out of his responsibilities. He declared that he wanted to lead the Bohemians back into the fold of the Roman Church. But they had fooled him with the offer of the crown, yet they had no intention to renounce the heresy (which they also never asserted to Vytautas).. At the end of March 1423, Korybut retuned to Poland via Moravia. Sigismund assured the safe conduct of the Crown Administrator. At the same time, the break between Jan Žižka and the Taborites had gotten so serious that he left the commu-

nity. The blind commander moved to the eastern part of the country and joined the Orebites. Žižka raised a new army and issued his famous War Directive into which he injected all his experience as a soldier.[234]

In the spring of 1423, it appeared as if two splits would occur within the Hussite movement. For one, Jan Žižka began a war against the Utraquist barons, and for the other the Prazans were turning against the Taborites. Therefore, at the end of March, the Taborites put themselves under the overall command of the blind army commander. When the Prazans began to besiege the Kříženec Fortress near Tábor, Žižka gathered his army at Havlíčkův Brod, in order to hurry to the aid of his hard-pressed brothers. However, on 20 April his field army and a levy of the East Bohemian nobles clashed at Hořic. As usual, Žižka's army took up a position on a steep hill and formed a *Wagenburg*. The horsemen of the nobles' levy had to dismount and storm the position on foot. On their way up the hill the attack lost its momentum while the losses increased from the firing from the *Wagenburg*. Finally the blind army commander ordered a counterattack that destroyed the enemy army. Shortly after that, a Taborite army under Bohuslav ze Švamberka (German: Bohuslav von Schwanberg) was able to relieve the Kříženec Castle.[235]

In the summer of 1423, Diviš Bořek z Miletínka, who had been one of the most important captains at Hořic, and Jan Žižka fell out with one another. Miletínka took over command of the Prazans' army, which he then led to East Bohemia. A first armed encounter by the "Lords' League" (*panská jednota*) against Žižka had already ended on 4 August with a victory by the radicals at Strachuv Dvur (Strauchhof) near Hradec Králové where the Orebites took 200 prisoners. Supposedly Žižka himself, using his mace, killed a captured priest from the Prazan''s army who had carried along altar bread.[236]

But the defeat only meant a temporary setback for the League. In the same month, two more Prazan armies advanced on Hradec Králové and *Čáslav*. Žižka had dug in there with the bulk of the Orebite armies. The Prazans began a drawn out siege. Žižka's allies, among them Mathias Lupák, decided to lead replacements there to relieve him. In order to stop them, the Prazans positioned a part of their army on the Elbe River near Kolín. On 22 August, the Orebite relief army arrived in Týnec, about thirteen kilometers (8 miles) north of Kolín on the Elbe. The Prazans made a surprise attack and slaughtered 300 Orebites, including Lupák. But they did not succeed in taking Čáslav. The Prazans' army had to break off the siege left a strong garrison behind in nearby Kutná Hora. Jan Žižka had suc-

230 PALACKÝ, Urkundliche Beiträge I, Nr. 243, p. 267;
   BEZOLD, Sigismund und die Reichskriege, pp. 100-122;
   BLEICHER, Das Herzogtum Niederbayern, p. 129.

231 The Vogtland is a region reaching across the present German free states of Bavaria, Saxony and Thuringia and into the Czech Republic (north-western Bohemia).

232 The House of Ascania (German: Askanier) is a dynasty of German rulers. It is also known as the House of Anhalt, which refers to its longest-held possession, Anhalt. The Ascanians are named after Ascania (or Ascaria) Castle, known as Schloss Askanien in German, which was located near and named after Aschersleben. The castle was the seat of the County of Ascania, a title that was later subsumed into the titles of the princes of Anhalt." Source: https://en.wikipedia.org/wiki/House_of_Ascania

233 CDS 1 B 4, Nr. 271, p. 165; PALACKÝ, Urkundliche Beiträge I, Nr. 265, p. 291-293; PALACKÝ, Der Hussitenkrieg 1419-1431, pp. 318-324;
   KROCKER, Sachsen und die Hussitenkriege, p. 6;
   ERMISCH, Schlacht bei Außig, p. 6;
   MEINHARDT, Im Dienste des Königs, pp. 115-117.

234 ŠMAHEL, Hussitische Revolution II, pp. 1277-1278;
   VERNEY, Warrior of God, p. 176.

235 PALACKÝ, Der Hussitenkrieg 1419-1431, pp. 331-333;
   ŠMAHEL, Hussitische Revolution II, pp. 1281-1284.

236 VERNEY, Warrior of God, pp. 191-192;
   BEZOLD, Sigismund und die Reichskriege, p. 13.

Sigismund Korybut Besieges a Town.
Depiction from the *"Geschichte Kaiser Sigismunds."*
Note the very curved sabre at Korybut's side.

ceeded in defending the independence of the Orebite alliance. A ceasefire established shortly hereafter ended the hostilities until March of 1424.[237]

In the fall of 1423, Žižka carried out a large operation into Moravia. His army advanced to Jihlava whose garrison, strengthened by Austrian mercenaries put up a fight but was badly beaten. But because the city was well fortified, the Orebites broke off the siege after a few days. But on 19 October they stormed Telč (Teltsch). The army probably even temporarily crossed the Danube to steal a herd of cattle from Austria. However, in did not come to a large scale raid into Austria and Hungary, as some chroniclers reported. Žižka never tried to carry the war over the kingdom's borders. His absence was however exploited by the Utraquists to gather new strength over the winter of 1423-1424.[238]

In October of 1423 at the Sankt-Gallus-Landtag (Diet of St. Gallen), the Utraquists adopted a new peace agreement (*Landfrieden*) that was clearly directed against the Taborites and Orebites around Jan Žižka. The decision presented a further attempt to obtain compromises with the Pope to end the war and at least to retain part of the Hussite reforms. However, the radicals, i.e., the Taborites and Žižka's field army, considered such efforts as treason.[239]

In the first months of 1424, Jan Žižka conducted several campaigns against the royalist barons and achieved a series of minor successes. After the ceasefire with the Lords' League expired in March, he attacked the Hostinné Castle that belonged to Krušina z Lichtemburka (German: Krushina von Lichtenburg) who had joined the League. But the Orebites were not able to take the castle. They moved on to the town of Mlazovice, which they completely destroyed. While Žižka destroyed Krušina z Lichtemburka's properties, the Prazans were gathering fresh forces.[240]

In April the Orebite army finally turned to the west to support the Taborites in an attack on the "public peace" of Pilsen. With that, however, Prague stood between Žižka's army and his East Bohemian bases of operation. Because only a very small part of the Taborites had joined the army, it could not risk an attack on Pilsen by itself and simply conducted an insurgency in West Bohemia. The Utraquist *Landfrieden* requested support from other royalist garrisons and in May received some cavalry as reinforcements from Karlštejn. The royalist forces offered the Orebites battle but Žižka withdrew to Louny. But because this town belonged to the Prague City League, the councilmen there considered an alliance of Louny with the Orebites as treasonous and mobilized their army. Žižka moved further to the east.[241]

In June 1424, a large army of Prazans and the Lords' League moved against Žižka, who had established his camp at Kostelec nad Labem (German: Kostelec an der Elbe, Elbekosteletz, and earlier also Elbkosteletz). The Orebite forces were surrounded. The royalists on the side of the Lords' League sent King Sigismund reports of a victory. But the skillful army commander withdrew to the east bank and pulled back from his enemy. Žižka looked for a suitable battlefield. He finally found one at Malešov (Maleschau) near Kutná Hora. Southwest of the town was a high hill that was enclosed on two sides by the Maleskova and Svadlenka creeks. The blind army commander informed his captain Jan Hvězda z Vícemilic about the advantages of the terrain. Žižka deployed his *Wagenburg* with its front facing Malešov. But this time he did not intend to barricade his forces behind it, instead he posi-

237 VERNEY, Warrior of God, pp. 192-193.

238 PALACKÝ, Der Hussitenkrieg 1419-1431, pp. 338-341;
ŠMAHEL, Hussitische Revolution II, pp. 1285-1303;
VERNEY, Warrior of God, p. 193; DURDÍK, Hussitisches Heerwesen, pp. 213-214.

239 PALACKÝ, Der Hussitenkrieg 1419-1431, pp. 337-338;
ŠMAHEL, Hussitische Revolution II, pp. 1285-1290;
DURDÍK, Hussitisches Heerwesen, p. 213.

240 VERNEY, Warrior of God, pp. 196-197.

241 VERNEY, Warrior of God, pp. 196-201.

Duke Albrecht of Austria Besieges a Castle in Moravia
(From *"Geschichte Kaiser Sigismunds"*)

tioned his infantry, flanked by the cavalry, in front of the *Wagenburg*. He placed many supply wagons loaded with stones behind the infantry.[242]

When the forces of the Lords' League passed through the deep valley of the Maleskova creek, they found that there was not enough room at the foot of the hill to deploy. While they were carefully and hesitantly assembling their forces, Žižka had his lines advance. The cavalry on the flanks swarmed out and suddenly the infantry let the heavily loaded wagons roll down the hill. The wagons cut wide swaths in the Prazans' ranks and caused great confusion. At the same moment, the howitzers in the *Wagenburg* fired a salvo that increased the chaos. Then Žižka ordered the attack on the entire line. The Hussites drove the Prazan army down the hill. The forward units fled in panic and caused confusion in the follow-on formations. Žižka's cavalry pursued the defeated enemies and killed many of them. Many cannon, wagons and weapons fell into the Hussites' hands.[243]

The Battle of Malešov (Maleschau) is an impressive example of the certainty with which the Hussite's individual branches operated together. Shortly thereafter, Jan Žižka captured Kutná Hora and a little later Havlíčkův Brod and Nymburk as well, which hardly put up any resistance.[244]

"King" Korybut

Because Sigismund could not hold Moravia with his own forces, he ultimately transferred the Margraveship as a fiefdom to Albrecht of Austria in October 1423. Meanwhile, since the King could not organize a new crusade, the Imperial princes formed a new alliance in Bingen (on the Rhine) on 17 January 1424. Its objectives were to protect the Empire from Hussite attacks and to eradicate the heresy.[245]

In the following years, the Empire was unable to organize a new crusade, so the Hussites concentrated their attention on the fighting in South Bohemia. Ulrich von Rosenberg remained their most dogged opponent there. In early 1424, Jan Hvězda z Vícemilic, called Bzdinka, unsuccessfully besieged Třeboň (Wittingau). Repelled by the garrison, he turned to the south and captured the Nové Hrady (Gratzen) Castle. Subsequently the Hussite units advanced as far as Upper Austria (Oberösterreich).[246]

The Hussite's Hassiko von Waldstein operated successfully in Moravia against the Bishop of Olomouc. But the conflict between the Taborites and the Utraquists pre-

vented the Hussites from conducting any major, joint campaigns. The Utraquists agreed to a ceasefire with the Catholic landed estates (*Landständen*) that Žižka was not ready to accept. He conducted a very destructive campaign in the north of Bohemia. On 9 September, his army reached the village of Libeň (now a district of Prague) from where the Orebites could see the Vyšehrad. But exactly during these weeks, Sigismund Korybut returned to Bohemia. The former Crown Administrator now tried to become the king even though his uncle Vytautas had warned him against doing so. Despite that, on 29 June, Korybut rode into Prague where the populace greeted him warmly. He exuberantly composed a letter of rejection to Sigismund and Duke Albrecht of Austria. In the letter's introduction, he referred to himself as "We, Sigmund, by God's grace, the Duke of Lithuania and of the Kingdom of Bohemia and the Margraveship of Moravia proclaimed and chosen King."[247] Yet no one had ever actually chosen Korybut. It is the only preserved, remaining document in which he is titled as such. In order to actually carry out these claims, a rapid treaty with the Orebites was needed. He actually was able to agree with Žižka to the so-called Treaty of Libeň on 14 September 1424. For Korybut this represented an overwhelming political success because now he had united all the Hussite forces under him and could conduct a new campaign to Moravia.[248]

Duke Albrecht of Austria was the only one to lead a new anti-Hussite campaign into Moravia in the summer of 1424. On 1 July, he gathered an army in Laa.[249] Sigismund supported this campaign with only 4,000 Hungarians. Despite that, the Duke successfully advanced into Moravia. The Austrians captured many Hussite castles and allegedly burned one hundred villages. Albrecht got South Moravia well in hand quickly and then decided to turn to Bohemia itself. He hoped to unite with the Utraquists there. Therefore, on 27 July, he wrote to Ulrich von Rosenberg that he wanted to call the moderate Hussite nobles to an assembly in Jihlava (Iglau). But in the meantime, the nobles had turned to Sigismund Korybut after he arrived in Prague. In fact Albrecht was able to advance as far as Olomouc in August but at this time the Lithuanian Administrator had united the various Hussite factions under the Treaty of Libeň. When Ulrich von Rosenberg also agreed to a ceasefire with the Hussites, Albrecht returned to Austria in September.[250]

242 PALACKÝ, Der Hussitenkrieg 1419-1431, pp. 348-349; ŠMAHEL, Hussitische Revolution II, pp. 1315-316; DURDÍK, Hussitisches Heerwesen, pp. 213-216.

243 PALACKÝ, Der Hussitenkrieg 1419-1431, pp. 349-350; DURDÍK, Hussitisches Heerwesen, pp. 217-221.

244 PALACKÝ, Der Hussitenkrieg 1419-1431, pp. 350-351.

245 PALACKÝ, Der Hussitenkrieg 1419-1431, pp. 351-352; STÖLLER, Österreich im Kriege gegen die Hussiten, pp. 23-24.

246 STÖLLER, Österreich im Kriege gegen die Hussiten, p. 24.

247 In MHG *"Wir Sigmund von gotes gnaden Littowscher herczog, vnd des Kunigreich zu Beheim vnd Marggraffschaft zu Merhern gevorderter vnd erwelter Künig."* Quoted from PALACKÝ, Urkundliche Beiträge I, Nr. 304, p. 356.

248 STÖLLER, Österreich im Kriege gegen die Hussiten, pp. 24-25; VERNEY, Warrior of God, pp. 206-209.

249 Laa an der Thaya is a town in the Mistelbach District of Lower Austria (*Niederösterreich*), near the Czech border in Austria.

250 PALACKÝ, Der Hussitenkrieg 1419-1431, pp. 356-358; ŠMAHEL, Hussitische Revolution II, pp. 1334-1345; STÖLLER, Österreich im Kriege gegen die Hussiten, pp. 25-28.

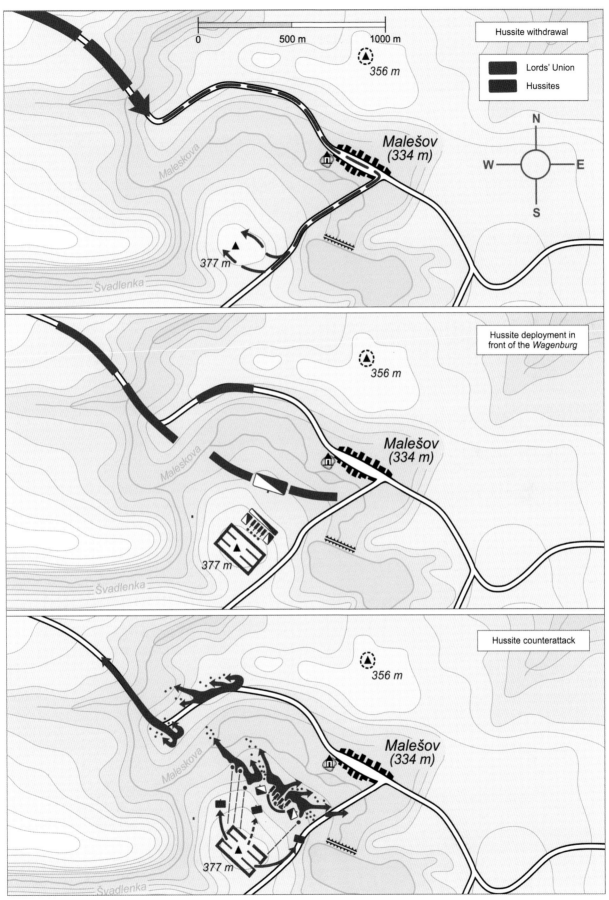

Battle of Malešov, 7 June 1424

Then it was the Hussites' turn to go on the offensive. On 29 September, Žižka and Korybut left Prague with their combined armies and marched to Přibyslav. On 11 October 1424, before the fortress fell and the Hussites destroyed it to its very foundations, Jan Žižka died, supposedly from plague. When the castle fell a little later, the Hussites burned all the defenders at the stake. At the end of October, the Taborites and Orphans, as Žižka's followers now called themselves, stormed the town of Ivančice (Eibenschitz), which they subsequently built up as a fortress. Then many of the Moravian Hussites, who had already paid homage to Duke Albrecht in the summer, joined the Taborites again. They captured the fortified town of Břeclav (Lundenburg) and from there they organized a devastating assault of Austria. So Duke Albrecht saw himself forced to mobilize the *Landwehr*. But new disputes broke out between the Taborites and Utraquists over the division of the spoils. As a result, Sigismund Korybut went back to Bohemia with the moderate Hussites while a smaller army captured more towns on the Austrian-Moravian border.[251]

Albrecht exploited the opportunity and advanced into Moravia again with his army that had been reinforced by the *Landwehr*. He went via Brno and Olomouc as far as Zábřeh (Hohenstadt), to where the Polish King had sent 5,000 horsemen to his aid. But Albrecht distrusted the offer and sent the Polish horsemen home. In November he marched his forces back to Vienna.[252]

At first there was a relaxation of inter-Hussite relations after Žižka's death. In the last months of his life, it was increasingly the blind army commander who had prevented a reconciliation with the King and with the Pope. Žižka left a void that Sigismund Korybut initially filled. Though Korybut was even able to bring the individual parties back to the negotiating table, no decisive results could be achieved.[253]

Another Imperial Assembly (*Reichstag*) was scheduled for 1425 in Vienna, but most of the princes did not attend. It was only the lack of consensus among the Electors that prevented Sigismund's removal from office as the "Roman King" at this point in time. In fact, it was the Imperial princes' disunity that allowed an Utraquist army to invade Upper Austria again in March. When Albrecht gathered the *Landwehr* at Laa, the Hussites marched northward again without having to engage in any major battles.[254]

But in the summer the Taborites took important fortresses in South Bohemia and prepared for a new invasion of Austria. While Albrecht put the border castles on alert, the Hussite attack collapsed due to the renewed internal differences between the Taborites with the Utraquists.

So the Duke of Austria was able to conclude an anti-Hussite alliance between Sigismund, himself and the Elector Frederick the Warlike on 25 July in Vác (Waitzen). Albrecht was then granted a claim to the Bohemian royal crown. Additionally, Frederick promised to give him his vote for the election as the Roman King in case of Sigismund's demise.[255]

In contrast, the Austrian army's deployment for the campaign this year stalled. Only on 6 October did Albrecht march into Moravia and unite with Sigismund's forces at Dalešice (Dalleschitz). The combined armies' objective was the Hussite occupied town of Třebíč (Trebitsch) that they besieged for the whole month.

Bzdinka's successor, Bohuslav ze Švamberka put up a successful defense. At the same time, the Moravian Hussites rose up against Albrecht who just like King Sigismund withdrew from Moravia so that the Hussites could besiege the castles loyal to the king without interference. So the main forces under Sigismund Korybut and Bohuslav ze Švamberka joined one another at Moravské Budějovice (Mährisch Budwitz) and advanced by way of Znojmo to Austria. On 12 November, the Hussites destroyed the Louka (Bruck) Monastery and following that besieged the town of Retz (in Lower Austria), which put up a stiff resistance. At first they did not succeed in overcoming in the town's walls, so they thoroughly despoiled the surrounding countryside. Albrecht, who was alarmed by this incursion, hurried to Vienna and tried to raise a relief army in great haste. The levies assembled in Laa and Eggenburg. Albrecht himself established his camp in Kreuzenstein, exactly between the two towns. This disposition suggests that the Duke initially was most concerned about protecting Vienna. However many Austrian cities and towns, especially Vienna itself, refused to send the needed levies. So Albrecht did not see himself in the position to relieve Retz. In the meantime during an attack on the town, Bohuslav ze Švamberka had died when he was struck in the face by an arrow. Then the Hussites undermined the town wall. In the night of 25 November, the Hussites stormed Retz through the resulting breach. Supposedly 6,000 people were killed and an equal number captured during the following pillaging. This number only seems credible if one assumes that a large portion of the surrounding countryside's population had fled to the town. The Hussites also took Pulckau shortly after that. Then they withdrew to Bohemia with their booty before Albrecht had assembled his army.[256]

After these moves an ever more profound division within the movement became apparent. The Taborites and the Orphans separated while the Prazans and Utraquists tried hard again for a reconciliation with the established church. Most of the East Bohemian Orebites'

251 STÖLLER, Österreich im Kriege gegen die Hussiten, pp. 27-29.

252 PALACKÝ, Der Hussitenkrieg 1419-1431, pp. 358-359;
STÖLLER, Österreich im Kriege gegen die Hussiten, p. 29.

253 PALACKÝ, Der Hussitenkrieg 1419-1431, pp. 375-379.

254 PALACKÝ, Der Hussitenkrieg 1419-1431, pp. 379-382;
STÖLLER, Österreich im Kriege gegen die Hussiten, pp. 29-32.

255 PALACKÝ, Der Hussitenkrieg 1419-1431, pp. 390-391; STÖLLER,
Österreich im Kriege gegen die Hussiten, pp. 31-32.

256 PALACKÝ, Der Hussitenkrieg 1419-1431, pp. 396-398;
STÖLLER, Österreich im Kriege gegen die Hussiten, pp. 34-36.

The illustration shows a typical **Hussite Footsoldier of the 1420s and 1430s** He wears a war hat and a gambeson. His armament includes a war flail with iron spikes and a long sword. Additionally he carries a pavis that is elaborately painted and shows the chalice, the Hussite symbol.

Lunyonov 2015

nobles split off and joined the Utraquists, while the small towns and peasants sympathized with the Taborites. The split essentially went back to Žižka's death, who had succeeded in uniting the individual groups. The rupture was less an expression of the power struggles that his successors conducted, than of the heterogeneity of the regional armies. This led to a downright civil war breaking out among the Orebites in the east of the country in 1425, which was less about religious than social issues between the nobles on one side and the townspeople and peasants in the other side.[257]

In contrast the Taborites and Orphans tried to take possession of the capital. On 31 March, units belonging to Jan Hvězda z Vícemilic, Jan Rohács of Duba and Bohuslavs ze Švamberka as well as probably also forces belonging to Jan Hertvíks of Ruśinov and the Hradec Králové Orphans marched up to the Prague New Town. In the approaching night, the Prazans tried to climb the walls but were driven back bloodied by the defenders. Therefore they moved to the north and, on 5 April, with levies from Žatec and Louny surrounded the town of Slaný that fell twelve days later. After they had captured a series of other towns and castles in the vicinity, the armies split up and cut wide swaths of destruction through West and East Bohemia.[258]

In the summer a heat wave and plague raged in the country, which also supposedly led to Čeněk von Wartenberg's death. In September, the Taborites surrounded the important Wožic Castle in the Pilsen district. The lord of the castle, Materna von Ronow, put up a strong resistance to the Hussites. Eventually they received reinforcements by the Orphans' army. The combined army then had enough strength that it could also send out a strong detachment against the moderate Prazans.

The siege lasted five weeks and the Taborite leader, Jan Hvězda, was wounded by an arrow during the fighting. On his deathbed, he received the news that Sigismund Korybut had arrived in the camp in order to negotiate a treaty between the individual parties. This actually came into effect on 18 October. Jan Hvězda was so happy about this that after the fall of Wožic he ordered the garrison to be spared. Because at this time the Pilseners could expect no assistance from King Sigismund, they also agreed to a ceasefire a little later. At the same time, a one-year ceasefire was concluded with Sigismund and the Pilsners. In the meanwhile only Duke Albrecht's forces remained before Trebitsch because Sigismund had withdrawn to Brno. So at the beginning of November, Sigismund Korybut turned toward Trebitsch to relieve the town. The Taborites and Orphans soon followed him. Shortly after that, *Jan Hvězda died near* Kamenice (Kamenitz).[259]

Until 1426, the Hussite Wars essentially were limited to campaigns in Bohemia. The movement only thought about defending their interests and not about reprisals against the princes' territories who attacked them, like in Meissen. Only Upper Austria was badly battered. In this phase, however, one cannot speak of a lot of fear of the Hussites in the Empire. The heretics were simply too far away for the common folk in the Empire.[260]

The towns of Most and Ústi, from which Frederick the Warlike launched his attacks on Bohemia were important objectives of the Hussite attacks. In the fall of 1424, a Hussite army encircled Ústi for the first time, but Frederick was able to break the siege ring with the help of the Lausitz Six Cities. In 1425, the Hussites were able to defeat a small Meissner army at Duchcov (Dux) and prepared a new siege of the two fortified towns, which prompted Frederick to strengthen their garrisons at the beginning of 1426.[261]

---

257 PALACKÝ, Der Hussitenkrieg 1419-1431, pp. 383-387;
ŠMAHEL, Hussitische Revolution II, pp. 1356-1358.

258 PALACKÝ, Der Hussitenkrieg 1419-1431, pp. 387-389;
ŠMAHEL, Hussitische Revolution II, pp. 1350-1352.

259 PALACKÝ, Der Hussitenkrieg 1419-1431, pp. 392-395;
ŠMAHEL, Hussitische Revolution II, pp. 1362-1364; Österreich im Kriege gegen die Hussiten, er, pp. 32-34. Oddly enough, Stöller treats Jan Hvězda and Jan Brzdinka as two different persons.

260 KROCKER, Sachsen und die Hussitenkriege, pp. 1-2, 6.

261 CDS II 8, Nr. 141, p. 94;
KROCKER, Sachsen und die Hussitenkriege, p. 7;
ERMISCH, Schlacht bei Außig, pp. 6-7; KRZENCK: Hussitenkriege, pp. 60-61.

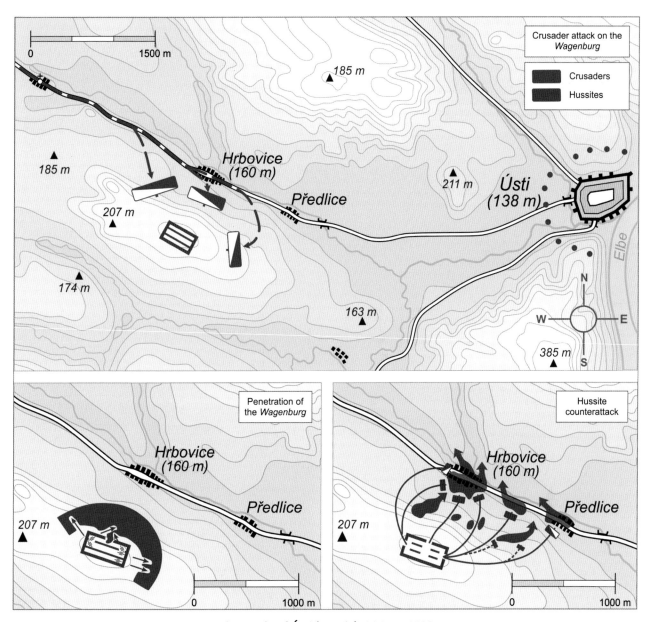

The Battle of Ústi (Aussig), 16 June 1426

Next double page: **The Battle of Ústi (Aussig)**
The depiction shows the turning point of the battle. The Saxon knights' attack on the *Wagenburg* has lost its momentum. The Hussite's transition into a counterattack. In small groups they overpower the horsemen and pull them from their horses with halberds or hooks. The group on the left carries a whole arsenal of polearms typical of the era: war flails, morning stars and awl pikes.

The Battle of Ústí (Aussig)

In January 1426, the Taborites attended an assembly that after lengthy negotiations recognized the Four Prague Articles. Additionally they decided there that war was still acceptable only as a means of defense[262] – a lip service because soon the cross-border "beautiful rides" would become pillaging campaigns necessary for survival.

In May and June 1426 at the Imperial Assembly (*Reichstag*) in Nuremberg, Sigismund demanded a new army of 6,000 *Gleves* (ca. 18,000 horsemen) be raised for a fourth crusade. But the princes protested. Such a huge army could not be put together in the Empire and could not be provisioned in Bohemia. These protests alone show that the inflated numbers for the earlier campaigns are unrealistic.[263]

Also during the negotiations, catastrophic reports arrived from northern Bohemia. The Hussites had taken up the siege of Ústí again. On 10 February, the town's commanders reported to the Saxon Elector Katharina "...*that the Orphans now are going to move next Friday from Schlaan* [Slaný] *to Laun* [Louny]*, and we have received actual messages that they will come in three days and want to storm and besiege us in Aussig* [Ústí]*, and have asked for help from Lutenbritz and Saatz* [Žatec] *and their other towns, which are now gathering and assembling at Laun.*"[264]

While the Elector Friedrich of Meissen was at the *Reichstag* in Nuremberg, he received letters from his wife warning him that the Hussites had taken Česká Lípa (Leipa) and were now headed to Most or Ústí in order to possibly attack Meissen from there. Actually several armies were streaming toward the two Saxon bulwarks. Česká Lípa was taken by a levy under Johann Rohacz of Duba, while Sigismund Korybut and Procopius the Bald (Prokop der Kahle) led their armies in that direction through the Cheb valley via Krupka (Graupen) and Teplice (Teplitz). At this time, Procopius the Bald was little known. But over the coming months, the priest would become one of the most important Hussite army commanders, Jan Žižka's true successor.[265]

At the news of the Hussite armies approach, a Saxon relief army was formed from the levies from Meissen's knights and towns, who gathered and were mustered in Gross Bobritzsch bei Freiberg in Saxony. The reports on this army's strength vary tremendously. Some chroniclers reported 100,000 men. But if it was impossible for the whole Empire to stand up such an army, how could it have been possible for a single prince to do so? More realistic estimates run between 8,000 and 25,000 men. The strength of the troops assembled at Gross Bobritsch probably amounted to 8,000 men. But the Saxon army consisted of three elements, which were joined by troops from the Six Cities (*Sechsstädte*) so that the total strength could feasibly have been 25,000 men. The Six Cities' levy under Hans von Kolditz had assembled at Grosshennersdorf in May. Their objective was actually the relief of the hard-pressed town of Česká Lípa. When the town fell, the Meissen-led force joined with the Saxon army.[266]

On 14 June, the army moved out accompanied for a while by the Saxon Electoral Princess. The Saxons marched in three army columns over the Erz Mountain passes to Krupka. In the meantime, the Hussite main army under Prince Korybut and Procopius the Bald had surrounded Ústí and Most. A third Hussite detachment observed the passes in the mountains. The Saxon commander, Bosse Vitzthum, planned to defeat these three forces in turn. However, the knights from Meissen who had arrived in Krupka postponed an immediate attack. They also wanted to wait for the Saxon army to unite with the Lausitzers' units. But this delay allowed the Hussites to gather their forces.[267] The Saxons were confident. A herald for the Bohemians, who was supposed to negotiate about the treatment of prisoners, was sent back with the declaration "We will kill them all without differentiating[268]

The Hussites formed their *Wagenburg* with an inner and an outer ring on a hill between the two villages of Předlice (Prödlitz) and Hrbovice (Herbitz), west of Ústí. It appears that shortly before the battle, Procopius the Bald was elected to the most senior commander of the various field armies. On 16 June, the decisive battle took place there. It was a hot summer day and the Saxons, who had just marched from Krupka and were already exhausted,

---

262 PALACKÝ, Urkundliche Beiträge I, Nr. 381, p. 430.

263 QUERENGÄSSER, Triumph for the heretics, p. 42;
PALACKÝ, Der Hussitenkrieg 1419-1431, pp. 405-407;
KROCKER, Sachsen und die Hussitenkriege, pp. 6-7;
BEZOLD, Sigismund und die Reichskriege II, pp. 81-82.

264 In MHG "...*das sich dy Weißen nu an deßem nesten fritage der haben vom Slan vnde czyhen vff Lunde, vnde vns eygentliche botschaft kummen ist, daz sy vor vns vnd vns berynnen vnd belegen wullen czu der Aswig in dryen tagen, vnde dy von Lutenbritz vnde Sacz vnd andern eren steten iczlicher stat dy helffte vff geboten ist, dy iczczunt alle czu czyhen vnd sammeln sich by Lune.*"
Quoted from CDS II 8, Nr. 142, p. 95, an enclosure to a letter dated 12 February 1426 from the Elector Katharina to the Council of the city of Leipzig.

265 QUERENGÄSSER, Triumph for the heretics, pp. 42-43;
PALACKÝ, Der Hussitenkrieg 1419-1431, pp. 407-408;
KROCKER, Sachsen und die Hussitenkriege, pp. 9-10;
ERMISCH, Schlacht bei Außig, pp. 6-7.

266 QUERENGÄSSER, Triumph for the heretics, pp. 4-443;
PALACKÝ, Der Hussitenkrieg 1419-1431, pp. 409-413;
KROCKER, Sachsen und die Hussitenkriege, pp. 10-16;
ERMISCH, Schlacht bei Außig, pp. 7-18;
KORSCHELT, Kriegsdrangsale der Oberlausitz, pp. 176-177;
KRZENCK, Hussitenkriege, pp. 60-61.

267 QUERENGÄSSER, Triumph for the heretics, pp. 44-45;
PALACKÝ, Der Hussitenkrieg 1419-1431, pp. 413-414;
KROCKER, Sachsen und die Hussitenkriege, pp. 16-18;
BEZOLD, Sigismund und die Reichskriege II, p. 82.

268 In modern German, "*Wir werden alle ohne Unterschied hinmorden.*" Quoted from ERMISCH, Schlacht bei Außig, p. 35.

Depiction der Battle of Ústi (Aussig)
(here called Bruck, i.e.,Brüx, a German name for Most, *"Geschichte Kaiser Sigismunds"*)

immediately attacked the *Wagenburg*. The defensive fires from the Hussites' cannon, handguns and crossbows tore large holes in the ranks of the Saxon knights.[269]

The knights who streamed back suffered from the heat, as one chronicler reported: *"And the people who had not been sent [engaged in the fighting] fled. In that same flight, the people suffocated in their armor from the great dust and heat and especially the good, upstanding knights who unhappily fled and had gladly done enough for their honor, were for the most part killed, while most of the [foot] folk fled back on that St. Vitis Day."*[270]

Nevertheless, the army succeeded in breaking into the first ring of wagons. But the Saxons' order had been so disrupted that Hussites' counterattack caused their attack to collapse. The flail-man pulled the knights, who were wedged between the wagons, off of their mounts and slew them. The Meisseners were said to have been the first to flee the battlefield, and the Thuringians the last. The defeated army streamed back to the safe forests of the Erz Mountains with the Hussites in hot pursuit. The flower of the Meissen-Thuringian knighthood was slaughtered, among them the last Burgrave (*Burggraf*) of Meissen, Heinrich von Hartenstein, as well as by some accounts eight to fourteen more counts, ten barons and over one hundred noblemen, and among them 21 just from the von Köckeritz family. The total loss figures vary so much, like the numbers for the army's strength – between 4,000 and 50,000 men. Using a Saxon army strength of 15,000 knights and men-at-arms, reports of 4,000 losses seem to be realistic.[271]

On the following day the Hussite army stormed Ústi and devastated the town so completely that it allegedly remained deserted for the next three years. The Saxon garrison and a large part of the population had been able to save themselves the day before the battle. Some of those fleeing thought they were safe in the nearby Střekov (Schreckenstein) Castle. But the Hussites also stormed it shortly thereafter.[272]

In Saxony, Elector Katharina prepared a defense of the border fortresses and towns of Königstein, Pirna, Freiberg and Dresden, but the Hussites still did not dare to cross the Erz Mountains. When Elector Friedrich returned from Nuremberg, he was not thinking about defending but about attacking again. Anyhow, the town of Most was still holding out against the Hussite siege. Elector Friedrich actually moved with a new army to Bohemia just eight weeks after the catastrophe at Ústi and beat back the Prazans' field army, which left 1,500 men and a large bombard, cast in Kutná Hora, on the battlefield.[273]

The Fourth Hussite Crusade

The Hussites were also active in South Bohemia again in 1426. They stormed many towns and castles and marched into Austria once more. But this time, Duke Albrecht was able to expeditiously assemble his army at Korneuburg so that the heretics had to withdraw.[274]

Duke Albrecht began with the siege of Břeclav (Lundenburg), an important Hussite fortress in South Bohemia. But despite various sources saying he had led almost 40,000 men to the field, the Hussites initially withstood his attempted attacks. In October, the Duke pressed for a decision, also because the Taborites' field army under Procopius was nearing the beleaguered fortress from the north. At the end of October, the Taborites from Eibenschitz were preparing for their attack. Duke Albrecht sent four letters to the city of Vienna, in which he urgently requested, this time angrily, reinforcements. But because the help was not forthcoming, the Duke had to break off the siege in the beginning of November and withdraw in front of Procopius' army.[275]

The Hussites moved into Austria again and pushed as far as the Danube. They pillaged many villages there and carried the stolen provisions back to Břeclav. At the same time, about 4,000 Hussites came from South Bohemia and invaded western Austria. On New Year's Eve of 1426, they appeared before the town of Zwettel, but it fended off all the attempted attacks. The enraged Hussites set fire to the Dominican monastery located outside the town and on 3 January 1427 they moved further to the north again.[276]

But the Taborites were so aggravated by the little town's stubborn resistance that on 12 March 1427 they were again standing in front of its gates, this time with 16,000 men. Although the town did not have any modern defensive walls, the Hussites were unable to take it in the first assault. To supply their army, they devastated the surrounding countryside and also went up the Krems Valley (Kremstal). Duke Albrecht assembled a relief army at Krems and on 25 March he attacked the Hussites' positions. The Austrians' first attack was crowned with success.

269 QUERENGÄSSER, Triumph for the heretics, pp. 44-45;
     PALACKÝ, Der Hussitenkrieg 1419-1431, p. 415;
     KROCKER, Sachsen und die Hussitenkriege, pp. 18-19.

270 In MHG *"Und das volck was noch ungeschicket unnd wart fluchtig. In derselben flucht erstickte das volck im harnasche von großem stoube unnd hitcze, unnd ditte was uff sente Vitis tag, sundern dy gutte redeliche ritterschafft, dy ungerne floen unnd den eren gerne hetten gnukg gethan, dy worden das meiste teil erslagen, wanne das volck das meiste teil gemeiniclich wedder zurucke floch."* Quoted from ERMISCH, Schlacht bei Außig, p. 41.

271 QUERENGÄSSER, Triumph for the heretics, pp. 45-46;
     PALACKÝ, Der Hussitenkrieg 1419-1431, pp. 415-416;
     KROCKER, Sachsen und die Hussitenkriege, pp. 19-20;
     ERMISCH, Schlacht bei Außig, pp. 20-31.

272 QUERENGÄSSER, Triumph for the heretics, p. 46;
     PALACKÝ, Der Hussitenkrieg 1419-1431, pp. 416-417;
     KROCKER, Sachsen und die Hussitenkriege, p. 23.

273 PALACKÝ, Der Hussitenkrieg 1419-1431, pp. 417-419;
     KROCKER, Sachsen und die Hussitenkriege, pp. 23-24;
     BEZOLD, Sigismund und die Reichskriege, p. 85.

274 STÖLLER, Österreich im Kriege gegen die Hussiten, pp. 39-40.

275 PALACKÝ, Der Hussitenkrieg 1419-1431, S.419-420;
     STÖLLER, Österreich im Kriege gegen die Hussiten, pp. 42-43.

276 STÖLLER, Österreich im Kriege gegen die Hussiten, pp. 43-45.

The Hussites were thrown back. During the subsequent pursuit, the *Wagenburg* was also stormed. However, instead of completing the victory, the Austrian forces fell apart. They plundered the Hussite camp and the Duke's mercenaries lost their cohesion. The Taborites used the opportunity, gathered a group of horsemen and they carried out a counterattack with loud shouts. They drove the Austrians out of the *Wagenburg* again. The Hussites killed many of the enemy during the following pursuit. Only a small part of the relief army reached the safety of Zwettel's walls. However, the Taborites' losses were also heavy and the town's garrison was strengthened by the Austrians who fled. So the siege was called off. The Bohemians moved to the east, parching the earth and burning, until they reached the Altenburg Monastery and from there they went to the north.[277]

After the Hussites' military successes and probably strengthened by their temporary political unity, in 1427, Sigismund Korybut tried to resume negotiations with King Sigismund in order to mediate a settlement between Hussites and Catholics. Now as before, Korybut was striving to get a crown for himself. Additionally, he started secret negotiations with the Pope, to whom he promised to bring the country back into the Church's fold. The Pope, as the highest judge, was supposed to decide on all unresolved theological issues. In response, Pope Martin V was supposed to withdraw his support for Sigismund's efforts to get back Wenzel's crown and instead to support the Lithuanian's candidacy. However, not only the Taborites saw these actions as treasonous. On 17 April 1427, the Prazans under Jan Rokycana, the university's new pastor, arrested and deposed the National Administrator and took him to the Valdshtejn (Waldstein) Castle in East Bohemia.[278]

Korybut's political isolation led to the nobles' and Prazans' voices temporarily losing their strength and the radical elements, namely the Taborites and the Waisen under Procopius' leadership gained in power. After the Battle of Ústi, Procopius had already called for the movement to be taken abroad. He was able to develop a good relationship with the Utraquists for a longer period, which may have been due to his fostering friendly ties with John of Rokycany[279] who increasingly took over the theological leadership position at the Charles University (*Karlsuniversität*) in Prague. For that matter, Rokycany belonged to the moderate part of this faction and saw considerably more commonalities between Utraquists and Catholics, than with the Taborites. Again it was only the issue within the Hussite movement of the chalice communion that gave it unity and that also welded Procopius and Rokycany.[280]

The crusade that had been decided upon in 1426 in Nuremberg only came into being the following year. The negotiations were tough, also because King Sigismund did not take any part in them. In June 1427, the Empire's levy assembled on the western border of Bohemia with Friedrich I of Brandenburg taking over its supreme command again. Friedrich the Warlike (of Meissen) remained in his sickbed and supposedly died half a year later. Instead, his son, Friedrich II, called "the Gentle" (*der Sanftmütige*), participated in this campaign.[281]

While many chroniclers estimated the German army to be from 160,00 to 200,000 men - which seems improbable just because of the feuds raging in the Empire between the Count (*Landgraf*) of Hessen and the Electors of Mainz and Cologne - authentic reports give the strength at 4,000 to 5,000 horsemen and many footsoldiers ("*viel fueßvoelcks*").[282]

The plan that was originally developed in Nuremberg envisioned four separate armies invading Bohemia. Friedrich of Brandenburg commanded the main thrust by the German contingent that gathered in Nuremberg. Friedrich of Saxony was to move with an army from Freiberg over the Erz Mountains, and the Silesian princes and the Six Cities move over the Riesen Mountains (Riesengebirge). Albrecht of Austria's and the Bishop of Salzburg's levies were to provide relief from the south.[283]

However, because it took some time until this army was assembled and had marched to the Bohemian border, the Taborites and Orphans used the opportunity to conduct their own campaign. In the middle of May, they marched over the Zittau Mountains into the Lausitz.[284]

In July, the crusader army moved to Tachov, where on 12 July it was jubilantly received. Friedrich of Brandenburg did not want to repeat the mistakes of the previous year. Instead of getting bogged down with besieging strategically insignificant towns, he planned a direct thrust against Prague. Therefore, he went to the Saxon army to get Friedrich II's cooperation. The Elector of Trier took over command of the main army, moved on toward Stříbro (Mies) and besieged the small mining town. The Saxon forces followed and also arrived in front of the town a little later. However Friedrich of Saxony became very ill and

277 Ibid., pp. 45-47.

278 Palacký, Der Hussitenkrieg 1419-1431, pp. 424-428.

279 John of Rokycany, also known as Jan of Rokycany, in Czech language Jan Rokycana, and Jan z Rokycan (c. 1396 in Rokycany, Bohemia - 21 February 1471 in Prague) was a Czech Hussite theologian in the Kingdom of Bohemia and a key figure in Bohemian church history. Source: https://en.wikipedia.org/wiki/Jan_Rokycana

280 Palacký, Der Hussitenkrieg 1419-1431, pp. 429-433.

281 Palacký, Der Hussitenkrieg 1419-1431, pp. 437-443; Krocker, Sachsen und die Hussitenkriege, p. 25; Stöller, Österreich im Kriege gegen die Hussiten, pp. 41-42; Durdík, Hussitisches Heerwesen, pp. 228-229.

282 Quoted from Krocker, Sachsen und die Hussitenkriege, p. 25.

283 Palacký, Urkundliche Beiträge I, Nr. 439, pp. 500-502; Bleicher, Das Herzogtum Niederbayern, pp. 140-141.

284 Palacký, Der Hussitenkrieg 1419-1431, pp. 434-436; Durdík, Hussitisches Heerwesen, pp. 231-233.

had to seek medical care in Tachov. The Germans had just completely encircled Stříbro when on 1 August the Hussite relief army under Procopius the Great approached.[285]

On the following day, Friedrich of Brandenburg sent out Heinrich von Plauen with 300 horsemen in order to stop the Hussites' advance, thus winning time for his army to form up again. Heinrich was courageous enough to attack the head of the column of the opposing army. His horsemen returned around midnight after lengthy, protracted skirmishes.[286]

On the morning of 3 August, as soon as the Hussites came into view, the German army fled back to Tachov. Friedrich of Brandenburg still reported very reluctantly to Sigismund about this defeat: *"So we lords including the named Cardinal in the council decided to withdraw to a mountain by Tachau [Tachov] and to move against the enemy further. So we came to the mountain and observed our people who had come the night before on horseback and on foot and also in wagons, with which they should have formed a Wagenburg according to war orders, which had been issued, but so much of the army was gone and had become so small that the Cardinal and the other princes and lords, according the opportunity were advised by most of the [captains – Hauptleuten] not to move against the enemy and to fight them at the Wagenburg."*[287]

Procopius let his troops rest, while in Tachov, Friedrich wanted to convince his knights to deploy for battle on a hill. On the next day when he mustered his army on this hill, so many knights and men-at-arms had already fled overnight that the remaining princes decided not at accept battle. In a fit of rage, the Papal Legate supposedly angrily ripped up the Imperial flag and threw it on the ground.[288]

The crusader army flooded back to the border without having engaged in any larger actions. Only a few knights fled to the town of Tachov, which after intense artillery shelling by the Hussites, was stormed on 11 August. The castle also fell three days later. A little later another cease-fire was concluded between the Hussites and the Pilseners who were still loyal to the king.[289] Thus, due to the disunity and numeric weakness of the German army, the Fourth Hussite Crusade failed without any major battles.

In February 1428, Procopius gathered the Taborites and Orphans and led them through the Morava Valley (*Moravský úval*, German: *Marchtal*) to the southeast. This time the Hussites' objective was Bratislava (Preßburg), from where they wanted to drive further into Hungary. But Bratislava withstood the Bohemians' first assault, so that Procopius already led his army back to Uherský Brod (Ungarisch-Brod) in Moravia at the end of February. He himself headed to Silesia while a small part of the army invaded Upper Hungary. This group initially pushed deep into the kingdom, but soon the tide turned. King Sigismund organized a countrywide levy and with the help of the Bratislavans was able to cut off the Hussites' way. Additionally, Duke Albrecht of Austria led an army to Znojmo. The heretics were threatened with encirclement. But the Hussites found a hole and escaped their pursuers by rapid marches to Bohemia from where they carried out a renewed invasion of Lower Austria in May.[290]

In the beginning of June, the Taborites and Orphans had gathered about 10,000 men around Břeclav and from there advanced to the Marchfeld basin on the Danube in Lower Austria. However, they did not risk crossing the river, but after devastating the villages and towns on the north bank, they returned to Bohemia.[291]

In July, the Hussites concentrated their attention on the siege of the small castle at Bechyně (Bechin), not far from Tábor. The courageous resistance by the castle's captain, Jindřich Lefl z Lažan (German: Henrich von Lazan), drew out the siege. Because the Taborites could no longer supply themselves in the town's vicinity, which had been stripped bare, they were forced to carry out long raids as far afield as Upper Austria. Only in mid-October did Lažan surrender the castle in return for withdrawing under safe conduct.[292]

The situation that Procopius operated on the country's periphery with the Orphans and Taborites, and that the war seemed to have no end, led to a strengthening of Sigismund Korybut's party. After Korybut's supporters learned of his whereabouts, they occupied Prague and on 9 September forced his release. But Korybut left Bohemia and returned to Poland from where he closely observed the events in the country.[293]

---

285 PALACKÝ, Der Hussitenkrieg 1419-1431, pp. 445-447;
     KROCKER, Sachsen und die Hussitenkriege, pp. 26-27;
     DURDÍK, Hussitisches Heerwesen, pp. 230-233;
     BLEICHER, Das Herzogtum Niederbayern, p. 143.

286 ŠMAHEL, Hussitische Revolution II, p. 1424.

287 In MHG *"Also wurden wir hern alle mit sampt dem egenanten Cardinal zu Rate vnd vns auf einen Bergk bey Tachaw zu ruken vnd fürder zu dem feinde zu zihen. Do wir also auf den bergk kamen vnd vnser volk schawten, do war des volks in der nachten davor zu rosse vnd zu fusse vnd auch der wagen domit man ein wagenburgh nach ordnung des streits gemacht solt haben, so dann bestalt vnd geordininirtt war, so vil wegk vnd das here clein geworden das den Cardinal vnd andern fürsten vnd hern nach gelegenheit der sachen von den meisten gerathen wurde, nicht gen den feind zu zihen vnd mit jn zu streiten ane wagenburg."* Quoted from PALACKÝ, Urkundliche Beiträge I, Nr. 472, Nr. 541-542.

288 PALACKÝ, Der Hussitenkrieg 1419-1431, p. 447;
     KROCKER, Sachsen und die Hussitenkriege, pp. 27-28;
     DURDÍK, Hussitisches Heerwesen, pp. 233-235;
     BLEICHER, Das Herzogtum Niederbayern, p. 144.

289 PALACKÝ, Der Hussitenkrieg 1419-1431, pp. 447-450;
     KROCKER, Sachsen und die Hussitenkriege, pp. 27-28;
     DURDÍK, Hussitisches Heerwesen, p. 235.

290 STÖLLER, Österreich im Kriege gegen die Hussiten, pp. 50-51;
     ŠMAHEL, Hussitische Revolution II pp. 1434-1436.

291 STÖLLER, Österreich im Kriege gegen die Hussiten, p. 51;
     ŠMAHEL, Hussitische Revolution II, pp. 1439-1440.

292 STÖLLER, Österreich im Kriege gegen die Hussiten, pp. 52-53.

293 PALACKÝ, Der Hussitenkrieg 1419-1431, pp. 453-454.

The year 1428 was supposedly the quietest of the entire war. King Sigismund and Pope Martin were unable to organize another crusade. In Bohemia the various Hussite parties attempted to find a theological compromise, which, however, also was a hopeless undertaking.[294]

In March 1429, despite his aggressive political-religious position, Procopius accepted an offer from King Sigismund to come to Bratislava and finally bring about an amicable agreement. The King had also invited some Silesian, Bohemian and Bavarian princes, as well as the Duke of Austria. Procopius and his retinue arrived in the city on 4 April. Sigismund was very cordial, but demanded the Hussites return to the Catholic faith. If they did not want to do so, then they could present their ideas at a Church Council that had been called for 1431 in Basel. Until then, the ceasefire should be maintained. But the Hussites did not want to be subject to the Church Council. Finally Procopius announced that his delegation was not empowered to make such an agreement with the King. To do that, a national assembly would have to be called into session in Prague. On 9 April, Procopius left Bratislava again. At the end of May, the national assembly took place. It finally agreed to send ambassadors to the Council and to maintain a ceasefire with Hungary, Austria and Silesia, but not with Saxony or Bavaria.[295]

In the spring of 1429, the Hussite field armies were broadly spread throughout South Bohemia and Moravia and carried out a series of pinprick attacks on Austria. In April they advanced to Eggenburg, besieged the town and pillaged the surrounding villages. However, a quickly raised relief army was able to force the Hussites to withdraw. In the meantime, the Taborites invaded the country and because a major part of the national levy was tied up at Eggenburg, they were able to advance as far as Krems. But the town, protected by the Danube and good walls, was able to resist long enough until the relief army hurried there and defeated the Hussites in a series of engagements. In July, they undertook another attack along the Linz Salt Road (Linzer Salzstraße) to Upper Austria. In all these attacks, the Hussites pulled back as soon as they met serious resistance. So it can be assumed that these raids were thought up as diversionary maneuvers for the campaign planned for 1429, in order to keep the Austrian forces away from Bohemia.[296]

This simplified depiction from the *"Geschichte Kaiser Sigismunds"* shows a cavalry attack on a *Wagenburg*. Although it is shown in a very idealized manner, it does show many authentic details about the knights' armor and weapons.

---

294 Ibid., pp. 457-460.

295 Ibid., pp. 475-482.

296 STÖLLER, Österreich im Kriege gegen die Hussiten, pp. 55-58.

THE "BEAUTIFUL RIDES"

Raids into Silesia[297]

In the spring of 1421, the Silesian lords and towns put together an army of allegedly 20,000 men with which they invaded the northeast of Bohemia. Between Police nad Metují, Trutnov (Trautenau) and Náchod (Nachod) they ravaged the villages and finally stormed the small town of Ostach, which the Silesians so thoroughly destroyed that it was never rebuilt. Therefore, the national council meeting in Čáslav (Caslau) decided to send its own army against the Silesians. The Silesians withdrew because they had no hope at this early time that King Sigismund, who was busy raising a levy for the Second Crusade, would come to their aid. Only quarrels among the Hussite army commanders in Náchod prevented a revenge operation also into Silesian territory that year.[298]

Despite that, in September, the Silesians chanced a second advance into Bohemia to relieve the crusader army stuck before the town of Žatec. On 19 September, they succeeded in defeating a Hussite army levy just outside of Náchod.[299]

In the summer of 1425, the Bishop of Breslau gathered an army and invaded eastern Bohemia. The Silesians made use of the disagreements within the Hussite movement and moved, torching places, as far as Trutnov and Náchod.[300]

In the spring of 1427, the Bohemians themselves went on the offensive. Under their new leader, Procopius, the Taborites and Orphans crossed over the border. In mid-May they marched over the Zittau Mountains into the Lausitz. They spared Zittau because it was well fortified and garrisoned, and instead, they marched to Görlitz where they crossed the Oder River and invaded Silesia. There they plundered the towns of Lubań (Lauban), Lwówek Śląski (Löwenberg), Złotoryja (Goldberg), Jawor (Jauer) and Bolków (Bolkenhain). When their army stood before Lwówek Śląski, Captain von Schweidnitz tried to lead a Silesian levy there as a relief force. But the Bohemians intercepted the army on the march, defeated it in open battle and drove many of the mercenaries into the Bober River (Polish: Bóbr; Czech: Bobr). In the beginning of June, they returned to Bohemia. The incursion had so frightened the Lausitzer Six Cities and the Silesian nobles that they only led one limited assault against Náchod that year.[301]

During the Fourth Crusade, the Silesians undertook another relief attack. They advanced over the mountains to Náchod. On 9 August, just short of the town, they clashed with an Orphans army under Jan Čapek von Sán. The Silesians only carried out a halfhearted attack on the Hussites and then feigned a retreat. When the Orphans impetuously began a pursuit, they wound up in an ambush and were badly beaten. However, because the Silesians got word little later about the Battle of Tachov, they again withdrew.[302]

In 1428, Procopius made another invasion of Silesia. On 13 March, his forces stormed Ober-Glogau (now Głogówek in Poland). In the meanwhile, the Bishop of Breslau assembled a levy of nobles and from the towns around Neisse (Nysa, Poland), where a battle took place five days later. There the Hussites scored a complete success, killed 2,000 of the enemy or drowned them in the Eastern Neisse River. Then they pushed into the town's outskirts and put them to the torch. This victory led to such panic among the population, that many people fled their towns and villages when the Hussites neared and the Bohemians found them deserted. Breslau, which the field armies' advance guard reached on 30 March, was the only place the Hussites did not approach. Instead they burned down Reichenbach (Dzierżoniów). The Bishop of Breslau did not remain idle in the meantime and assembled a new army in April. But the Hussites also received reinforcements from Bohemia that swelled their army to 24,000 men. Procopius soon learned that the new Silesian army was gathering at Liegnitz (Legnica). When he united his forces there and wanted to accept battle, the Germans scattered. The Hussites marched on Breslau once again. Allegedly in those days 100,000 Silesians had fled to the city. Many of the towns that Procopius' army passed on the march tried to pay off the Hussites with one-time tribute so they would not burn them out. In mid-May, Bohemians' transport wagons were so packed full of booty that Procopius led his forces back over the border without having attempted to attack Breslau.[303]

In September of the same year, the Orphans returned and set up a camp near Glatz (Kłodzko) where they expected a Silesian levy's attack. This occurred on 27 December under Duke Johann von Münsterberg. But the defensive fires from the Hussites barricaded behind their wagons weakened the attack. When the cannon opened fire, the Silesian horsemen panicked and fled. The Duke with his horse and in his heavy armor got stuck in a

297 Silesia is now within Poland, so place names are given in German and Polish.

298 MACHILEK, Schlesien, pp. 126-129;
PALACKÝ, Der Hussitenkrieg 1419-1431, pp. 245-246.

299 MACHILEK, Schlesien, pp. 128-129;
PALACKÝ, Der Hussitenkrieg 1419-1431, p. 254.

300 MACHILEK, Schlesien , pp. 129-130;
PALACKÝ, Der Hussitenkrieg 1419-1431, p. 392.

301 MACHILEK, Schlesien, p. 130;

PALACKÝ, Der Hussitenkrieg 1419-1431, pp. 434-436;
DURDÍK, Hussitisches Heerwesen, pp. 231-233.

302 MACHILEK, Schlesien, p. 130;
PALACKÝ, Der Hussitenkrieg 1419-1431, p. 451.

303 MACHILEK, Schlesien, pp. 131-133;
PALACKÝ, Der Hussitenkrieg 1419-1431, pp. 462-464.

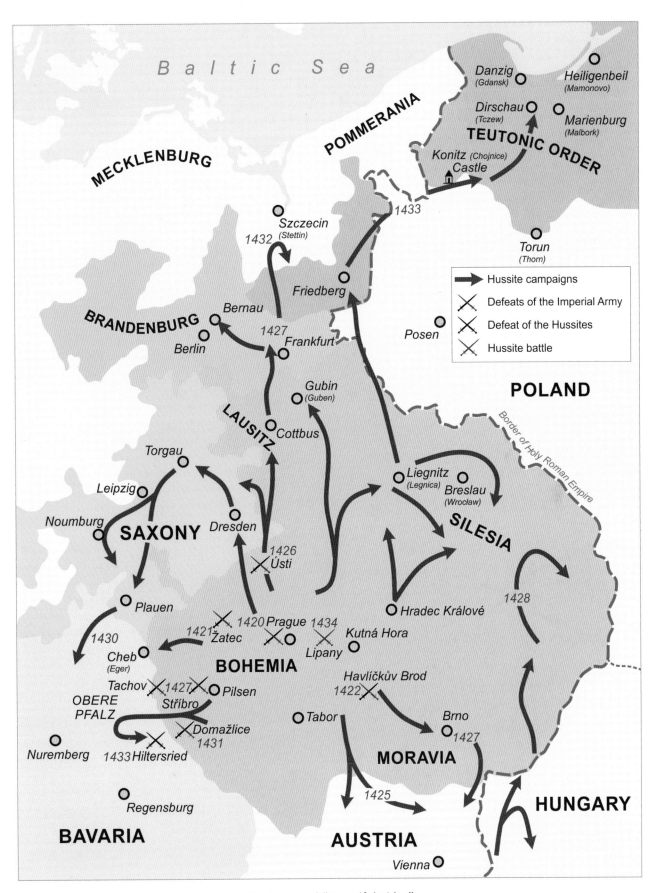

The Hussites' "Beautiful Rides".

swamp and was killed, as were 350 of his men. The Hussites continued the pursuit during the night and burned several villages. They devastated the land for ten weeks before they returned to Bohemia loaded down with booty.[304]

In 1430, the Hussite armies carried out another operation into Silesia breaking the ceasefire they had worked out with King Sigismund. It was led by one of Sigismund Korybut's supporters. The Hussites captured Brzeg (Brieg) and Niemcza (Nimtsch), which they were said to have occupied in the following years and from where they spread the movement into Silesia.[305]

In the summer 1430, Niemcza was still besieged by a Lausitzer levy and subjected to bombardment by heavy cannon. They caused serious damage to the town's walls, but the Hussite garrison was able to hold out. Finally two armies, one led by Procopius the Great, moved from Bohemia to relieve the town.[306]

In 1433, after the Hussites had pulled out large portions of their Silesian garrisons for an operation to Galicia (German: Galizien), the Duke of Troppau was able to retake the village of Odrau (Polish: Odry) on 28 April. However, he was quickly driven off by Boček Puklice z Pozořic (German: Bocek Puklice von Pzorice). Boček started a campaign deep in Silesian territory to relieve Landsberg (Gorzów Wielkopolski), which was besieged by several levies. But before he reached the town, the garrison had laid down its weapons. Boček himself was defeated on the way there and retreated to Odrau, which he defended until the autumn of 1434. The garrison of Niemcza also had to resist various attacks but likewise held out until 1434.[307]

Raids into the Lausitz

Along with Austria, the Lausitz region belonged to the Hussite's' preferred objectives from the very beginning. The so-called Six Cities (Sechsstädte) and the Lausitz Margraveships were part of Bohemia's kingdom and proved to be immune to the Hussite preaching. So King Sigismund's admonition to the city of Bautzen on 15 March of *"how grievously the Wycleffists, who are called Hussites, have committed disbelief, nonsense, misdeeds and unspeakable works, that they have done for a long time and do daily with destroying churches and many other inhuman acts contrary to Christian belief, the Holy Roman Church,"*[308] was hardly necessary to get the Lausitzers on his side.

In September 1420, a small army was already advancing as far as Zittau. In June, the town informed Görlitz's councilmen that a major invasion by the Hussites was about to occur and that *"if it is the evildoers' intent that they want to soon begin it, and they go with theirs with care, if we hear that it will not be otherwise, as that we will with God's help may resist them, with Your help, if we call you day or night or would send a messenger that we are in need."*[309] Because the town was well fortified and the heretics apparently did not have the necessary siege equipment, they moved on to Oybin.[310] But they could take neither the mountaintop castle nor monastery. After then burned down the associated farmhouse and some nearby villages, the Hussites headed back to Bohemia.[311]

This first operation had indeed put the Lausitzers on alert. Bautzen, Görlitz and Zittau renovated their city walls and prepared modern cannon. In 1421, the Lusatian League concluded a five-year mutual defense treaty with Friedrich the Warlike.

Initially the crusades tied up considerable Hussite strength in Bohemia. For example, in 1422, small raiding parties again and again moved along the Zittau Mountains. But they did not risk going into the Lausitz because they were too weak to attack Zittau and could have easily been cut off along their withdrawal route. At the beginning of the year, smaller Hussite units operated in the vicinity of Zittau and occupied Neuhaus, whereupon King Sigismund requested the Lusatian League, *"to help one*

304 MACHILEK, Schlesien, p. 133;
     PALACKÝ, Der Hussitenkrieg 1419-1431, pp. 470-472.

305 MACHILEK, Schlesien, p. 130;
     PALACKÝ, Der Hussitenkrieg 1419-1431, pp. 505-506.

306 MACHILEK, Schlesien, pp. 133-134;
     PALACKÝ, Der Hussitenkrieg 1419-1431, pp. 509-510.

307 ŠMAHEL, Hussitische Revolution II, pp. 1577-1578.

308 In MHG *"... wie gar grösslich der Wicleuisten die man anders Hussen nennet, vnglaube, vnsinne, vbeltate, vnd vnredliche werke, die Sy mit zerstörung kirchen, vnd mannichen andern vnmenschlichen dingen, langezijt begangen haben vnd teglich begeen, wider Christenn glauben, die heilig Romisch kirche..."* Quoted from PALACKÝ, Urkundliche Beiträge I, Nr. 15, pp. 22-23.

309 In MHG *"...wenne der bozewichte meynunge ist daz sie in kurcz das begynnen wollen, vnd das Ir euch mit den ewern vnde sie ec. Also in achtunge doryn setzcen wenn wir lo horen das es anders nicht seyn will, als das wir von gote gehulffen In widersteen mogen, mit ewir hulffe so wir euch anruffende tag oder nacht oder ander botschaft vnd das is not were tun wurden."* Quoted from PALACKÝ, Urkundliche Beiträge I, Nr. 116, p. 119.

310 Oybin - Ruins of a castle and monastery remain at Mount Oybin, which is located near Zittau and is about 45 kilometers or 28 miles from Görlitz.

311 KORSCHELT, Kriegsdrangsale der Oberlausitz, p. 174.

another. Therefore with this letter we [the King] request you all and each of you earnestly and firmly [help] the Zittauers, to rebuild that same Neuhaus and occupy and hold it."[312]

In April 1423, a band of just 400 men attacked the west of the Lausitz and burned some villages. The Lusatian League and some of the region's nobles decided on a counterstroke against Rumburk (Rumburg) in Bohemia. But the Lausitzers were badly beaten there. The Hussites mutilated or burned many of their allies. However the rest of 1423 remained peaceful.[313]

The following year, a Hussite army of 8,000 footsoldiers and 700 mounted men under Pezko of Poděbrad (Pezko von Podiebrad) neared the border. The Zittauers, who hoped for support from their Lusatian League partners, occupied the Karlsfried Castle so they could better protect the border. On 25 January, the Zittauers bravely marched against the enemy but were decisively defeated. The Hussites sent back 15 of the 16 prisoners with severed thumbs and noses to frighten the town. Karlsfried was stormed quickly and then destroyed. Poděbrad set up his quarters in Hartau and turned his focus to the castellans (*Burggrafen*) von Dohna at Grafenstein and Zittau. The Hussites were able to destroy many villages, but the well-fortified town as well as the castle, which was on the heights, both withstood their assaults. Afterward, Poděbrad withdrew. The Lusatian League's help arrived in the border region too late, but still undertook retaliatory operations in Bohemia in February. The Lausitzers also took advantage of the small villages there.[314]

Finally the Hussite movement also spread to the Lausitzers. In 1425, the influential lords of Wartenburg joined with the Bohemians. They owned the Tollenstein, Tetschen, Kamnitz and Demnin castles that henceforth served as deployment bases for raids on Lausitz towns. At Easter of 1425, Johann von Wartenberg went from Tollenstein with his band through the Lausitz as far as Marienthal. Wartenberg stole a large herd of cattle that he hoped to sell profitably in Bohemia. On the way to Rumburk he got into a battle at the village of Spitzcunnersdorf with a Zittau levy, which was badly beaten by Wartenberg's force. Their commander, Nicol of Ponikau, was taken to Tollenstein as a prisoner.[315]

In the summer of 1425, a Taborite army advanced over the border. The reason for this may have been the anti-Hussite alliance that King Sigismund had concluded on 25 July with the Duke of Austria, the Elector of Saxony and also the Lusatian League. The Hussites burned down the towns of Weisswasser (Běla Woda), Mimoň (Niemes) and Jablonné (Gabel). An attack on the town of Löbau was repulsed, but its outskirts were severely damaged. The area around Kamenz (now Kamjenc in Poland) was also devastated. Finally the Hussites were joined by the Lausitz nobleman Sigismund von Wartenberg at Děčín (Tetschen) and by Vilém z Lípa (Wilhelm von Leipa) at Ronov nad Doubravou (Ronow) and then headed for Löbau again. The city of Görlitz sent some handgunners to reinforce the town's garrison. In the end, Löbau withstood the siege.[316]

Aside from the "renegades," the Lausitz knighthood and the towns displayed great unity. Albrecht von Kolditz, appointed as the Land Steward (*Landvogt*) by Sigismund in 1425, decided that the League should employ a mercenary army long term.

After a large part of the Lusatian League's army was destroyed at Ústí, Wartenberg's men again attacked the villages in the late summer of 1426. Johann blockaded the city of Zittau with 400 horsemen, while his brother Heinrich stole huge herds of cattle between Dittersdorf and Cunnersdorf. As the thieving knights were trying to take their booty over the border, they were surprised by a Zittau levy, attacked and thoroughly defeated.[317]

In 1427, the Hussites carried out another major incursion in the Lausitz. Procopius the Great and Welek Kaudelink (Wenzel von Kaudelink) had assembled large armies in the Zittau Mountains. To protect the threatened border city, the *Landvogt* transferred many of the Teutonic Order knights to Zittau. Görlitz also sent a large contingent to help. The Hussites began the siege at the beginning of April. But the garrison withstood all the attempted assaults and after fourteen days the Bohemian army headed to the north. They devastated Hirschfeld, the Marienthal Monastery and Ostritz. However, the Hussites balked at a siege of the Oder River city of Görlitz, which had already prepared a strong defense. Instead, they appeared at Lauban on 15 May. The town's citizens were even able to beat Bohemians with an initial sortie. During a second sortie, however, they were defeated by the Hussites. When the Laubaners fled back into the town, the Hussites followed them and pushed through the open gates. The town was plundered for two long days and then burned to the ground before the Hussites moved on.[318]

The spring and summer of 1428 initially remained peaceful. But in November, Welek Kaudelink returned with an army and stormed the Frýdland (Friedland) Castle. From there, the Hussites moved to Görlitz, which they again bypassed and from there went on to Löbau, which they completely put to the torch. In the west, another band joined with the lord of Wartenberg to steal cattle in the western Lausitz. On 11 November, both forces returned to Rumburk, pursued by the *Landvogt's* levies.

312 In MHG *"...einander zu helffen. Daromb gebieten wir ewer allen und ewer yglichen ernstlich und vesticlich mit diesem brieue, dass Ir den czittawern, dasselbe Newehaus wider zu bawen das zu beseczen zu behalden."* Quoted from PALACKÝ, Urkundliche Beiträge I, Nr. 285, p. 324.

313 KORSCHELT, Kriegsdrangsale der Oberlausitz, p. 174.

314 Ibid., pp. 174-175.

315 Ibid., p. 176.

316 Ibid., pp. 175-176.

317 Ibid., pp. 176-177.

318 Ibid., pp. 177-178.

Five later, fighting took place at Chrastava (Kratzau). The Lusatian League succeeded in scattering the Hussites with their second attack, causing the latter to lose not only their booty, but also 600 dead and 400 prisoners. At Machnín (Machendorf) many of the Bohemians drowned attempting to swim across the Neisse River. Others were driven into barns by the Lusatians and burned. The victory caused a great sensation in the Upper Lausitz.[319]

But Hussitism was still not extinguished. In the spring and summer of 1429, smaller Hussite raiding parties moved through the Lausitz, before almost the entire united power of the Bohemians under Procopius the Great was to follow in the autumn (see following section).[320] When the Hussites finally advanced over the Erz Mountains in October, the Lusatian League feared the next major attack. In this regard, Görlitz's Council requested news from Dresden: *"We have heard that the damned heretics may have encamped in the country of Meissen. [Therefore,] we ask thee [tell us] what thou hast heard of their plans, where they are bound and also will turn, and what their intention is."*[321]

After their major campaign, the Hussites again went back into the Lausitz in the summer 1430. They occupied Löbau, from where Sigismund von Wartenberg carried out a series of raids on Děčín (Tetschen) and its vicinity. He even threatened Görlitz, but then he passed by it with his army and marched on Rózbork (Rothenburg). In December, an Orphans' army passed over the Zittau Mountains and moved toward Bernstadt. The inhabitants, who had already brought all their possessions behind the tall walls of the church for safety, surrendered without any resistance and were therefore spared. The Bohemians occupied the town and then moved further west. Besides Bernsdorf, they also occupied Altbernsdorf, Cunnersdorf, Dittersbach and Cástá (Kiesbach). The inhabitants received written passes and in return had to promise never to take up arms against the Hussites. Additionally, they were supposed to no longer pay their hereditary taxes to their lords, but to the Bohemian brothers instead. In fact, the hill by Reichenbach, where the letters were issued is still called the *"Ketzerberg"* "Heretics Hill" today. In the meantime, the peasants from the surrounding villages had fled to Reichenbach. Its inhabitants decided to oppose the Hussites. They dug a deep moat around the church's walls and put up their defense behind them. The Orphans first pillaged the half deserted town and then began their assault on the fortified church. The first attack was repulsed in a hail of crossbow bolts and handgun projectiles. But then the Hussites were able to climb over the north wall of the church complex. What followed was a bloody slaughter. The remaining defenders fled into the solid church building. They threw hot tar from the clock tower onto the attackers and repelled the assault. The Orphans tried to storm the house of worship for another fifteen days. When the Lausitz levies under Thimo von Kolditz and Hans von Polenz appeared before Reichenbach on 10 January 1431, the Orphans set fire to the town and withdrew.[322]

But in February, a new army of Taborites and Orphans under Procopius' leadership moved from Silesia toward Görlitz. In the meanwhile, the city had further improved its fortifications and had its own strong body of mercenaries. Therefore, the Hussites bypassed Görlitz and marched on Bautzen. The city leaders offered Procopius a one-time payment of tribute if he would immediately move on with this army, but he refused. The Bautzeners had to burn down their suburbs, which they had just rebuilt, and pulled back behind their walls for protection. On 21 February, the Hussites had drawn up heavy cannon at two different locations and began to bombard the city. After nine hours, Procopius started an assault that was, however, driven off. Then the Hussites immediately broke off the siege and moved on to Löbau, which they captured without difficulty and occupied with 400 men. They exhausted the villages of the surrounding area and finally marched to Grosshennersdorf. An attack on Zittau, which was fired upon with heavy cannon, also failed so that Procopius led his army back to Bohemia.[323]

At Penacost, Procopius again appeared before Zittau and began a traditional siege of the town. But its garrison had been significantly reinforced by levies from the Lusatian League, so that the Hussites did not risk attempting to storm the town. So Procopius divided his army, sent a part to Frýdlant (Friedland) and used the other part to releave Löbau's small garrison, which in the meantime was under dire pressure by the Lausitzer levies. Subsequently this element moved on to Silesia. The group that had been sent to Frýdlant under Zapko von Zaan also turned toward the north and stopped at Lauban (now Lubań, Poland). Its populace fled to a nearby Franciscan monastery that at first refused any demands to capitulate. Initially, they were able to fend off many attacks by the Hussites. But then the Hussite artillery was able to shoot a breach in the walls through which Zaan's soldiers forced their way into the monastery. The defenders were killed or burned without any considerations.[324]

Because Löbau's Hussite garrison repeatedly carried out pillaging raid in the vicinity, in July the Oberlausitzers decided to retake the town. Löbau fell after a twenty-six day siege. Subsequently, the Steward (*Vogt*), Albrecht von

---

319 Ibid., pp. 178-179.

320 Ibid., p. 178.

321 Quoted from CDS II 5, Nr. 179, p. 149. In MHG *"Wir habin vornomen, wie das die verdampten ketzcere ire legir vmbe uch im lande zcu Miessin sullin habin. Bitten wir uch, was ir vornemet von irer gelegginheit, wo sie sich hyn meinen zcukeren und adir wendin und was dorynne ir vorsacz sey."*

---

322 KORSCHELT, Kriegsdrangsale der Oberlausitz, pp. 180-182.

323 Ibid., p. 182.

324 Ibid., pp. 182-183.

CCXlix

Hie lagent die Hussen vor Görlitz mit grosser machte
vnd das wart hans von bollentz gewar mit dem lant volk
vnd gewan den Hussen an ir wagenburg vnd erstochent
su alle tot

A Lausitz Levy Storms a Hussite *Wagenburg*
(From *"Geschichte Kaiser Sigismunds"*)

Kolditz, recommended, *"that one burn it out, throw down and plow under the town walls, towers and defenses, and fill in the moats."*[325]

After that, the greatest threat to commerce and peace in general was from Nicol von Keuschberg, a Hussite supporter. He had Grafenstein and Hamrštějn (Hammerstein) firmly in his hands and had turned the church in Chrastava into a veritable fortress. He even dared to attack Görlitz. After an indecisive fight with its garrison before the city's gates, he was however forced to withdraw. Keuschberg remained a permanent threat. In January 1433, the Görlitzers and some Lausitz nobles finally were able to lure Keuschberg's troops into an ambush near Frýdlant and badly defeat them. They lost 60 dead, 9 wounded and 14 prisoners, most of whom were later executed in Görlitz. The victorious levies subsequently moved on to Chrastava and captured the robbers' nest.[326]

In the same year, Grafenstein was betrayed by Ralsko von Wartenberg auf Roll to the *Landvogt* who captured the castle with a levy from Görlitz. Ralsko himself was taken captive by the Zittauers a little later and executed, whereupon the family swore bloody revenge against the city. After that, Johann and Sigismund von Wartenberg executed any Zittauers who fell into their hands during their raids. They even were so bold as to attack Zittau's weavers' suburb, which they burned to the ground. In 1434, a skirmish took place between a Zittau levy and the Wartenbergs at Rosenthal bei Hirschfeld. The Zittauers got the short end of the stick and retreated. The victors marched home with six wagons loaded with booty. Starting in 1434, no further large Hussite forces entered the Lausitz, but the war between the Lusatian League and the Wartenbergs and Keuschbergs supposedly lasted another ten years.[327]

The Great Hussite Campaign of 1429-30

The dramatic, unglamorous failure of the Fourth Crusade showed the Hussites the weakness of the Empire and made a sortie from Bohemia seem very promising. Procopius the Great's image had so increased from his victory at Ústi and the successes at Stříbro and Tachov that he could temporarily unite the quarrelling Hussite factions. And finally, Friedrich the Warlike, one of the most dangerous enemies of the heretics' movement, died on 4 January 1428.[328]

A thrust into the central German area seemed a military necessity at this time. Despite the Hussites' military successes, the lengthy war, which had been conducted almost exclusively in Bohemia, exhausted the country. In April 1427, Gottfried von Rodenberg already reported

to the Teutonic Order's Grand Master (*Hochmeister*) about the rising prices for food in Prague: *"Also, gracious, dear Master, according to Lord Johann von Wartenberg, the sale of all kinds of food from time to time gets more expensive in Prague, especially a bushel of salt which one must buy for a Schock and 20 Groschen."*[329] The country was even reliant on imports for essentials like salt because it was not naturally present in Bohemia.

An incursion into densely populated Saxony and the Lausitz regions promised the prospect of booty, above all in the form of foodstuffs. Up to then, only small bands had gone over the Erz Mountains. They had met only relatively minor resistance and had taken rich booty.[330]

Since the defeat at Ústi, at least in Saxony they were conscious of the danger of an invasion by the Hussites. In the summer of 1429, the new Elector Friedrich II regularly received warnings from the town of Most, which his forces were still defending. But Procopius' campaign was initially directed against the Oberlausitz region. A large army under Johann von Koluch and Johann von Wartenberg advanced over the mountains along the border. The Hussites overran Oybin, which was thoroughly plundered. A little later, another army under Procopius the Small (der Kleiner) followed with 4,000 men on foot and 400 mounted accompanied by 130 war wagons. They moved to Löbau, captured the town and devastated Ebersbach and Gersdorf. At Frenzelberg bei Warnsdorf the Hussites and the Lausitzers were said to have waged a major battle with 1,000 casualties. On 3 October, the Hussites appeared before Görlitz. But the city withstood their attack so that only some suburbs fell victim to the flames. The armies then marched to the west, devastated the area around Bautzen as well as the towns of Bischofswerda, Pulsnitz and Königsbrück. The Marienstern Monastery was burned down. Kamjenc (Kamenz) withstood the enemy army's onslaught for five days. When the besiegers were able to break down the Castle Gate (*Burgtor*), they pushed into the town. More than 1,200 people were killed in the ensuing pillaging. On 13 October, another army element had appeared in front of Bautzen that was defended by the Land Stewart (*Landvogt*) Thimo von Kolditz. On the first day, the defenders were still able to repel all the assaults. But on the following day, several fires broke out in Bautzen that destroyed almost a quarter of the city. On the third day of the siege, when the Hussites tried to storm the walls on ladders they had obtained from the surrounding villages, their leader Molesto was fatally struck by two arrows. Discouraged, the Hussites gave up the siege. Allegedly they had bribed the towns' scribe, Peter Prischwitz, who was to spoil the gunpow-

325 In MHG *"... das man sy auszbrante, Stadmawir, Türme vnd dy Weren zu würffe vnd zu flügei vnd die Graben fülte."* Quoted from PALACKÝ, Urkundliche Beiträge II, Nr. 795, p. 274.

326 KORSCHELT, Kriegsdrangsale der Oberlausitz, p. 183.

327 Ibid., pp. 183-184.

328 KROCKER, Sachsen und die Hussitenkriege, p. 28.

329 In MGH, *"Ouch gnediger liber her meister zo saget her John von Wartenberg daz allerley spyse koff czu male tawir sey in Prag sunderlich eynen scheffel salcz mus man kouffen vm eyn schock vnd XX groschen."* Quoted from PALACKÝ, Urkundliche Beiträge I, Nr. 434, p. 497.

330 KROCKER, Sachsen und die Hussitenkriege, pp. 28-29.

der and set fire to the town to distract the defenders. On 6 December, Prischwitz was therefore placed inside a cow's hide and dragged through the town, disemboweled and quartered. The four parts of his body were then hung up in the locations on the town wall where the Hussites had tried to storm it.[331]

On 18 October, Procopius the Great appeared in the Oberlausitz with another 5,000 men. The commander had skillfully pushed past the Saxon border castles and fortresses in the East Erz Mountains (*Osterzgebirge*). The Hussites were able to overrun Altendresden (present day Neustadt). They pillaged and set fire to the place, but left the considerably better fortified town on the east bank as they did later for Meissen. Instead, they marched along the river's east bank far to the north (supposedly almost to Magdeburg, but which is doubted today) and carefully plundered that area. Subsequently, the force turned to the east and invaded the Lower Lausitz (*Niederlausitz*) where the Hussites pillaged the Neuzelle Monastery and the town of Gubín. On their return march by way of Silesia, the Hussites appeared again before Görlitz and demanded the handover of the city. In response, the burghers stuck the envoy in a sack and threw him in the Neisse River. Procopius had the Görlitz suburbs burned, however, he did not risk an attack on the city. From there they surprisingly turned to the west. It wasn't until mid-November that their army returned to Prague.[332]

But in mid-December, a much stronger Hussite army under Procopius' leadership, estimated to be up to 40,000 footsoldiers, 4,000 horsemen and 2,500 war wagons, again made its way into Saxony. On 14 December, the commander left Prague, four days later he reached his troops who had assembled at Krupka, and on 20 and 21 December, the Hussites streamed over the Nollendorfer Pass and advanced on the city of Pirna.[333]

Elector Friedrich sent the imperial princes many letters requesting help, but no one came to his aid. He moved with his small army – unfortunately reliable estimates are completely lacking – back inside the walls of the small city of Leipzig where he prepared for a siege by burning the suburbs. Procopius' army cut a swath of destruction through West Saxony.[334]

Only then did the Empire assemble levies; indeed, only the Elector of Brandenburg among the great princes agreed to help. The young Margrave Johann led that army,

actually between 10,000 and 20,000 men, to Oschatz, while the Saxon army deployed between Grimma and Leipzig.[335]

But the Hussites attacked before both armies could unite. On 29 December, they captured Oschatz and burned down the town. Margrave Johann retreated to Leipzig. The Bohemians took and torched the towns of Strehla, Torgau, Riesa and Belgern over the New Year's period. Then they advanced on Wurzen, burned the town and moved up the Mulde River, supposedly to cross it at Nerchau on 6 January 1430. The Saxon army appears to have put up no resistance there. Subsequently the Hussites moved on Leipzig. They plundered the surrounding villages, but left the commercial city in peace, probably because they did not want to engage the unified Saxon-German army there with a siege. A battle was not the objective of this campaign.[336]

Before Leipzig they divided their army into five columns and marched on a broad front to the south. On 12 January one of the groups captured Altenburg, ransacked the town, but failed in an attempt to capture the fortified palace.[337]

On 25 January, the Hussites stormed Plauen in a "*battle here at the castle, the Bohemians killed holy and secular, noble and common, burgers and peasants together with many honest people and [have} destroyed and plundered everything,...*"[338] In the small town, which in 1388 still counted 3,400 inhabitants, an estimated 500 to 1,000 people were killed and many had their hands and feet hacked off.[339]

The army moved from the *Vogtland* into the Franconian territory on a route parallel to the mountains along the Bohemian-German border and attacked the Hohenzollern possessions there. The town of Hof was taken and burned as they marched by. Kulmbach and Bayreuth also fell into their hands. Only well fortified castles that put up stubborn resistance remained spared. On this campaign, the Hussites were out for quick booty and avoided tough fighting. Then it was the Elector Friedrich of Brandenburg who was asking the Empire's estates for assistance with defending his hereditary lands, but he was also essentially ignored. Nuremberg was threatened to be the next to fall victim to the storm, so the Hohenzollers decided to buy

331 PALACKÝ, Der Hussitenkrieg 1419-1431, pp. 486-489; KROCKER, Sachsen und die Hussitenkriege, pp. 29-30; KORSCHELT, Kriegsdrangsale der Oberlausitz, p. 179.

332 KROCKER, Sachsen und die Hussitenkriege, pp. 29-30; KORSCHELT, Kriegsdrangsale der Oberlausitz, pp. 179-180.

333 PALACKÝ, Der Hussitenkrieg 1419-1431, pp. 489-490; KROCKER, Sachsen und die Hussitenkriege, pp. 30-31; BEZOLD, Sigismund und die Reichskriege, pp. 28-29.

334 KROCKER, Sachsen und die Hussitenkriege, pp. 31-32; GUNDRAM, Döbeln und die Hussiten, pp. 8-9.

335 KROCKER, Sachsen und die Hussitenkriege, pp. 32-33; GUNDRAM, Döbeln und die Hussiten, pp. 9-10; KRZENCK, Hussitenkriege, p. 67.

336 PALACKÝ, Der Hussitenkrieg 1419-1431, pp. 490-491; KROCKER, Sachsen und die Hussitenkriege, pp. 33-34; Döbeln und die Hussiten, p. 10; KRZENCK, Hussitenkriege, pp. 67-68.

337 KROCKER, Sachsen und die Hussitenkriege, p. 34; GUNDRAM, Döbeln und die Hussiten, pp. 10-13.

338 In MHG "*... schlacht, so die behemen alhier aufn schloß geistlich und weltlich, edel und unedel, buerger und pawern und samt viel redlicher leut erschlagen und alles zerstort und geplundert.*" Quoted from GRINTZER, Zerstörung der Stadt Plauen, p. 142.

339 GRINTZER, Zerstörung der Stadt Plauen, pp. 143-144; KROCKER, Sachsen und die Hussitenkriege, p. 34.

their way out of danger by making a considerable tribute payment. The towns of Bamberg and Forchheim provided 12,000 *Talers* for that, as did Nuremberg, while Elector Friedrich paid 9,000 and Johann of Bavaria contributed 8,000 *Talers*.[340] On 11 February, the Elector and Procopius, along with the most important Hussite captains, met at the Böheimstein Castle[341] and signed a treaty according to which the Hussites would return to their homeland after payment of the "contribution." It was the first treaty in which the Bohemian heretics were treated as an equal negotiating partner. The treaty bears signatures of the captains of the five major army columns: Jakob Kromesin of Brezovic commanded the Taborites' field army, Ondřej Keřský z Řimovic commanded Old Tabor, *Jiří* of Řečici led the Orphans' army, Sigmund Manda z Kotenčic headed the Prazans' levy and Jan Královec z Hrádu commanded the forces from the remaining Bohemian towns. In mid-February, the Hussites finally returned to their homeland by way of the Fichtel Mountains and the Bohemian Forest.[342] On 21 February, the army arrived in Prague with hundreds of wagons full of booty.[343]

Beforehand, the news of the heretics approach caused unrest in the Bishopric of Bamberg. A chronicler reported: *"300 bold knaves came together there, forced their way into the town hall and other houses, and the [women's] cloister, took whatever they wanted with great lewdness, for which there was no help or consolation."*[344] The Waldensian communities in Franconia had been sympathetic to the Bohemian heretics since 1418. However, Bamberg's plundering cannot be viewed as a medieval, popular revolt as Marxist journalism liked to portray it. When the news arrived that the Hussites were approaching, the majority of the population left the city. The few people who remained in Bamberg almost exclusively belonged to the lower social classes and simply used the opportunity to enrich themselves in the deserted burgers' and councilmen's houses.[345]

The Raid into the Mark Brandenburg in 1432

At a *Landtag* in Prague in February 1432, the quarrelling Hussite parties agreed to undertake a major "ride" to Brandenburg. Supposedly they were endeavoring to financially hurt the Elector of Brandenburg. Friedrich I had led the Empire's armies on three crusades into Bohemia, the last time in 1431. At this point in time, the Hussites possibly were already conducting peace negotiations with the Electorate of Saxony and hoped that a successful incursion into the Mark would also prompt Brandenburg to leave the alliance with Sigismund. Besides that, an operation in a so far unscathed area held the prospect of rich booty.[346]

The "ride" began in March with two armies. One Taborite ca. 5,000-man army under Otík z Lozy (German: Otik von Loza) marched over the Iser Mountains (Isergebirge) to the North Bohemian town of Friedland. The town was plundered and burned. Then the army pushed into Lower Silesia and occupied Bunzlau (Bolesławiec, Poland) and Świebodzice (Freiburg). The Taborites split up there. A unit advanced on Gubín in the Lower Lausitz, the other turned to the south and marched on Görlitz, where it awaited the arrival of the Orphans' army.[347]

This Orphans' army under Jan Čapek assembled in eastern Bohemia and in the second half of March first marched northward in two columns. A group moved directly toward the Taborite element before Görlitz, the other followed Lozy's route of march through Silesia and joined his army before Gubín on 6 April. Shortly thereafter the army from Görlitz arrived before the town so that the Hussites could bring together a force of almost 10,000 soldiers there. In view of the overwhelming numerical superiority, the town council voluntarily opened the gates and declared themselves to be ready to pay a large "contribution."[348]

In mid-April, the Hussites carried out assaults from Gubín into Brandenburg with smaller units. One group advanced as far as Seelow and plundered the countryside. But on the Hussites' return march, a levy from the city of Frankfurt (an der Oder) attacked the Bohemians at Müllrose and wiped them out. The Bohemians lost about 300 to 400 men. The city council wrote to the Görlitz city council about the battle: *"We inform you that with the help of God we have slain and have burned almost 400 heretics at Melrosen in Stettin. .. the next Tuesday [15 April] .. captured more than 40 horses."*[349] So the main army broke up its camp at Gubín on 13 April and moved on Frankfurt. But

---

340 A Taler was a silver coin used in some areas within the Holy Roman Empire and it is the term from which the English word "dollar" is thought to have been derived.

341 The Böheimstein Castle, now ruins, is located in the town of Pegnitz in Upper Franconia in Bavaria.

342 The Fichtel Mountains are called the *Fichtelgebirge* in German and in Czech *Smrčiny*, while the Bohemian Forest is known in German as the *Böhmerwald* and in Czech as *Šumava*.

343 PALACKÝ, Der Hussitenkrieg 1419-1431, pp. 491-496; KROCKER, pp. 34-35; MACHILEK, Hussiten in Franken, pp. 28-30; BEZOLD, Sigismund und die Reichskriege, pp. 32-35.

344 In MHG *"do kamen bei 300 küner buben zusamen, stiessen das rathaus vnd ander hewser auff, vnd die frauenkloster, namen was In gefiel, mit grosser vnzucht, des war kein hülf oder trost."* Quoted from PALACKÝ, Urkundliche Beiträge II, Nr. 644, p. 104.

345 MACHILEK, Hussiten in Franken, pp. 27-28.

346 TRESP, Hussiten vor Bernau, p. 144; JECHT, Zug der Hussiten nach der Mark, pp. 31-32.

347 TRESP, Hussiten vor Bernau, p. 144; JECHT, Zug der Hussiten nach der Mark, pp. 32-34.

348 TRESP, Hussiten vor Bernau, p. 144; JECHT, Zug der Hussiten nach der Mark, pp. 35-39.

349 In MHG *"Thun wir euch wissen, das wir mit der Hülffe Gotis der Ketzir na by 400. Tot geslagin und vorbrant haben zur Melrosen im Stetchin. Dorzu unser G. H. den nehsten dinstag [15 April] vorgangin in ouch mehr denn 40. Pferd vnd gefangin haben."* Quoted from PALACKÝ Urkundliche Beiträge II, Nr. 799, p. 279.

This depiction from the "*Geschichte Kaiser Sigismunds*" shows the Hussite attack on the town of Bernau.

Previous Double Page:
On their "Beautiful Rides," the Hussites preferred to attack small towns that could not adequately defend themselves. It often happened that the citizens in such towns retreated into walled churches and put up a defense there, as shown in the illustration.

the city was well fortified and withstood their attempts to storm it. The Hussites avoided a drawn-out siege, pillaged the outskirts of the town, burned it to the ground, and finally move to the west. Over the following days, many groups of them devastated the land between the Oder and Spree Rivers, and attacked Fürstenwalde and Altlandsberg. They stormed Müncheberg, Buckow and Straßberg and almost completely burned down these towns. The Hussites' most northerly detachment advanced as far as Gersdorf near Eberswalde. That is where the son of the Elector, the Margrave Johann, gathered the Brandenburg army. However, he needed time, which the Hussites did not give him. Brandenburg was, therefore, dependent upon its towns' ability to defend themselves.[350]

On the evening of 22 April, the Hussites appeared before Bernau. It is not certain whether it was their entire army or only a reinforced unit. In any case, on their "beautiful rides" the Hussites always stripped the areas bare and did not occupy the towns or cities for long. So a complete concentration of forces against a town or city would have been unlikely. Bernau was an excellently fortified town with walls up to eight meters (26 feet) high interspersed with 42 towers. On 23 April, the Hussites attempted to storm the town. The valiant population defended itself with all means available and poured "*Treiber*," a thick brewer's byproduct, from the walls. Eventually they were able to fend off the attack. The Hussites returned to their camp, licked their wounds and ended the siege the next day. During the Hussites' withdrawal, the Bernauers kept a watchful eye on them and fell upon a number of their stragglers. But the Bohemians' planned major battle never took place.[351]

In the end, the Taborites and Orphans withdrew from Mark Brandenburg in good order. The two armies went their separate ways at Gubín. The Taborites went back to Bohemia by way of the Lausitz while the Orphans took the route via Silesia. At the beginning of May, the two armies arrived in their homeland.[352]

Hussites in Poland

The Grand Kingdom of Poland-Lithuania initially took a wait-and-see, even partially a protective approach to the Hussites. The reason for this was obvious: King Wladislaw Jagiello had grown up in Lithuania's pagan culture. His conversion to the Christian faith was for political reasons. On one hand, it was so he could marry to the Polish king's daughter, Hedwig. And on the other, he wanted to take away the religious justification for the existence of the Teutonic Order's State, which was geographically surrounded by Poland-Lithuania. He was definitely not firm

in his Christianity. And the house of Luxembourg was a thorn in his side because Sigismund ruled not only Hungary and Bohemia but also the Empire. So the Hussite revolution presented a welcome means to weaken his competition for the Bohemian crown. Hussites going to Poland were not persecuted in the kingdom; and for example, on 28 February 1421, Kaiser Sigismund angrily wrote to Friedrich I of Brandenburg: "*So the King of Poland and his cousin Vytautas take in the heretics from Prague and their companions, and as is the common talk, Vytautas wants to give them aid and to move against us with force; and to accompany them, against God and the Christian faith, and to oust us as the king of the Bohemian crown; and us, as if we do not trust in God, but instead abandon [our] complete hope in God to bring all of Christendom to disgrace and ruin: and it is indeed foreseeable that the King of Poland will not leave his brother.*"[353]

In 1421, Sigismund sent a letter to the Grand Master of the Teutonic Order. In it, he directed him to attack the King of Poland "*if it should happen that the King of Poland and Duke Vytautas want to side with and help the heretics.*"[354]

Only after growing pressure from Sigismund and also from the Pope, did Wladislaw's stance toward the Hussites become more hostile. Therefore, on 1 April 1424, he issued an edict against the Hussites in his own land and demanded that all Poles who had gone with Sigismund Korybut to Bohemia must return otherwise he would consider them as heretics.[355] That year, the Polish King increasingly distanced himself from Korybut and declared that he wanted to raise an army against the Hussites, but claimed that he lacked the money to do so.

Lithuanian Grand Prince Vytautas died in 1430. For a long time there had been tensions between the united Polish-Lithuanian Kingdom's two peoples that then erupted. There were various pretenders to the Lithuanian throne. One of them was Sigismund Korybut. In March, the aged King Wladislaw called a meeting of the estates of the realm in Cracow (Kraków) at which the religious issue

---

350 TRESP, Hussiten vor Bernau, pp. 144-145;
     JECHT, Zug der Hussiten nach der Mark, pp. 40-43.

351 TRESP, Hussiten vor Bernau, p. 145;
     JECHT, Zug der Hussiten nach der Mark, pp. 42-46.

352 TRESP, Hussiten vor Bernau, p. 145;
     JECHT, Zug der Hussiten nach der Mark, pp. 45-47.

353 In MHG, although most likely originally written in Latin: "*So nympt ouch der kunig von Polan vnd Witold seyn vetter auf die ketzer von Prag vnd ire beyleger, vnd als die gemeyn red ist, der Witold meynet in hulffe zu tun vnd sich myt macht wider vns zusetzen, vnd in beylegen, wider got vnd christen glawben, vnd vns als eynnen kunig der cronn Behem zudrucken, vnd vns, als verre als das an im were, des wir gott nicht getrawen, sunder gantze hoffnung in got setzen, der nyderzulegen, der ganczen kristenheit zu schande vnd schaden: vnd ist wol versechlich, das der kunig von Polan seynen bruder nicht verlassen wurde.*" Quoted from PALACKÝ, Urkundliche Beiträge I, Nr. 66, p. 65.

354 In MHG "*... were es der Sache, das der kunig von Polan und Herzog Wytold den Keczern zulegen und helfen wollten.*" Quoted from PALACKÝ, Urkundliche Beiträge I, Nr. 146, p. 156.

355 PALACKÝ, Urkundliche Beiträge I, Nr. 288, pp. 331-333; Nr. 290, pp. 333-334;
     ŠMAHEL, Hussitische Revolution III, pp. 1936-1937.

was also to be discussed. If Korybut's following actually succeeded, then Hussitism also threatened to gain a foothold in Poland.[356]

However, as a consequence of the military cooperation between the Hussites and the Poles against the Teutonic Order in 1433 and in Bohemia itself in 1438, close personal contacts between the Bohemian and Polish petty nobility had arisen. It led to a moderate form of Utraquism spreading in Poland. After the Hussite Wars had abated in Bohemia itself, their brothers in Poland held on relatively long. In fact, after the failed candidacy of a Polish magnate for Bohemian crown, the Bishop of Cracow, Zbygniew Olesnicki, attempted to form a confederation to fight against the Utraquist nobility. On 4 May 1439, an army of Polish Hussites under Spytko of Melsztyn was wiped out by the Confederates at Grotniki and with that blow, the movement in Poland was decisively weakened. Spytko von Melsztyn died in the battle.[357]

The Great "Beautiful Ride" of 1433

During the major Hussite campaigns in central Germany in 1429-30, the Grand Master of the Teutonic Order had already informed his commanders (Komture) that the Hussites *"also want to invade and damage our lands."*[358] The rumors were not completely out of thin air, because the Komtur of Kalau (present Kaława, Poland) received a letter from his cousin informing him extensively about the Hussites' sweep through the Margraveship of Meissen and closed with: *"Also prisoners and others at the court and from the other ends [of the land] have said that they suppose that [the Hussites] will come to you in the Prussian land, that you indeed know how to act, that you should examine such talk and threats that they have made against your Order, so you must speak with the Grand Master for my sake."*[359] The Hussites headed to the west, but when the Taborites' army invaded Silesia in March, the Grand Master heard renewed rumors about a possible move against Poland.[360]

The Hussites began their largest "beautiful ride" in 1433. On 22 March, the Taborite army under Jan Pardus z Vratkova (also called Jan Pardus z Hrádku, or in German Jan Pardus von Hrádek) started to march. The Hussites marched through Silesia, where they gathered another

3,000 to 4,000 men from their garrisons. At the end of March, they camped in the vicinity of Rybnik and supplemented their provisions. From there, they marched on Pless (Pszczyna), where on 10 April messengers from the Polish King met them. Wladislaw could not persuade the Hussites to take part in his war against the Order, but because they had turned to Galicia, he could be sure that Sigismund would not attack him in the rear from there if he attacked the Order's State. Because he had also guaranteed the Hussites the right to free transit through his kingdom, he was able to break their political support for Swidrygello, who was still fighting about Vytautas' succession. At the end of May, Pardus´ army ravaged Galicia and in three weeks traveled back the enormous distance of 1,300 kilometers (about 800 miles).[361]

In contrast, at the end of April, an Orebite army and a unit of the Hradec Králové Orphans under the joint leadership of Jan Čapek moved in two columns into Prussian Pomerania and the Neumark which both belonged to the Teutonic Order. However, the Hussites experienced an initial setback at Frankfurt an der Oder where their attempt to cross the Oder River was fended off by a levy from the Lausitz. The Hussites headed back to Gubín and then on to Glogau (Głogówek), where they made it to the Oder River's right bank and reinforced their army with local levies that increased their forces to 700 horsemen, 350 war wagons and 5,000 to 7,000 footsoldiers. Then they made a quick advance through Greater Poland (Wilkopolska) into the Neumark, where they occupied Friedeberg (Strzelce Krajeńskie) in mid-June. During the subsequent pillaging of that town, three clerics, including a refugee from Bohemia, were stuck into barrels painted with tar and burned.[362]

The Hussites continued their advance. After their demonstration of strength at Friedeberg, many towns voluntarily opened their gates and paid "contributions." These were mostly limited to money and food because the army lacked the transport capacity to move bulky spoils. The Steward (Vogt) of Neumarkt urgently pleaded to the Grand Master for reinforcements for his numerically weak forces. The Komtur of Elbing (Elblag) attempted to equip an army as quickly as possible, but in the meantime the Hussites pushed inexorably forward, took Woldenberg (Dobiegnew), Landsberg (Gorzów) and Soldin (Myślibórz). No Hussite army campaign had such a strong foreign component as this one, because in the meanwhile a Polish army had also joined the Bohemians. The incursion into the Order's lands above all served the interests of the Polish King who was continuing his war against the Teutonic Knights.[363]

---

356 PALACKÝ, Der Hussitenkrieg 1419-1431, pp. 509-514,

357 ŠMAHEL, Hussitische Revolution III, pp. 1942-1944.

358 In MHG *"och vnser lande wellen obirczihn vnd beschedigen."* Quoted from PALACKÝ, Urkundliche Beiträge II, Nr. 618, p. 72.

359 In MHG *"Auch haben gefangen vnd andere zum Hoffe vnd andern enden gerett das sye ye vermainen auch auff euch In das prewsszen landt zu zcihen, do wist Ir euch wol nach zu richten, vernemt Ir ein sulchs das sie sulchen reden vnd drawen nach volgen wollten, so sie der ewern Orden getan haben, so mucht Ir wol mit dem Hoemeister regen von meinen wegen."* Quoted from PALACKÝ, Urkundliche Beiträge II, Nr. 665, p. 129.

360 PALACKÝ, Urkundliche Beiträge II, Nr. 670, p. 137 provides a letter from Duke Konrad of Oels to the Grand Master informing him about the Hussite military operation.

361 ŠMAHEL, Hussitische Revolution III, pp. 1575-1576.

362 ŠMAHEL, Hussitische Revolution III, pp. 1578-1579; KOROWSKI, Die Marienburg, p. 273.

363 ŠMAHEL, Hussitische Revolution III, p. 1579; ZIMMERLING, Der deutsche Ritterorden, pp. 273-274; KOROWSKI, Die Marienburg, p. p. 273.

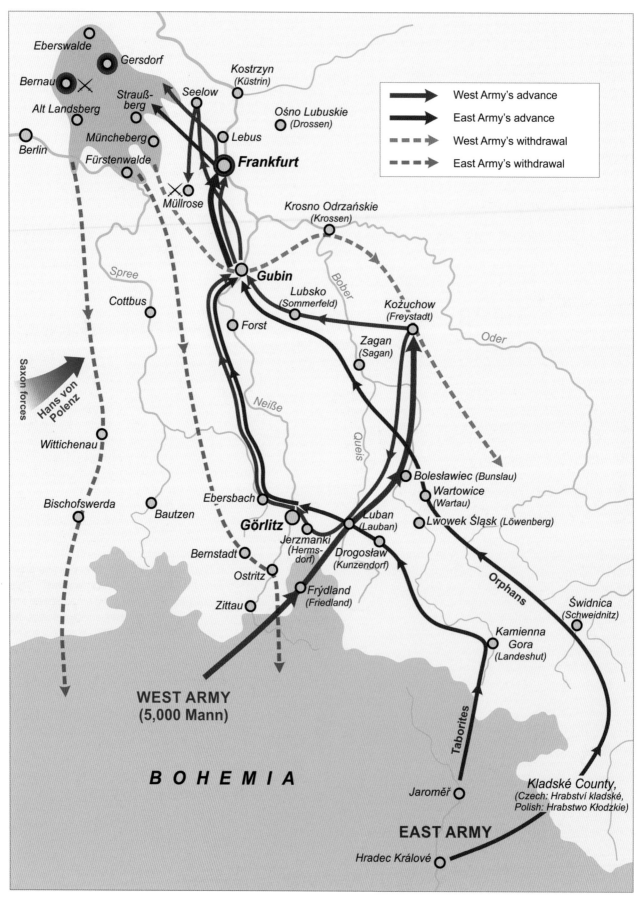

The Great Raid into the Mark Brandenburg in 1432

Legend:
- West Army's advance
- East Army's advance
- West Army's withdrawal
- East Army's withdrawal

Map labels:
Eberswalde, Gersdorf, Bernau, Alt Landsberg, Strauß-berg, Seelow, Kostrzyn (Küstrin), Ośno Lubuskie (Drossen), Berlin, Müncheberg, Fürstenwalde, Lebus, Frankfurt, Müllrose, Krosno Odrzańskie (Krossen), Spree, Gubin, Lubsko (Sommerfeld), Bober, Kożuchow (Freystadt), Oder, Cottbus, Forst, Zagan (Sagan), Saxon forces, Hans von Polenz, Neiße, Wittichenau, Queis, Bischofswerda, Bolesławiec (Bunslau), Wartowice (Wartau), Ebersbach, Bautzen, Lwowek Śląsk (Löwenberg), Görlitz, Jerzmanki (Herms-dorf), Łuban (Lauban), Bernstadt, Drogosław (Kunzendorf), Ostritz, Frýdland (Friedland), Orphans, Świdnica (Schweidnitz), Zittau, Kamienna Gora (Landeshut), WEST ARMY (5,000 Mann), Taborites, BOHEMIA, Jaroměř, Kladské County, (Czech: Hrabství kladské, Polish: Hrabstwo Kłodzkie), EAST ARMY, Hradec Králové

Since the Teutonic Knights' defeat at Tannenberg and following Treaty of Torun (*Thorner Frieden*), the Brothers had to watch how their power on the Baltic Sea coast shrunk. They lacked the money to hire mercenaries to defend against the Hussite-Polish threat. The Grand Master was overwhelmed with complaints from all his Commanderies (*Komtureien*). Meanwhile, the Hussites pushed on to Konitz (Chojnice) and Tuchel (Tuchola). Konitz was only a small castle, but was stubbornly defended by the energetic *Komtur* Erasmus Fischborn. Exerting all his energies, he put his defenses in readiness. The knights had hardly any prospect for relief since most of the towns in the Kulmer Land (now Chełmno Land, Poland) had refused to the Grand Master's call to military service. But Konitz proved to be too hard a nut for the Hussites to crack. For six weeks, they and their Polish allies stood before the castle. Čapek urged the Polish commander, Janusz of Michalów, to move on to other objectives. But the Poles absolutely wanted to take the castle. On 22 July, Michalów gave his troops the order to storm the place. But because the artillery was still unable to make any breaches in the thick brick walls, the assault failed. A Hussite had already tried to drive a mine under the fortress wall, however, the tunnel caved in prematurely. Water from a nearby fishpond flooded the tunnel so that many of those digging were killed. Four Hussites were rescued by the besieged. The Order Knights had those four attackers bathed and then released them. In thanks, Čapek released a hundred of the Order's mercenaries from captivity and also sent the *Komtur* the clothing that he had lent the four rescued men. Eventually the besieging army was having increasing difficulty provisioning itself. On 18 August, the Orphans' army broke camp and headed to Dirschau (now Tczew, Poland). The Poles followed soon afterward.[364]

Dirschau was far less well prepared to withstand an attack. Because the citizens refused to tear down the sprawling houses on the outskirts of the town's walls, the Hussites set them ablaze. The wind spread the sparks to the town and ignited a serious fire there. Dirschau almost completely burned down. When the town opened its gates to the besiegers, the Bohemians carried out a bloodbath among the population. The Poles simply stood by and watched, and allegedly even handed over their prisoners to the Hussites. Bohemian exiles were burned at the stake. When atrocities took the upper hand, the Castellan of Cracow finally put an end to them by force of arms.[365]

Subsequently, the army moved on to Danzig (Gdansk), but its walls proved to be too strong like those of Konitz. While the citizenry had refused the Grand Master's command to do military service, the city's levy was still strong.

The Hussites assailed the city for four days, but were always repulsed with heavy casualties. Eventually they also gave up on this worthwhile target.[366]

Instead, the Bohemians plundered the nearby monastery of Oliva (Oliwa) and moved through the Vistula River's estuary to the beaches of the Baltic Sea. There the most senior commander, Čapek, called together his bands and proudly announced he had led them to the ends of the world. Only the sea had been able to limit the Hussites. Two hundred Polish nobles and Čapek were knighted on the beach. Many Hussites filled their water bottles with the salty seawater, which they wanted to take back to their homeland as trophies.[367]

On their way back, the Hussites continued to devastate the land. Wladislaw Jagiello had accomplished what he desired. On 13 September 1433, a preliminary treaty was concluded in the Polish camp near Jeßnitz (Jasienica, Poland) that initially was valid until Christmas. Only the king's death, on 30 May, delayed the further negotiations, and the talks finally ended on New Years Day 1435 with the lasting Treaty of Brzesk. However, by that time, the Hussites had long since left the Order's lands again.[368] The campaign to the Baltic Sea was the last of the "beautiful rides." In the meantime, the political situation had drastically changed. The time of the radical-minded field armies was coming to its end.

The Fifth Hussite Crusade

At the end of April 1430, Velek z Březnice, a captain of the Orphans, moved into western Slovakia with an approximately 10,000-man levy from the Prague New Town and the Orphans. The Hussite advance started very favorably until on 23 April they ran into the resolute Hungarian army under Sigismund's own command. The King led the defense of his country from the Schintau (Šintava, today Slovakia) Castle, while his army commanders lured the Hussites into a swampy area at Tyrnau (Trnava, present Slovakia). On 28 April, they attacked the Bohemians. Under the leadership of the army commander, Stibor of Stiborze, they penetrated the enemy *Wagenburg*. Velek fell in the ensuing fighting. Yet the Hussites were able to push the Hungarians out of their positions and to withdraw under the cover of darkness. They were helped by the circumstance that Stibor's deputy, János Maróti, who had arrived late and then thought the battle lost, pulled back with his knights and opened up a path for the Hussites' retreat. The estimates, according to which 6,000 Hungarian fighters were killed in the battle, indeed seem exaggerated.[369]

364 ŠMAHEL, Hussitische Revolution III, pp. 1580-1581; ZIMMERLING, Der deutsche Ritterorden, p. 274.

365 ŠMAHEL, Hussitische Revolution III, p. 1581; ZIMMERLING, Der deutsche Ritterorden, pp. 274-275; KOROWSKI, Die Marienburg, p. pp. 273-274.

366 KOROWSKI, Die Marienburg, p. p. 274.

367 ŠMAHEL, Hussitische Revolution III, pp. 1581-1582; ZIMMERLING, Der deutsche Ritterorden, p. 275.

368 ŠMAHEL, Hussitische Revolution III, p. 1582; KOROWSKI, Die Marienburg, p. pp. 274-275.

369 ŠMAHEL, Hussitische Revolution II, pp. 1490-1491; PALACKÝ, Der Hussitenkrieg 1419-1431, pp. 506-507.

Procopius the Great operated with another army in Moravia. The Hussites blockaded the city of Brno there and were able to capture the Šternberk (Sternberg) Castle.[370]

The fear of a return by the Hussites was acute, especially in Saxony. Leipzig improved its walls in the summer of 1430. But the Bohemian heretics did not risk any further major advances into central Germany. Therefore, Sigismund was able, even if with a lot of effort, to organize a new crusade in 1431. This time, the Electors were to also put - along with the standard mounted levies – large numbers of wagons, cannon and flail-men on the Hussite model into the field. But the undertaking frighteningly mirrored the campaign of 1428. A small German army moved to Tachov and from there to the small town of Domažlice.[371]

After Procopius had gathered his army, which according to various sources numbered 40,000-50,000 men and 5,000 wagons, he moved against the crusader knights. They were camped on the heights around the town. On 14 August, the Hussites moved against them in good order. When Procopius' army got close to the crusaders, Friedrich of Brandenburg ordered the army elements camped to the north of the town to shift to the east and to form a *Wagenburg* to protect the potential retreat routes. But he fatally forgot to inform the other commanders about the deployment. Then when the papal legate Cardinal Cesarini and the other army commanders heard the Hussites' loud battle songs and at the same time observed how the Brandenburger's wagons were rolling faster and faster in the direction of the border, they thought that their commander in chief meant to retreat. Panic broke out among them and their knights and they fled into the mountains. The horsemen and the footsoldiers streamed into the woods, the wagons followed them at a gallop, whereby the men tending the supply train threw all the provisions into the road to move forward more quickly. The Cardinal tried to reestablish a *Wagenburg* in the woods to prevent a pursuit by the Hussites. Battle-hardened Italian mercenaries defended this position. But the pursuers had already gotten too close to their enemies and stormed the ring that had not yet been completely closed. Yet the Italians were able to hold off the Hussites until nightfall. There was complete chaos "*and those who could flee quickly, were well off. The people who got away quickly, and the army had all separated and everyone went back home.*"[372]

Heinrich von Plauen, who had already distinguished himself in the Fourth Crusade, rescued the shaken Cesarini with his cavalry. The Hussite cavalry pursued the crusader knights to the border. The losses were probably small but the Hussites claimed to have at least captured 2,000 wagons and 300 guns from the crusader army. Along with that were chests full of treasures, richly filled tents and the possessions of many well-heeled nobles that had been abandoned with the wagons. The Battle of Domažlice demonstrated in an impressive manner that it was not enough to copy the Hussite *Wagenburg* as a tactical method. To win out over a disciplined, well organized army like that of the Hussites, the crusaders needed an essentially better coordinated organization.[373]

Albrecht of Austria opened his campaign very late, as he had done in previous crusades. In August, he marched from Eggenburg via Iglau into Bohemia. The Hussite forces remaining there retreated in the face of his numerically superior army. Mid-month – where is unknown - he struck a supposedly 14,000-man Utraquist army that is said to have lost 6,000 men in the engagement. But when Procopius the Great moved to the south with the bulk of the Taborites and Orphans after the battle at Domažlice, Albrecht also halted his campaign at the beginning of September.[374]

Therefore, the Hussites became active again in the autumn. A large Taborite and Orphans army invaded Hungary. Jan Čapek led forces there from Silesia and joined Procopius the Great and Prokupek's levies in the Váh Valley (Waagtal). However, a little later, the Taborites under Procopius returned because a disagreement had arisen with Čapek about booty. He continued his campaign with the Orphans from Hradec Králové and Prague New Town's levies, plundered many towns and in November turned toward home with rich booty. But when crossing the Waag River on 9 November, his forces were attacked by a Hungarian levy. The Bohemian artillery was able to fend off the first attack. But the cold autumn rains had softened the trail and turned the stream's banks into a swamp. The heavy wagons got stuck in the mud. And the Hungarians continued their attacks day by day. After ten days of hard fighting, Čapek was only able to save seventy of the wagons loaded with the most precious booty. His army supposedly lost two thirds of its 7,000 soldiers.[375]

In September, another army, of about 5,000 men with 360 wagons, under Jan Sokol z Lamberka (Nikolaus Sokol von Lamberg in German) drove into the Austrian Waldviertel.[376] The campaign initially went well. The Hussites pil-

370 PALACKÝ, Der Hussitenkrieg 1419-1431, p. 507.

371 PALACKÝ, Der Hussitenkrieg 1419-1431, pp. 520-524; ŠMAHEL, Hussitische Revolution II, pp. 1513-1518; KROCKER, Sachsen und die Hussitenkriege, p. 37; DURDÍK, Hussitisches Heerwesen, pp. 236-238.

372 In MHG "*unde wer da vaste hat geflien mogen, deme ist wol gewest. Doch die lute dannoch vaste davone komen sind, unde daz her haid sich alliz zcutrennet, unde yderman zyuhet wider heym.*" Quoted from PALACKÝ, Urkundliche Beiträge II, Nr. 764, p. 242. See also ŠMAHEL, Hussitische Revolution II, pp. 1519-1521; Turnbull,

Hussite Wars, p. 40; and BEZOLD, Sigismund und die Reichskriege, pp. 149-153.

373 PALACKÝ, Der Hussitenkrieg 1419-1431, pp. 531-547; KROCKER, Sachsen und die Hussitenkriege, p. 37; DURDÍK, Hussitisches Heerwesen, pp. 238-240.

374 STÖLLER, Österreich im Kriege gegen die Hussiten, pp. 67-68.

375 PALACKÝ, Böhmen und das Baseler Konzil, pp. 20-21.

376 The Waldviertel (Forest Quarter) is the northwestern region of

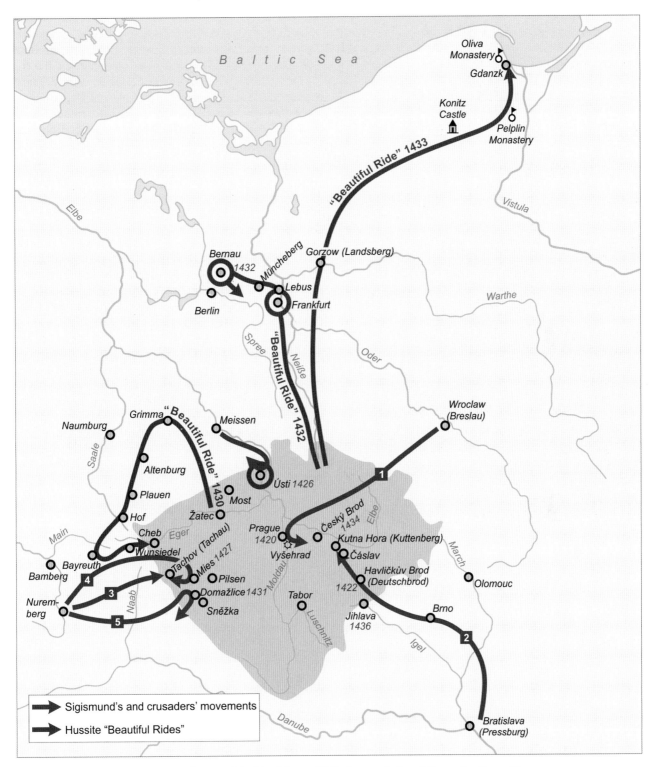

The Hussite "Beautiful Rides" (*spanilé jízdy* or *rejsy*) and Crusader Operations

laged Altenburg and Pernegg and got ready to march back with their fully loaded wagons. But then on 14 October 1431, an Austrian national levy caught up with them and beat them badly at Kirchberg. Sokol was only able to save a part of his army. The field standards captured from the enemy were later displayed in the Viennese Court Chapel (*Hofkapelle*).[377]

But the Hussite success at Domažlice, the increased resumption of the "beautiful rides" and possibly the war weariness of the most important German princes, especially the Elector of Saxony, led to the conclusion, on 23 August in North Bohemian Frýdštejn (Friedstein), of a two-year peace treaty between the Saxon dukes on one side and the Taborites and the Orphans on the other. For centuries, it was said there had been a renewed Hussite invasion of Saxony in 1433. That such an attack in which the town of Taucha in northern Saxony was plundered, really occurred has been seriously cast in doubt by research, if nothing else because of the existing treaty.[378] It is possible that smaller bands crossed over the border, but there was certainly not a larger operation like that of 1429-1430.

The Council of Basel

After the defeat at Domažlice and Sigismund's renewed serious problems raising a new army at the *Reichstag*, the Cardinal Legate, Cesarini, suggested a diplomatic solution to the King. They decided to invite the Bohemians to the upcoming Church Council at Basel. This recommendation was accepted differently by the Hussites. While the Prazans agreed to attend, the Taborites rejected any negotiations. But the Orphans, who had argued with the Taborites about the division of the booty during the last campaign in Hungary, also agreed; so the necessary majority was reached at the national assembly (*Landtag*). Then initially a delegation was sent to Cheb to discuss the negotiating modalities with the Council's delegates.[379]

Based on these negotiations, the fighting temporarily eased in Bohemia's north and west. The fighting in Bohemia's south also abated, and only the partisan war on the border continued to increase. In the spring of 1432, smaller Taborite bands carried out further advances to Upper Austria where they plundered the monasteries of Waldhausen and Baumgartenberg two times. On 2 May,

in response, Duke Albrecht of Austria started a campaign against the Hradisch Monastery, the Moravian Hussites' main base. It fell to him after a short siege.[380]

At the same time the Hussite representatives agreed with the Council's representatives in Cheb about the negotiating modalities and on a guarantee of safe passage for the Bohemian delegates. However, an attempt to establish a general treaty for the land failed due to the Taborites' rejection.[381]

In order to keep their willingness to negotiate from being seen as a sign of weakness, shortly thereafter, the Taborites assembled their army under Procopius the Great and carried out new "beautiful rides" into Silesia, Hungary and Austria. In Hungary they captured the Tyrnau Fortress that would remain in their possession for a long time.[382]

After smaller Hussite bands were repeatedly defeated by Austrian levies in the last months of 1432, the Taborites invaded the land with a large army in February 1433 and captured the important Rosenburg Fortress.[383]

In the meantime the first Utraquist delegation arrived in Basel on 4 January. The Bohemians presented their demands in the early negotiations. But no noteworthy results were achieved until April because both the representatives of the Catholic Church, as well as the Hussites insisted on their own positions. But the Church representatives showed themselves to be more diplomatically skillful. They sent a delegation to Prague that was to ensure that the negotiations would not be halted. Also Sigismund, who had been crowned Emperor in the meanwhile, was able to work out an approach between the Pope and his delegates who had been working hard for a reconciliation.[384]

But Basel was not the only place where a future ceasefire was being debated. It was also heatedly discussed in June at the *Landtag* in Prague. The Church delegates from Basel as well as some delegates from Duke Albrecht of Austria also participated. But Andreas Procopius' word still had weight and he vehemently spoke out against the ceasefire. When the delegates from Basel left Prague on 3 July, they were indeed aware that they would have to make concessions to the Hussites in order to get at least the moderate wings to come to an agreement.[385]

In Basel even Cardinal Cesarini showed himself to be willing to compromise. Therefore, moderate forces increased in importance. The Utraquists joined with the Catholic towns in Bohemia. At the Council of Basel, they had at least been able to get the communion with

the northeast Austrian state of Lower Austria.

377 STÖLLER, Österreich im Kriege gegen die Hussiten, pp. 68-69;
      PALACKÝ, Böhmen und das Baseler Konzil, p. 19;
      ŠMAHEL, Hussitische Revolution III, pp. 1525-1527.

378 KROCKER, Sachsen und die Hussitenkriege, pp. 38-39;
      PALACKÝ, Urkundliche Beiträge II, Nr. 819, pp. 304-306;
      ŠMAHEL, Hussitische Revolution III, pp. 1550-1551.

379 ŠMAHEL, Hussitische Revolution III, pp. 1530-1540;
      STÖLLER, Österreich im Kriege gegen die Hussiten, p. 73.

380 STÖLLER, Österreich im Kriege gegen die Hussiten, pp. 74-75;
      ŠMAHEL, Hussitische Revolution III, pp. 1544-1550.

381 STÖLLER, Österreich im Kriege gegen die Hussiten, p. 75.

382 Ibid., pp. 75-77.

383 Ibid., p. 77.

384 ŠMAHEL, Hussitische Revolution III, pp. 1560-1575;
      STÖLLER, Österreich im Kriege gegen die Hussiten, pp. 77-78.

385 ŠMAHEL, Hussitische Revolution III, pp. 1575-1591;
      STÖLLER, Österreich im Kriege gegen die Hussiten, p. 78.

A Hussite Handgunner
The gunner uses a hooked culverin (*Hakenbüchse*) that he supports on his pavis and his shoulder,
which provide a relatively stable shooting platform.

the chalice to be permitted in the kingdom again. Then the Taborites and the Orphans sent their representatives to Switzerland, among them, Procopius the Great. But the priest and his supporters did not want to agree to any compromises and soon departed disappointed. But through an agreement with the Utraquists, a solution to the Hussite question was signed for the Pope and Kaiser on 30 November 1433.[386]

The Downfall: Lipany

In the 1430s, the Bohemian economy was exhausted. The war had drained the country and commerce was dangerously weakened. Prices rose drastically while the currency was devalued. Two important commodities, salt that was not mined and wine that was not produced, were normally obtained by merchants from Austria. But the Duke there forbade the export of these goods to the "Ketzerland" ("Heretics' Country").[387] Therefore, these goods also were coveted booty during the "beautiful rides."

In the summer of 1433, the Hussites' main focus was on the siege of Pilsen. In conjunction with it, larger detachments repeatedly undertook incursions into the Oberpfalz to pillage for food and money.[388] In mid-September, Procopius tasked the captains Jan Pardus and Jan Ritka of Bezdedice to carry out such a raid in the Oberpfalz with 500 horsemen and 1,500 men on foot. The Hussites advanced to Cham and brutally ravaged the land. On 21 September 1433, their forces were finally attacked and decisively defeated at Hiltersried by a considerably smaller army belonging to the Palatine Count (Pfalzgraf) Johann von Pfalz-Neumark (who was actually not present at the battle; the levy was commanded by Heinrich Pflug). The blame for this defeat was allegedly born by a single wagon driver who had negligently left a gap in the Wagenburg. The Pfalzgraf's mercenaries pushed through this gap and are said to have then killed 1,200 Hussites and captured 300. Pardus and Ritka returned with only a handful of men to the army besieging Pilsen.[389]

The defeat triggered a revolt by the Taborite field army. Procopius, who had been restricted to a sick bed for a long time, was the target of the attacks, as were the two defeated captains. At the end of September, he and Pardus were relieved of their positions and imprisoned for a short time. Soon the situation calmed down again, but it showed that the Taborites' unity was no longer so unshakable as it had been a few years earlier. A little later when Jan Čapek arrived with the Orphans' army in front of Pilsen, he took over command of both field armies. Čapek's men, who had just returned from their foray to the Baltic Sea, proudly presented their comrade a looted camel.[390]

But the Hussites did not enjoy their booty very long. In December, the besiegers made a half-hearted assault on the city that was repulsed. When the defenders made a sortie against the Orphans' camp, they were even able to take the camel.[391]

In early 1434, while the Taborites and Orphans were still besieging Pilsen, the solidarity of the individual Hussite factions fell apart for good. Kaiser Sigismund, by using significant financial resources, was able to unite the majority of the Bohemian nobles on his side. Furthermore, the Landtag accepted the Basel and Prague Compacts. The moderate Bohemian nobles formed a new "Herren-Liga" ("Lords' League") and together with the bulk of the Prazans came over to the King's side. The radical Taborites and Orphans, who still refused as before, became isolated with one stroke.[392]

With that, both field armies found themselves in a militarily precarious situation. While Pilsen's siege bound them together in the most westerly part of the kingdom, the Utraquists were gathering an army in the vicinity of Kutná Hora. From there, the Utraquists could attack either Hradec Králové, or heavily fortified Tabor. In West Bohemia knights loyal to the King, and lords as well, formed small bands to intercept the besieging army's foraging troops. In Prague, the residents of the Old Town who were loyal to the king got ready for a siege of the New Town, which was still radical. On 2 May, Čapek met with some of his captains in the city on the Moldau. In the threatening situation, Procopius the Great was asked to take over command of the armies again. Procopius agreed and prepared the defense of the Prague New Town. But the Lords' League was faster. On 5 May, the army loyal to the King appeared before Prague and occupied the New Town one day later.[393]

Procopius then wanted to mobilize the Homeland Army in Tabor and join with the field armies. But on 5 May at Pilsen, the faction loyal to the King enjoyed a spectacular success when a huge grain convoy got past the besieging army and entered the city. Additionally the Hussites received news that the army of the Lords' League was preparing to depart Prague and if possible attack them from the rear. Because starving out Pilsen was now increasingly unlikely, Prokupek, the Orphans' Administrator, broke

---

386 ŠMAHEL, Hussitische Revolution III, pp. 1597-1621; DURDÍK, Hussitisches Heerwesen, p. 242; STÖLLER, Österreich im Kriege gegen die Hussiten, pp. 78-80.

387 STÖLLER, Österreich im Kriege gegen die Hussiten, p. 7.

388 The Oberpfalz is located in eastern Bavaria opposite the current Czech border and includes the towns of Cham, Neukarkt and Weiden among others.

389 MACHILEK, Hussiten in der Oberpfalz; pp. 211-215; ŠMAHEL, Hussitische Revolution III, pp. 1594-1595; RIEDER, Die Hussiten, p. 225; Schmidt, Die große Schlacht, pp. 23-24.

390 ŠMAHEL, Hussitische Revolution III, pp. 1596-1597; RIEDER, Die Hussiten, pp. 225-226.

391 ŠMAHEL, Hussitische Revolution III, pp. 1620-1621; RIEDER, Die Hussiten, p. 227.

392 ŠMAHEL, Hussitische Revolution III, pp. 1625-1631.

393 ŠMAHEL, Hussitische Revolution III, pp. 1630-1632; RIEDER, Die Hussiten, p. 227.

This picture supposedly shows **a battle from the time of the Hussites.** The ox's head on the flag on the right is, however, a Moravian insignia, wherefore it can be assumed that it depicts fighting during a Turkish campaign. Nevertheless, it provides interesting details about the equipment.

off the siege on 9 May and marched via Hostovice to the Moldau. A few days later, he joined with Procopius' hurriedly raised forces. The army of the *Pilsner Landfrieden*[394] assembled and arrived in Prague on 26 May where the forces of the Lords' League were preparing for an advance on Český Brod. The commander of this army was Diviš Bořek z Miletínka, an old brother-in-arms of Jan Žižka's. The experienced commander clearly understood that he did not have to look for Procopius' army, but that it would show up as soon as the Lords' League started the siege of Český Brod.[395]

On 27 May 1434, the army's lead elements arrived at the town located about 30 kilometers (19 miles) east of Prague. One day later reconnaissance forces reported the approach of the Taborites and Orphans. On 30 May, both armies ran into one another at Lipany near Český Brod.[396]

Procopius the Great's army included just 10,000 men, of which 700 were horsemen. He had more than 360 wagons. The Utraquist Union led 20,000 men with 660 wagons into the field. The Taborite field armies had approached the battlefield in a rapid march and had established a *Wagenburg* on a hill west of Lipany. With Diviš Bořek z Miletínka, the Utraquists also possessed an experienced field commander who had likewise learned his handiwork under Žižka. Miletínka was familiar with the Hussite standard tactics: waiting for the opponents' attack and the immediate counterattack as soon as the enemy had been repelled from the *Wagenburg*. He planned the coming battle accordingly. He supposedly arranged his wagons in eleven rows. Between 3 and 4 o'clock in the afternoon, the Lords' League army marched toward Procopius' *Wagenburg*. A

fine springtime rain began and caused fog to rise from the moist meadows. When the Utraquists were in range, they fired the four cannon that had been moved up to the front and then veered to the right. The column of wagons marched around the hill and presented its right flank to the Taborites' left.[397]

A Chronicler described the following fighting in detail: "*Our captains sent four cannon to the point [of the force]. And the other cannon [were placed] all on the side. When our point ran into the Taborites' point, then our [troops] fired the forward cannon into the Taborites' point. And ceased [fire] after a short duration. And they acted as if they were dismayed. They turned as if they wanted to leave the field. Then the Hussites fired all their guns at ours. Then Lord Nikolaus returned to our point at that hour. And he had the men on our side [of the column] fire guns upon the side [flank] of the Hussite army. But then Lord Nikolaus turned and pulled back a little as if he wanted to give ground. When the Hussites saw that, then they opened their Wagenburg and wanted to chase after us. Then Lord Nikolaus had our people turn around again and stormed the Wagenburg with them and fought with the enemies for a long time when they had closed the Wagenburg. So our lords, Meinhardt von Neuhaus, von Rosenberg and other lords who were the best armored men, penetrated the Wagenburg and helped ours. Meanwhile ours overpowered the enemy and overturned the wagons in the Wagenburg so our troops could come in to assist. They held the field and slew all the enemy.*"[398]

---

394 These were the forces that were united by the agreement or treaty (*Landfrieden*) at Pilsen.

395 Šmahel, Hussitische Revolution III, pp. 1634-1637.

396 Šmahel, Hussitische Revolution III, pp. 1636-1637; Durdík, Hussitisches Heerwesen, p. 242; Stöller, Österreich im Kriege gegen die Hussiten, p. 80.

397 Šmahel, p. 1639; Durdík, Hussitisches Heerwesen, pp. 243-245.

398 In MHG "*Da haben vnser lawt vier puchsen an den Spitz zu geschickt. vnd die andern puchsen all neben auf die Seitten. Da si ze samen ritten vnser spitz mit der Thaber spicz. da haben die vnsern mit den vordristen puchsen in Irn Spicz geschossen. Vnd haben dernach ein klein weil aufgehort. Vnd haben getan als si getrubt gewesn sein. vnd haben sich gewendet, als sie aus dem veld haben wellen. Da haben die Hussen alle Ir püchsen auf die vnsern abgeschossen. Also ist Herr Niclaus zu stund wiedervmb*

This contemporary engraving shows a scene from the **Battle of Hiltersried**.
Some researchers believe that its was done in the 1430s. If that is the case, it would be about the oldest picture of
a Hussite howitzer (center of picture).

However, the picture's entire composition points to its creation in the second half of the 15$_{th}$ century.
(bpk / RMN - Grand Palais / Philippe Fuzeau)

pmeditat̄Æ:paucos poſt dies mltis cū munerib⁹(vt ipe ſpabat)
placatū regm hūgarie trãſiluanas traducere fecit in partes.
De electione dn̄i iohãnis wayuode in gubernatorē:⁊ de ta/
lione per eunde a drakul wayuoba exacta.

Oſt hãc tãdē belli tēpeſtatē: poſtq̃z regis wladiſlaiu/
gubzem unteritū:ne quis in regno in alterius offenſã
moueretur:per dominos pzelatos ⁊ barones regni in
terdictum eſt.⁊ nihilominus vt adueniente feſto pē/

János Hunyadi was a Transylvanian nobleman and
important commander. He got his first military
experiences at the end of the Hussite Wars as a
mercenary in the hire of Emperor Sigismund. This
contemporary depiction shows in detail a suit of armor
from the first half of the 15th century.
The large horseman's *tartsche* shield (*Reitertartsche*) is
interesting.

After the wagons of the Lords' League's had turned,
there was a short but intensive artillery duel. Gunpowder

*zu Iren Spicz kömen. vnd hat die herren auf vnser Seitten haissen
schiessen in der Hussen heer auf die Seitten mit den püchsen, Da
hat sich her Niclaus aber gewendet vnd ein clain weg von In gezo-
gen als er hiet weichen wellen. Da das die Hussen ersehen haben,
da haben sie Ir Wagenburg aufgetan. vnd den vnsern nacheilen
wellen. Da hat sich her Niclaus mit dem Volk wider vmbkert. vnd
hat mit In in die Wagenburg gesprungen vnd hat mit den veinden
gefochten als lang das Si in di Wagenburg verschlossen haben.
Also haben die vnsern von herrn Mänharten vom Newenhausz
der von Rosenberg vnd ander herrn pest gewappnet lewt. vnder
den vnsern vmb die Wagenburg hin ein gehebt vnd geholfen. die
weil haben die vnsern die veindt gestürmpt vnd die wägen in der
Wagenburg nider geworffen, das sie den vnsern hin ein ze hilf
kömen sein. das si das veld also behabt vnd die veindt all nider
gelegt haben."* Quoted from PALACKÝ, Urkundliche Beiträge II, Nr.
912 B, pp. 416-417, in MHG, but probablly originally written in
Old Czech.

smoke sunk over the valley and robbed the Taborites and
Orphans of visibility. However, they could recognize that
the Lords' League's wagon column had made a 180° turn
and had marched back toward Lipany. When it got further and further away, Čapek thought that Miletínka had
accepted defeat and he ordered a pursuit. The *Wagenburg*
was opened and the cavalry and the footsoldiers stormed
after the Utraquists. But the Utraquists were expecting
the attack and were able to exploit their numeric superiority on the open battlefield. Step by step the radicals
gave way back to their *Wagenburg*. In the meantime, the
point of the Utraquist wagon column had turned around
and attacked the opponent in the flank and rear. Many
sources claim also that Miletínka held cavalry ready in the
flank of the *Wagenburg* and he had it go over to the attack
when the radicals broke out. These groups eventually
pushed their way into the *Wagenburg*. Yet the Hussites
were able to close the gaps in the ring of wagons and to
bottle up the Utraquists' lead assault element. But more
and more footsoldiers pushed after them and so a second final assault on the *Wagenburg* succeeded. Procopius
and Prokupek were both killed during the following fierce
hand-to-hand fighting. Jan Čapek heard the desperate sig-
nals that ordered him back, but he was himself so hard
pressed that he had to rush to the *Wagenburg* for help.
He fled with part of his cavalry to the fortified town of
Kolín, for which he was later often accused of treason.[399]

The Utraquists' victory was complete. Only a small part
of the Taborites and Orphans were spared and went over
to the Utraquists. The remainder were executed on the
battlefield. About 900 were said to have been burned in
barns near Český Brod.[400]

The Battle of Lipany broke the backbone of the radical
Hussites' field armies. Admittedly the conflict with smaller
groups lasted a while longer, but the few battles that still
occurred were mostly unsuccessful for the radicals.

On 4 May 1434 in Brno in Moravia, Duke Albrecht
concluded a countrywide peace treaty (*Landfrieden*),
to which the Hussite nobles also consented. The radical groups indeed continued their war and undertook
another incursion into Austria in June. The Hussites drove
as far as Krems and at the end of the month returned
home laden with booty. However, this attack made it
easier for Albrecht to get his own *Landtag* to approve the
means for a new campaign in Moravia, but it also brought
no significant results.[401]

399 ŠMAHEL, Hussitische Revolution III, pp. 1639-1640;
    DURDÍK, Hussitisches Heerwesen, pp. 245-247.

400 DURDÍK, Hussitisches Heerwesen, p. 247.

401 STÖLLER, Österreich im Kriege gegen die Hussiten, pp. 80-81.

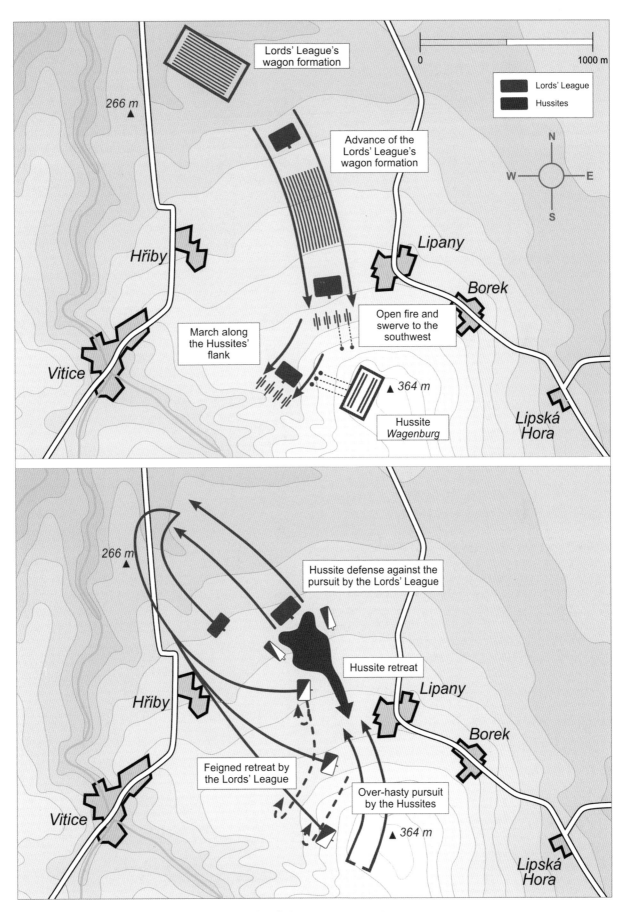

Lords' League's wagon formation

Advance of the Lords' League's wagon formation

Lords' League

Hussites

266 m

Hřiby

Lipany

Borek

Open fire and swerve to the southwest

March along the Hussites' flank

Vitice

▲ 364 m

Hussite *Wagenburg*

Lipská Hora

266 m

Hussite defense against the pursuit by the Lords' League

Hussite retreat

Hřiby

Lipany

Borek

Feigned retreat by the Lords' League

Over-hasty pursuit by the Hussites

Vitice

▲ 364 m

Lipská Hora

The Battle of Lipany, 30 May 1434

THE HUSSITE KING

Sigismund of Luxembourg was certainly an unlucky ruler. His reign was shaped by the most serious church crisis of the Middle Ages. He himself proved to be a reformer ready to make compromises. While the Utraquists were unable to realize their demands for the implementation of the Four Prague Articles at the Council of Basel, they were ultimately allowed, with Sigismund's consent, to have the communion with the chalice. Prague received an Utraquist bishop. The King sealed this promise in the so-called Compacts of Jihlava (German: *Iglauer Kompaktakten*). In 1436, the Bohemian Landtag recognized the Luxembourger as king. Then Sigismund declared the Hussite Revolution as ended. He died a year later.[402]

For his successor, he chose his son-in-law, Albrecht of Austria, who was actually also elected king by the Bohemian estates and who entered Prague in 1438. He also died after a year, on 27 October 1439. In these years, the last of the radical Hussites' armies were destroyed. Jan Roháč z Dubé, who survived the Battle of Lipany, barricaded himself with some Orphan fighters in his Dubé Castle, which was also besieged by King Sigismund. After the castle fell on 6 September 1437, Jan and 53 of his comrades-in-arms were hanged in Prague. Another Hussite army was wiped out on 23 September 1438 by a Saxon levy at *Želenice* (Sellnitz) near the town of Most.[403]

After Albrecht II's death, a long period of turmoil about succession to the throne began in Bohemia. Two parties struggled for dominance in the country: one was the Catholics centered around the still active Ulrich von Rosenberg, and the other was the Utraquists around Meinhard von Neuhaus (Czech: Menhart z Hradce). Eventually in the 1440s, a young man stepped forward from between them and succeeded in reuniting the fragmented parties. Jiří z Poděbrad (German: Georg von Podïebrad) came from one of the noble families that had joined the Hussites early in the movement. His father was supposedly a close friend of Žižka, who was also Jiří's godfather. At the age of 14, the young squire had taken part in the Battle of Lipany. In 1448, Jiří, in the meantime also the leader of the Utraquists, was elected to be the National Administrator. Then the Catholic Party occupied Prague. In response, Jiří raised a fine army in the north of the country. In September 1448, he marched to the Moldau with less than 1,000 men and occupied the capital without significant difficulty. Meinhard von Neuhaus, the *Burggraf* (Burgrave) of the Hradschin, was arrested and taken to the Poděbrady Castle. Because Jiří refused to release Meinhard and wanted to place him before a court exercising criminal and civil justice, eventually a civil war broke out in Bohemia, from which Jiří emerged the victor.[404]

Subsequently, he participated in the Saxon Fratricidal War (1445-1451) on the side of William the Brave (Wilhelm der Tapferen).[405] Bohemian armies once again pushed into Saxony. Jiří's move was seen as a new "Hussite" invasion.

In 1451, Kaiser Friedrich III named Jiří to be the Bohemian Marshal of the Land (*Landesmarschall*), and shortly thereafter the estates elected him to be the National Administrator (*Landesverweser*). Two years later the Bohemians elected the young Austrian Duke Ladislaus Postumus as king but who died 1557. On 27 February 1458, Jiří emerged from the resulting new elections as the victor thanks to his large number of supporters within the Utraquist landed nobility. But this election was not acknowledged in the south of the country. Jiří moved with an army against the town of Jihlava, which he besieged for four months before it accepted his rule. The city of Wrocław also had to be compelled with force to pay homage to him.[406]

Starting in 1459, Jiří was able to overcome the effects of the Hussite Wars. That year the Treaty of Eger (German: *Vertrag von Eger*, Czech: *Chebský mír*) between him and the Wettiners established the Bohemian-Saxon border that is still recognized today. The country thrived again under his rule. It took a lot of effort, but he normalized relations with the Holy See, because he suppressed the most radical Hussite factions, which Papacy still repudiated. Jiří settled on implementing the Compacts of Jihlava and as King, protected the Hussite Utraquists and the Catholics. Nevertheless the conservative Pope Paul II excommunicated him in 1466. Then the Catholic party joined the Alliance of Zelená Hora (of Green Mountain)[407] and although Friedrich III and also Hungarian King Matthias Corvinus had maintained good relations with Jiří up until then, they began to act against the Hussite King militarily under pressure from the Papacy. The Hungarians occupied large parts of Moravia, where Matthias Corvinus had himself crowned as the new King of Bohemia in Olomouc on 3 May 1469. In 1470, Jiří (Georg von Podïebrad) was able to reconquer extensive parts of the country. Despite the papal ban, the majority of the Bohemians still supported the charismatic king. But his unexpected death on 22 March 1471 ended the war. Then Matthias Corvinus and the son of the Polish King Kasimir, Wladislaw II, quarreled over the Bohemian crown. Both were professed Catholics. Wladislaw eventually prevailed and so the Polish Jagiello family ruled in Bohemia until 1526.[408]

---

402 ŠMAHEL, Hussitische Revolution III, pp. 1622-1640; RIEDER, Die Hussiten, pp. 230-233; Macek, Revolutionäre Bewegung, pp. 166-169; HÖNSCH: Geschichte Böhmens, pp. 148-149.

403 ŠMAHEL, Hussitische Revolution III, pp. 1687-1690; RIEDER, Die Hussiten, pp. 236-241; Macek, Revolutionäre Bewegung, pp. 166-167; HÖNSCH, Geschichte Böhmens, pp. 149-151.

404 HÖNSCH, Geschichte Böhmens, pp. 154-158.

405 The Saxon Fratricidal War (German: *Sächsischer Bruderkrieg*) was a war fought from 1446 to 1451 between the two brothers Frederick II, Elector of Saxony and Duke William III over areas ruled by the House of Wettin.

406 BACHMANN, Georg von Podïebrad, pp. 602-606; PALACKÝ, Georg von Poděbrad I.; RIEDER, Die Hussiten, pp. 244-253.

407 The Alliance of Zelená Hora (German: *Grünberger Allianz*, also *Grünberger Bund, Grünberger Union, Grünberger Einung*; Czech: *Jednota zelenohorská and Zelenohorská jednota*) was a Bohemian Catholic union of nobles formed to depose the Utraquist King Jiří/ Georg of Podiebrad. It existed from 1465 until 1471.

408 HÖNSCH, Geschichte Böhmens, pp. 158-163; BACHMANN, Georg von Podïebrad, pp. 606-612; PALACKÝ, Georg von Poděbrad II.; RIEDER, Die Hussiten, pp. 253-288.

The illustration shows the Meissener **Knight Friedrich von Dohna**. His father was one of the last Burgrave (*Burggrafen*) of Dohna. Until 1402, the family owned a not inconsiderable domain south of Dresden, but lost it in a war with the Margrave of Meissen. After that, Friedrich supposedly served as a mercenary. In 1410, he fought for the Teutonic Order. In 1426, he participated in the Saxon army's campaign to Ústi where he ultimately was killed.

His armor consisted of a *Hundsgugel* bascinet, and coat-of-plates and leg armor, which were increasingly being used in Central Europe at that time. His shield, showing the crossed stag antlers – the Dohna's coat-of-arms, has a notch in the upper right corner for resting the lance.

Lunyakov 2015

THE HUSSITE REVOLUTION AS THE BOHEMIAN REFORMATION

One of the greatest strengths of the Hussite movement, the national element, ultimately became a decisive weakness, because it made extending the movement outside the country considerably more difficult. As the Bohemians diverged more and more from a confessional standpoint, the failure of the radical wing became inevitable. Only the negotiations of the Utraquists, who were open to compromises, could preserve the Hussite ideas.

In 1435, with Sigismund's support, the Bohemian estates even chose Jan Rokycana as a new Hussite Archbishop. But Rokycana never received Papal recognition. In contrast to Rome, Sigismund and his successors were, however, very supportive of a reconciliation of the religious factions. On 5 July 1436, he ratified the Compacts of Jihlava, which essentially confirmed the Compacts of Prague and permitted the Prazans a Calixtine bishop. But this agreement never got Papal recognition. In 1462, Pope Pius II nullified the compacts again and demanded a unification of Bohemia's churches.

After Jiří of Poděbrad's death, with the establishment of a Catholic dynasty with the Jagiellos, the new kings' policies concerning the Hussites changed very little. Wladislaw II also worked hard for Papal recognition of the Compacts. In 1485, he again confirmed them at the *Landtag* in Kutná Hora and allowed his subjects in Bohemia the free choice of their religion between Catholicism and Utraquism. The Religious Peace of Kutná Hora (German: *Kuttenberger Religionsfrieden*) was significantly more tolerant, than the 1555 Religious Peace of Augsburg in the Empire between the Catholics and Lutherans, or the 1598 Edict of Nantes between the French Catholics and Huguenots. The provisions were recognized at a further *Reichstag* in 1512.

Hussitism's radical values also gained renewed strength in the 15th century. Again it was the Waldensian theology that led to the spin-off of the Bohemian and Moravian brothers. In 1459 they officially created their own church, but were persecuted for a long time. It was only when religious diversity increased in the course of the Reformation that the brothers achieved at least official tolerance in 1574-75 in the *Confessio Bohemica*. The *Confessio Bohemica* served as the recognition of the Protestants in the country, and with it obtained an extension of the Religious Peace of Kutná Hora to their congregations. In the second half of the 16th century, the Utraquists and Protestants reached a settlement. It is hardly surprising that even Luther himself wrote: "*I had already, without thinking it, learned everything from Hus [...] simply that we are all Hussites, without knowing it.*"[409] In 1609, Rudolf II granted the Bohemians the right to exercise religious freedom in his Majesty's Letter (*Majestätsbrief*). This letter was torn up by his successor, Ferdinand II, after the Catholic armies defeated the rebellious Bohemians in 1620 at the Battle of White Mountain (*Schlacht am Weißen Berg*). Through the following Counterreformation, both the Protestants and the Hussites were driven out of Bohemia or forced to go underground. It was only with the end of Habsburg rule in 1918 and the subsequent establishment of an independent Czechoslovakia that saw the founding of the Evangelical Church of the Bohemian Brothers (1918) and the Czechoslovakian Hussite Church (of 1420), which were both closer to Utraquism than to Lutheranism. Today both Churches have about 154,000 members.[410]

---

409 "*Ich habe schon bisher, ohne es zu ahnen, alles von Hus gelehrt [...] kurz wir sind alle Hussiten, ohne es zu wissen.*" Quoted from: LUTHER, Gesammelte Werke, p. 1541.

410 HÖNSCH, Geschichte Böhmens, pp. 419-525.

EFFECTS OF THE HUSSITE MILITARY SYSTEM ON OTHER EUROPEAN ARMIES

Duke Albrecht of Austria was one of the first European princes to modernize his army based on the influence of the Hussite movement. He was especially impressed by the size of the Hussite levies. As a result, he initially determined how many able-bodied males between the ages of 16 and 70 were in his own country. Additionally, he demanded that the cities, towns and castles provide exact inventories of their on-hand military equipment. Because Austria represented one of the Hussites' first objectives outside Bohemia, the Duke also made great efforts to improve his border fortifications.[411]

After Albrecht's bad experiences with the *Landwehr* units in the 1424 and 1425 campaigns, he issued a national defense order in February 1426 that firmly ensured him an army of 1,000 horsemen from the knight's class and the cities, as well as from the Church's institutions. Additionally, the cities should pay 24,000 florins and the priesthood should pay 43,000 florins to finance these forces. Also, the fortifications of some cities were modernized.[412]

---

411 STÖLLER, Österreich im Kriege gegen die Hussiten, pp. 17-18.

412 Ibid., pp. 37-38.

On 28 April 1431, the Duke issued a new army directive closely following the Hussite model. Every tenth man of the sedentary population was to be enlisted for the coming campaign. Every twenty men were to man a wagon and could elect a ""*Führmann*" (leader).[413]

Encouraged by his successes in 1431, Duke Albrecht reduced the mercenary portion of his army to a minimum of 1,000 men and relied increasingly on the country-wide levy and the knights. He divided his country into six "quarters" (Czech "*čtvrť*", German "*Viertel*"), whose levies would be trained by four Quarter Captains ("*Viertelhauptleuten*"). A senior captain ("*oberster Hauptmann*") stood at the head of the army. The army's smallest tactical unit was 200-man "infantry group" ("*Infanteriehaufen*") and one wagon. In case of a need to defend the country, the nobility had to appear "with servants, horses, armor, weapons and other things",[414] and for campaigns outside the country with 500 horsemen.

From the beginning, the six Lausitzer cities relied considerably more heavily on levies from the citizenry and peasantry than others participating in the wars. In a 1421 agreement about a joint levy with the Silesian princes, it stated that, among other things, for every ten men there should be an accompanying wagon. "Namely each wagon should have a chain, which is called a *Landzucht*, two planks, two grave-shovels, a shovel, two saws(?), a hatchet or two. And each should bring along his best weapons, as in pikes, crossbows and wares that he likes best".[415]

In July 1424, the Margraves of Meissen also decided to establish a *Landwehr*, "for the sake of better peace, use and protection".[416] The proportion of handgunners and also the artillery in the Saxon levies increased significantly. Like in Bohemia, the cities' financial power made acquisition of expensive weapons possible. For example, on 26 May 1426, the Elector (*Kurfürstin*) Katharina wrote to the City Council of Leipzig about the cities' forces that should go to Ústi as a relief army, "we earnestly demand that you come on horse and on wagons with all forces to Dresden on the Tuesday after Saint Boniface's Day (5 June) with handguns, trestle guns, gunpowder and other equip-ment as well".[417] The war flail also gained great popularity in the 1430s and 1440s in Meissen and became a standard weapon for footsoldiers.[418]

In 1430 when the Imperial Assembly (*Reichstag*) in Nuremberg decided to raise an army to restore peace in Bohemia, it said "The Bishop of Mainz, the Bishop of Cologne, the Bishop of Trier, the Count of the Palatine on the Rhine shall have an army and a *Wagenburg* and put aside their disputes…"[419] Also the Dukes of Saxony and Braunschweig (Brunswick), the landed Counts of Thuringia and Hessen, the Electoral Prince of Brandenburg, the Bishops of Würzburg, Hildesheim, Halberstadt, Maitburg and Bobinburg, the Swabian and Franconian knights and the Silesian and Lausitz princes, the Imperial Cities and the Duke von Austria were explicitly instructed to provide *Wagenburg*s. Additionally, composition of the infantry according to the Hussite model was precisely controlled: "Also whatever each prince, lord or city provides as footsoldiers or armored horsemen, they shall be evenly one half handgunners and one half crossbowmen having bolts, lead, powder and whatever pertains to that. Furthermore, they shall give a captain for each ten footsoldiers and a captain for every hundred and a captain for every thousand".[420] At the same time the call-up established how many cannon the individual princes had to provide. The Duke of Saxony, as one of the most powerful imperial princes was to bring 14 stone-firing cannon and an incendiary firing cannon on the campaign. In this case "*camer buchsen*" *were* explicitly mentioned.

Similar to the situation in Bohemia, the cities in the Empire played a decisive role in providing cannon that the princes themselves usually could not afford. In 1420 King

---

413 Ibid., p. 66.

414 In MHG, "*mit diener, pherten, harnasch, wer und ander natturften …*" in modern German, "*Mit Diener, Pferden, Harnisch, Wehr und anderer Natturften (=things)…*" Quoted from Ibid. , p. 71.

415 In MHG, "*Nemlich itzlich waijn sol haben eine kethe, die man nennt eine landzocht, zwey brethe, zwei grabescheit, eine schauffel, zwu zcoe, eine haue adir zwu. Vnd itzlicher sol seine beste were mit jm nehmen, also spisse, armbroste vnd suste so er beste mag*". In modern German, "*Nämlich jeder Wagen soll haben eine Kette, die man eine Landzucht nennt, zwei Bretter, zwei Grabenscheite (eine Art Spaten), eine Schaufel, zwei Sägen(?), eine Haue oder zwei. Und jeder soll seine beste Wehr mitnehmen, also Spieße, Armbrüste und Waren, so er am besten mag*". Quoted in PALACKÝ, Urkundliche Beiträge I, Nr. 150, p. 150.

416 In MHG, "*umb besser frides, nuczes und schirmes willen*". In modern German, "*um des besseren Frieden, Nutzen und Schutzes willen*". Quoted in CDS I B 4, Nr. 360, p. 229.

417 In MHG, "*[d]ououn begern wir ernstlich, das ir geritten vnde vff waynen mit ganczir macht vff den dinstag nach Bonifacii gein Dresden komet vnde hantbuchsen vnde tarrasbuchsen, puluer vnd andere gerete dorczu*". In modern German, "*darum begehren wir ernstlich, dass ihr beritten und auf Wagen mit ganzer Machst auf den Dienstag nach Bonifazius (5 June) gen Dresden kommt und Handbüchsen und Terassbüchsen, Pulver und andere Geräte dazu*". Quoted in CDS II 8, Nr. 152, p. 100.

418 DOLÍNEK/DURDÍK, Historische Waffen, p. 152.

419 In MHG, "*Item der bischoff von mencz, der bischoff von kolln, der bischoff von Tryren, der falczgraffe vom Reyne sullin eyn hehr vnd eyn wagenburg haben vnd yren streit bestellen*". In modern German "*Auch der Bischof von Mainz, der Bischof von Köln, der Bischof von Trier, der Pfalzgraf bei Rhein sollen ein Heer und eine Wagenburg haben und ihren Streit beilegen*". Quoted in PALACKÝ, Urkundliche Beiträge II, Nr. 731, p. 198.

420 In MHG, "*Item was eyn yczlicher furste, hirre ader stad fussgenger ader wepener brenget, dy sullen gleich halb buchsen, halb armbrost haben mit pheylen, pley, puluer vnd was dazu gehoret. Also sul man vber X fussgenger eynen hewptman geben, vnd vber hundert eynen hewptman, vber tawsint eynen hewptman*". In modern German "*Auch was ein jeder Fürst, Herr oder Stadt Fußgänger oder Gewappnete aufbringt, die sollen gleichmäßig die Hälfte Büchsen, die Hälfte Armbrüste haben mit Pfeilen, Blei, Pulver und was dazu gehört. Also soll man über 10 Fußgänger einen Hauptmann geben und über hundert einen Hauptmann, über tausend einen Hauptmann*". Quoted in PALACKÝ, Urkundliche Beiträge II, Nr. 731, p. 199.

Sigismund was already demanding for the upcoming crusade that the Lausitzer Six Cities should "send and load your largest cannon that you have in your cities".[421]

From the very beginning, artillery played a great role in the crusader armies, at least for sieges. In the summer of 1421 when the Second Crusade reached the town of Maštov (Maleschau), a Nuremberg mercenary reported how the army commander "coveted our guns and also the equipment for them".[422] In the document joining the forces of the Silesian princes and the Six Cities in 1421, an already powerful artillery arsenal is mentioned: "Also the Schweidnitzer lands and towns shall take along a large cannon, 15 trestle guns (Terassbüchsen), and 100 Pischullen [pistols and handguns, author's comment]. Additionally, the other princes, lands and towns shall bring along whatever is at their disposition. Summa summarum of the guns, 20 large cannon with which one can collapse walls, 300 trestle guns and 2,000 Pischullen (handguns)".[423]

For the Fourth Crusade in 1427, a total of 211 guns of all kinds were to be made ready. The lion's share - almost one third - were supplied by the Imperial City of Nuremberg, which impressively underscores its economic potential. In contrast, Munich proved just a single cannon.[424]

In January 1430, Electoral Prince Friedrich I of Brandenburg asked the city of Nuremberg for large cannon and personnel to crew them. "And as your princely grace has requested of us two cannon and master gunners (Büchsenmeister), therefore we wish to loan your grace two cannon and one Büchsenmeister and many stones (cannonballs)".[425]

Despite that, it must be kept in mind that the other lands did not directly or permanently employ the Hussites' most important technical innovations, the war wagon and the massive use of firearms. In the 16th century, the war wagon was outperformed because Europe's armies strongly oriented themselves on Swiss Landsknechts, the massed formations that possessed great offensive power. In the second half of the 15th century, the field artillery system, except for that of Charles the Bold's Burgundian army, lost the significance it had possessed with the Hussites.[426]

The Hussite movement also had a significant influence on how castles were constructed. German architects either were oriented on the Bohemian examples or developed their own ideas, to make the defenses in the Empire more resistant against the Hussite armies that were equipped with strong cannon. This was recognizable above all from the integration of round, D- or horseshoe-shaped corner towers into the walls. Additionally, scientific investigations have proven that the introduction of various forms of loopholes or embrasures in castles for hook culverins (Hakenbüchsen) occurred earlier in the Empire than previously accepted, namely in the 1420s and 1430s. Those included shovel-shaped, round and keyhole-shaped as well as T-shaped loopholes, sometimes combined with one another. These loopholes are sometimes placed in a very steep manner in the tower and partially staggered ("abgetreppt") in small steps in order deflect penetrating missiles.[427]

In the Bavarian region, the measures were already evident very early. The Königstein Fortress on the Danube was erected about 1410 to protect the Duchy of Bavaria. Because of the Hussite threat, the expansion of the complex was significantly accelerated between 1421 and 1424 and a "Zwinger"[428] among other things, was constructed.[429] In 1429, Duke Ludwig VII of Bayern-Ingolstadt began the massive strengthening of the city fortifications of Schärding, which incorporated the fortification findings of that time.[430]

---

421 In modern German, "… ihre grösseste Büchse, die sie in ihren Städten hätten, aufladen und sich dazu schicken". Quoted in PALACKÝ, Urkundliche Beiträge I, Nr. 13, p. 21.

422 In MHG, "vnser püchsen vnd zewgs auch darczu begerten". In modern German, "unsere Büchsen und Zeug auch dazu begehrten ….". Quoted in PALACKÝ, Urkundliche Beiträge I, Nr. 135, p. 145.

423 In MHG, "Item die Sweidnitzer land vnd stete sullen mit jm nehmen eine grosse bochse, 15 tarrasssteinbüchsen vnd 100 pisschullen. Item die andern fursten vnd land vnd stete werden och mete nehmen iglicher nach seinem anslage. Summa summarum der bochsen, 20 grosse bochsen, damite man mawren fellen mag, 300 tarrasssteinbüchsen, 2000 pisschullen". In modern German, "Auch die Schweidnitzer Landschaft und Städte sollen mitnehmen eine große Büchse, 15 Terasbüchsen und 100 Pischullen [pistols and handguns, author's comment]. Außerdem werden auch die anderen Fürsten und Landschaften und Städte mitnehmen, jeder nach seiner Anlage. Summa summarum der Büchsen, 20 große Büchsen, damit man Mauern fällen kann, 300 Terassbüchsen, 2000 Pischullen". Quoted in PALACKÝ, Urkundliche Beiträge I, Nr. 140, pp. 150-151.

424 BLEICHER, Das Herzogtum Niederbayern, pp. 141-142.

425 In MHG, "Vnd als ewr fürstenlich gnade zweyr püchsen vnd püchsenmeysters von vns begert hat, also wellen wir ewern gnaden zwo püchsen einen puchsenmeister vnd etwieuil steyn vnuerzogenlich leihen". In modern German, "Und als eure fürstlichen Gnaden zwei Büchsen und Büchsenmeister von uns begehrt hat, also wollen wir euer Gnaden zwei Büchsen, einen Büchsenmeister und etlich viele Steine unverzüglich leihen". Quoted in PALACKÝ, Urkundliche Beiträge II, Nr. 634, p. 94.

426 LUGS, Handfeuerwaffen I, p. 15.

427 ZEUNE, Hussitenzeitliche Wehrelemente, pp. 130-132, 150-152.

428 Translator's note: A Zwinger is an open area between two defensive walls that is used for defensive purposes. Zwingers were built in the Middle Ages and Early Modern Period to improve the defence of castles and town walls. Source: https://en.wikipedia.org/wiki/Zwinger

429 BLEICHER, Das Herzogtum Niederbayern, pp. 186-187.

430 Ibid., p. 188.

THE SIGNIFICANCE OF THE HUSSITE MILITARY SYSTEM FOR MILITARY HISTORY

A number of West European historians are of the opinion that the Hussite military system made no lasting contribution to the further development of Late Middle Ages armies, and the *Wagenburg* hardly lasted beyond the Hussite Wars as a tactical system. For example, the German military historian Siegfried Fiedler came to the conclusion: "Their one-and-one-half decade long wars (1419-1434) had a lasting impact on the environment, however, they brought about no fundamental, revolutionary changes in the broader course of military developments".[431]

He is contradicted by the Hungarian historian László Veszprémy, who was more strongly focused on the influence of the Hussite military system in Eastern Europe: "Also of great importance was the Hussite struggle in Bohemia in the fifteenth century, which became one of the motors of military modernisation in the region. The Hussites managed to defeat German imperial troops for many years, and Hussites served as mercenaries in every country in the region".[432]

Nevertheless, it must be put on the record that the Hussite innovations had little influence on West European armies. Their modern employment of artillery again made a place for its conservative use, primarily limited to sieges, for another 100 years, until Charles the Bold's Burgundian army made mobile field artillery a standing component of modern armies. And also, if Bohemian mercenaries were very much in demand even in the Empire in the 15th century, the "Infantry Revolution" emanated from the Swiss mercenaries' mass formations, with their meters-long pikes, that developed considerably more shock power than the Hussites' comparatively short polearms.[433]

---

431 *"Ihre anderthalb Jahrzehnte dauernden Kriege (1419-1434) waren von nachhaltiger Wirkung auf die Umwelt, doch haben sie im weiteren militärischen Entwicklungsgang keinen grundlegend revolutionären Wandel verursacht".* FIEDLER, Taktik und Strategie, p. 190.

432 *"Ebenfalls von großer Bedeutung waren die Hussite Unruhen in Böhmen im 15. Jahrhundert, welch zum Motor einer militärischen Modernisierung der Region wurden. Den Hussites gelang es, die German Reichsheere viele Jahre lang zu schlagen und Hussites dienten als Söldner in jedem Land dieser Region".* VESZPRÉMY, State and military affairs, p. 99.

433 ROGERS, Tactics, pp. 204-208.

MILITARY LEADERS

To fully understand their armies, a handful of the Hussites' most important military and political leaders should be briefly introduced. A complete lexical compilation of all of the field commanders from this warlike time has not existed up to now. The following, therefore, only presents a few important officers who are representative of a certain period or kind of Hussite military leadership.

A later depiction of Jan Žižka
The helmet and armor correspond to ancient examples.
Graphic from volume No. 1 (*Klebeband Nr. 1*)
of the Fürstlich Waldeckschen Hofbibliothek Arolsen
Source:
http://digi.ub.uni-heidelberg.de/fwhb/klebeband1
Wikimedia Commons, licensed under
CreativeCommons-Lizenz CC-BY-SA 3.0 DE

Jan Žižka

Jan Žižka came from the petty Bohemian nobility and was supposedly born around 1370 in Trocnova, in the southwest of the country. But in 1384 he sold his patrimonial lands and went to Prague, where he served in the court of King Wenzel. He probably became blinded in one eye in his early youth. His epithet "Žižka" ("*der Einäugige*" – "the one-eyed") already appears in the sources in 1378. He was married twice, and both times the woman was named Katharina. Regarding the first wife, little more than her name is known and that she died during childbirth. As for the second wife, the sources only give her name. Žižka's daughter married in a way that was fortunate for the family politically. As the wife of Peter of Dubá, she married into one of the most important Bohemian families at that time.[434]

In Prague, Žižka climbed to the position of a Master of the Hunt (*Jagdmeister*) at the King's court. Although he no longer owned any land, the most important criterion by which nobles were measured at that time, his new role underscored a certain closeness to the King. But eventually Žižka got pulled into the Bohemian internal disputes. Wenzel's reign was anything other than stable. Žižka joined one of the groups loyal to the King that sparked an insurgency in the country's southeast. Žižka gained important military experience in that conflict. He made the acquaintance of Jan Sokol from Lamberg, a talented soldier who recognized Žižka's talents and advanced him further. The one-eyed commander eventually got into a feud with the Moravian city of České Budějovice (Budweis) that beheaded his brother in 1400. The feud only ended in 1409 with King Wenzel's intervention.

A year later, Žižka followed Jan Sokol with a Bohemian levy to Poland. The Polish King, Wladislaw Jagiello, was making war against the Knights of the Teutonic Order. On 15 July 1410, the supposedly largest battle of the Middle Ages took place in the vicinity of the villages of Tannenberg-Grunwald. Whether Žižka participated is not completely certain. If he did so, then he certainly did not fight in the most forward lines and did not lose his eye there as some later stories claim. Regardless, his participation gave him important insights into the way modern knights' armies fought then. Žižka along with others could have seen what penetrating impact the Teutonic Brothers' attack on the Polish-Lithuanian right wing could have had against lightly armed troops. At the same time, he could have been convinced that the Polish knights had some problems in their assault on the Order's baggage train that had formed a *Wagenburg*, which was already a practice at that time.[435] It is certain that after the battle, Žižka was stationed with a Bohemian garrison in the captured Order's Radzyn Castle on the Vistula River, and they defended it against attempts by the German knights to retake the castle.

After the 1411 Peace of Torun (*Frieden von Thorn*), he returned to Prague as a respected soldier and war hero. His mentor, Jan Sokol died from a plague shortly thereafter. Žižka became a kind of captain (*Hauptmann*) of the Royal Bodyguard and it is at least known that he accompanied Queen Sofia to Jan Hus' sermons in the Bethlehem

---

434 Verney, Warrior of God, pp. 12-13.

435 For a description of the course of the battle, see Iselt, Tannenberg 1410 (Heere & Waffen Number 7 in German, English translation to be published)..

Chapel. In 1414, he purchased a house in the Prague New City. In that year, he was added to the city's registers as a "*portulanis regius*", a Royal Door Guardian. Žižka appears to have been one of Wenzel's closer confidants until the King's death. Given that, it is completely conceivable that he could have studied the latest works about military science, like Kyeser's "*Bellifortis*" in the Royal Library. After the First Prague Defenestration, he was chosen by the new city council to be one of the captains of the Prague city militia. With that, he began his ascent to become the movement's most important military leader. In 1421 at the second siege of the Rabi Castle, he lost vision in his good eye and became completely blind. Nonetheless he proved, admittedly also thanks to his officers' advice, to have a remarkable skill at choosing his battlefields. That same year, he was promised a small wooden Teutonic Knights' castle, the *Ordensburg* Triebsch (*Třebušín).* Žižka had the castle significantly expanded and renamed as "Chalice". After that he called himself Jan Žižka of Trocnova and the Chalice (*Jan Žižka z Trocnova a Kalicha).*

Žižka was considered a completely headstrong commander with strict principles. However, on religious issues, he always relied on the Prague Magister's advice. During his lifetime, he avoided taking the Hussite revolution abroad and conducted a purely defensive war. His death in 1424 finally gave the conflict a different aspect.[436]

Žižka was initially buried in the Peter and Paul's Church in Hradec Králové (Königgrätz). In 1437, after the city fell into the hands of Diviš Bořek z Miletínka, his body was moved to Čáslav. But even here, the commander did not find a final resting place. Almost two hundred years after his death, in the aftermath of the Catholic victory in the Battle of White Mountain (1620)[437] and the Counterreformation carried out in Bohemia, his grave was destroyed. According to legend, his remains were buried again at the city gallows, but nothing is known about where his body actually lies.

Jan Želivský

Little is known about Jan Želivský's birth or early life. He first appears in sources as a monk in the Order of Canons Regular of Prémontré after Jan Hus's death. After he had preached for a period in southern Bohemia, he went to Prague in 1418 where he seized upon the teachings of Hus and within the shortest time became one of the movement's most radical representatives. Želivský linked religious ideas to social demands that eventually aimed at the elimination of the classes. His preachings were well received by his listeners. Jan Želivský advanced as a kind of plebeian tribune.

On 30 July 1419, he led the attack on the Prague City Hall and, with that, was decisively involved with the outbreak of the Hussite Revolution. Although Želivský had no military experience, he was elected to be the captain of a Prague levy and soon after that also to be a councilman. After that, relying on his solid popularity with the simple people, he began more and more to push his opponents in the national assembly to the wayside. What Jan Želivský was seeking is not completely clear. It is certain that he was always part of the radical wing on the movement whose views were not held by the majority of the population. Whether he only wanted to protect the interests of his fellow believers, or he was personally striving for a form of religious-political dictatorship, similar to what Oliver Cromwell did in England 230 years later, cannot be determined for certain.

In 1420 for the first time, Želivský commanded a levy of the Prazans and Orebites during a campaign in eastern Bohemia. He showed little skill as a field commander. Nevertheless, one year later he went to war again and attempted to capture the north Bohemian town of Most (Brüx). There, on 5 August 1421, the Hussites had to accept their first serious defeat against the Meissen army under Friedrich the Warlike. This defeat was Jan Želivský's political undoing. His opponents in the national assembly won the upper hand and in 1422 charged him with having committed various acts of violence during his regency. On 9 July 1422, he was beheaded in front of the Prague City Hall. Želivský was still very beloved among his adherents. Bloody riots broke out in the Bohemian capital that among other things unleashed a pogrom against the Jews.[438]

Mikuláš of Hus (Mikuláš z Husi)

Little is known about Mikuláš z Husi's background. Originally, he called himself after the Pístný manor, so it is suspected that he was born there. In German he is called Nikolaus von Hus. Mikuláš enjoyed a solid education that helped him to become a lawyer at the Prague High Court of Justice (Czech "*pražský dvorský soud;*" German "Prager *Hofgericht*"). He received a lien of the Vyšehrad Castle County and in 1404, he became the Count of Hus near Prachatitz. How his rule went is also not known. He developed good contacts with Heinrich von Rosenberg and served as a mercenary for the Dukes of Austria. From 1414 to 1417, he often stayed in Prague and established close contacts with the Hussite movement. However, he did not join into the Bohemian nobles' protest letter about the reformer's burning at the stake. But shortly after that he renounced King Wenzel and was banished which would explain Mikuláš' split with the House of Luxembourg. In 1418, the banishment was lifted, yet Mikuláš apparently

---

436 For a biography, above all see Tomek, *Jan Žižka* and Verney, *Warrior of God.* Verney however, relies on much information from outdated literary descriptions and can only be viewed with caution.

437 Translator's note: The Battle of White Mountain (Czech *Bitva na Bílé hoře*; German *Schlacht am Weißen Berg*), on 8 November 1620, was fought near Prague in Bohemia. The battle marked the first major victory of the Roman Catholic Habsburgs over the Protestant Union, a military alliance among the Protestant states of Germany, in the Thirty Years' War (1618–48).

438 PALACKÝ, Der Hussitenkrieg 1419-1431, pp. 50-286.

subsequently joined the Hussite movement and became one of the first three important Taborite commanders. Nominally he was even senior to Jan Žižka. Mikuláš was a talented organizer whom people would willingly follow. At the same time, he was, however, arrogant and hotheaded, which undermined his position throughout his life.[439]

In June 1420, he led a small army of horsemen and defeated the Austrian forces besieging Tabor. He subsequently did not return to Prague that was being threatened, and it has been considered by many as a sign of the opposition to Jan Žižka's growing authority. Only in October, when Žižka had already left the city did Hus return to the Moldau city with his cavalry troop, in order to take part in the siege of the old hilltop castle. When Žižka arrived back in the city in December, an open conflict ensued between him and Hus about how to continue the war. When Hus, who felt insulted, wanted to leave the city, he fell from his horse, broke a leg and suffered serious injuries to his ribcage. Although he feared that the Prazans wanted to kill him, he was given the best treatment. The doctors could fix his leg, but they could not heal the serious injuries to his torso from which Mikuláš died on Christmas Day 1420.[440]

Andreas Procopius (Prokop)

One of the best-known leaders of the national-Bohemian movement had, of all things, German roots. Andreas Procopius' father was the German merchant Jan Cach, who had settled in Prague. Andreas supposedly was born about 1380 in the vicinity of the later city of Tabor. He studied theology at the Prague University and later became a pastor in the capital. There he soon became attached to Jan Hus' teachings. After the reformer's death, Andreas Procopius developed into a more radical exponent of Hussitism. After Prague's citizens agreed to a ceasefire with the King's garrison, he left the capital and in 1420 moved to Tabor. Procopius became one of Jan Želivský's protégés. When the young priest was arrested during the Picarde unrest, it was Želivský who got him freed. Up until Žižka's death in 1424, little is known about his activities. But that year he appeared as the Taborites' field commander. He was also called "the Bald" (Old Czech: *Prokop Holý*, Latin: *Procopius Rasus*, German: "*der Kahle*") because he went against Hussite priests' tradition by not wearing a beard, i.e. shaving (and not because of his monk's tonsure, as sometimes claimed).

Until 1426, Andreas Procopius was establishing himself as the movement's new military leader. Žižka was actually always opposed to priests taking on military tasks, but Procopius proved that he had not approached him in tactical and strategic skills, but even exceeded him in political caginess. He achieved a series of spectacular victories in 1426 at Ústi (Aussig), in 1427 at Zwettel (in Austria) and

Tachov (Tachau) that even overshadowed Žižka's successes. But unlike the blind army commander, Procopius not just protected Bohemia, but thought to take Hussitism abroad. Starting in 1427, the Taborites, Orphans and Orebites under his leadership increasingly undertook large campaigns into Poland, Silesia, the Lausitz, Saxony, Bavaria, Austria and Hungary. These "*spaniel jizdy*" ("beautiful rides", German "*herrlichen Heerfahrten*") were, however, also born out of economic necessity because Bohemia had been stripped bare by several crusades and was hardly in the condition to keep many field armies supplied.[441]

An early modern depiction of Andreas Prokop
Contemporary portraits of the Hussite leader unfortunately do not exist.

After Procopius defeated a crusader army again at Domažlice in 1431, King Sigismund attempted to end the prolonged war by inviting Hussite representatives to the Church Council in Basel. Andreas Procopius also appeared in the Swiss city as a speaker for the Taborites. However, during the negotiations, he showed himself to not be ready to compromise and because staying in the city was very expensive, he left Switzerland after a few weeks. He did not recognize the so-called Prague Compacts worked out by the Utraquists. In 1434, when pacified Hussites assembled an army and went to the field against the radical Taborites and Orphans, Procopius stood up his numerically inferior force for battle at Lipany on 30 May. But Pro-

---

439 ŠMAHEL, Hussitische Revolution I, p. 248.

440 ŠMAHEL, Hussitische Revolution II, pp. 1090, 1116.

441 ŠMAHEL, Prokop, p. 45.

copius was able to outwit the Prazans' leader, Diviš Bořek z Miletínka and to storm the *Wagenburg*. Yet Andreas Procopius was killed during the ensuing hand-to-hand fighting. His death and the Taborites' defeat marked an important endpoint for the movement.[442]

Jan Čapek ze Sán

As a member of the Bohemian petty nobility, Čapek ze Sán first comes to light late in this history. He came from an eastern Bohemian family and was owner of the small Slány estate. Supposedly he was born between 1390 and 1400. He first appears in sources as a captain in a Hussite army that attacked Silesia in 1427. During that campaign, Jan Čapek ze Sán was badly defeated at Náchod. That battle revealed character traits that the commander would display again and again in the following years. Jan Čapek did not lack courage or thirst for action, but was short on tactical prudence. Four years later he commanded an Orphans' field army that together with the Taborites under Procopius advanced into Slovakia. However, there the two commanders argued about the dividing of the booty. Procopius left and Jan Čapek continued the campaign alone. The Orphans did take rich booty, but on the return march they were pursued by Hungarian levies and badly defeated. They lost almost two thirds of their men.

In 1433, despite these military setbacks, Jan Čapek ze Sán led an Orphans army into the Neumark, where he joined with a Polish army and attacked the Teutonic Order's state. Under his leadership, the Hussites advanced to the shores of the Baltic Sea where Jan Čapek was knighted. Unlike just about any other Hussite commander, Čapek used the "beautiful rides" above all for his personal gain. During them, in this time of brutality and religious fanaticism, he stood out by his marked cruelty.

On the return from his campaign to the Baltic Sea, Čapek joined the Hussite forces besieging Pilsen. After a larger foraging force from this army was decisively defeated during a movement in the Oberpfalz at Hiltersried, an uprising ensued during which the Taborite leader Procopius was temporarily imprisoned. For a time, Jan Čapek took over command of the besieging army but could not get Pilsen to fall. In the summer of 1434, he reunited his army with the Taborites under Procopius who had been reinstated and he fought in the Battle of Lipany. Like at the Battle of Náchod, he let his forces be lured out of the secure *Wagenburg* too early in order to pursue the supposedly fleeing enemies. When the Lords' League (Czech *panská jednota*; German *Herrenbund*) forces had finally stormed the *Wagenburg* and Procopius had been killed, Jan Čapek fled the battlefield, which afterward was interpreted as his committing treason. The Lords' League in the Prague New City later confiscated 5,000 "*Schock*" Groschen that Jan Čapek had looted during the "beautiful rides". For that time it was a considerable amount.[443]

Jan Čapek had to leave Bohemia. In 1438, he obtained the East-Moravian Hukvaldy Castle from which on his own initiative he carried out raids into Hungary and Poland. In 1443, he took part in a campaign against Hungary as a retainer of the Polish King Wladislaw III. In the following year Čapek fought in a crusade against the Turks at the Battle of Varna in eastern Bulgaria. Afterward he joined the service of the Hungarian *Voivode* Jan Jiskra of Brandeys (Jan Jiskra z Brandýsa). In 1445 he married Hedwig Petřvaldská. It was already his second marriage. From his first marriage he had a daughter, who at the same time married Jan Talafús of Ostrov, a retainer of Jan Jiskra. Hedwig had also been married once before and bore two sons. Jan Čapek supposedly died in his Hukvaldy Castle in 1452.

Diviš Bořek z Miletínka

Diviš Bořek z Miletínka belonged to Bohemia's poor landed nobility. He was already familiar with the teachings of Jan Hus during the reformer's lifetime. When the Hussite Wars broke out, he joined Jan Žižka's army. It is not known whether Miletínka already had prior military experience, but during the prolonged campaigns he gained a deep insight into the blind commander's way of operating.

With Žižka's growing radicalization, Diviš Bořek z Miletínka became alienated from him. For his entire life he remained a moderate Utraquist. In 1421, he moved to East Bohemia and restored the Kunětická Hora castle ruins into his ancestral seat. In the following months he conducted several campaigns in East Bohemia and Moravia that were in part aimed at the radical Taborites and Orebites. In April 1423, at the side of Jan Žižka he defeated a Catholic army at the Battle of Hořice (Horschitz). He led the Hussite cavalry in a merciless pursuit of the now fleeing former pursuers and almost annihilated them. But just a few months later the two commanders had a falling out. Apparently Diviš tried to establish his brother Jetrich as the administrator in Hradec Králové (Königgrätz). The councilmen were unhappy with this choice and asked Žižka for support. Jan Žižka ejected Jetrich and in doing so drove Diviš into the camp of the Lords' League, which was forming at that time. A short time later, however, Miletínka was badly defeated by his old teacher at Strážnice.[444]

---

442 Ibid., p. 245.

443 DURDÍK, Hussitisches Heerwesen, p. 247. Translator's note: Per Ziemann, Adolf, *Mittelhochdeutsches Wörterbuch zum Handgebrauch*, p. 366, in mediaeval German-speaking lands, the "*Schock*" or "Schog" was normally a term for sixty, but someplaces it meant 24, 20 or 12 handfulls. So theoretically the sum could have been as great as 300,00 Groschen, which seems highly unlikely.

444 ŠMAHEL, Hussitische Revolution II, pp. 1293-1294.

However, this defeat did his reputation no harm. Miletínka continued to operate in the kingdom's east and became the captain of Chrudim und Litomyšl (Leitomischl). In 1427, the burghers of Kolín called to him for help when Procopius the Great's army was nearing the town. Miletínka was able to defend Kolín for three long months. But when food was becoming scarce, some citizens betrayed the commander and forced him to agree to capitulate. Through diplomatic skill he was, however, able to negotiate safe conduct for himself and his followers in exchange for paying a ransom.

After the bulk of the Utraquists had reconciled with King Sigismund through the Prague Compacts and gone to the field, they elected Miletínka to be their field commander.

It was a fortunate choice, because using his experience, on 30 May 1434, he was able to lure Andreas Procopius into a trap and decisively defeat him at Lipany. Miletínka, along with the Margrave of Meissen, Friedrich the Warlike, was the only army commander of this period who was able to capture a Hussite *Wagenburg* in a large battle in the field. In thanks, Sigismund awarded him estates around his Kunětická Hora Castle and at Pardupice (Pardubitz). Diviš Bořek z Miletínka, who was possibly the canniest commander of this time next to Jan Žižka, died in 1437.[445]

---

445 PALACKÝ, Der Hussitenkrieg 1419-1431, pp. 101-450.

PRIMARY SOURCES

Documents taken from later editions are always quoted in the text first with the edition number and then with the relevant page number.

Codex Diplomaticus Saxoniae Regiae I B 4: Die Urkunden der Markgrafen von Meißen und Landgrafen von Thüringen 1419-1427, ["The Diplomatic Codex of the Saxon Kings I B 4: The Documents of the Margraves of Meissen and the Count of the Land of Thuringia 1419-1427"], (Leipzig- Dresden: Otto Posse, 1941) [quotes are shown shown as: CDS I B 40].

Codex Diplomaticus Saxoniae Regiae II 5. Urkundenbuch der Städte Dresden und Pirna ["The Diplomatic Codex of the Saxon Kings II 5, Book of Documents of the Cities of Dresden and Pirna"] (Leipzig: Karl Friedrich von Posern-Klett, 1875) [quotes are shown shown as: CDS II 50].

Codex Diplomaticus Saxoniae Regiae II 8. Urkundenbuch der Stadt Leipzig ["The Diplomatic Codex of the Saxon Kings II 8, Book of Documents of the City of Leipzig"] (Leipzig: Giesecke & Devrient, 1868) [quotes are shown shown as: CDS II 8].

Die Hussiten. Die Chronik des Laurentius von Brezová 1414-1421. Aus dem Lateinischen und Alttschechischen übersetzt, eingeleitet und erklärt von Josef Bujnoch ["The Hussites: The Chronicles of Laurentius of Brezová 1414-1421. Translated from the Latin and Old Czech, introduced and annotated by Josef Bujnoch"] (Graz, Vienna and Cologne: Styria, 1988 [quotes are shown shown as: *Laurentius-Chronik*].

Hassenstein, Wilhelm, *Das Feuerwerkbuch von 1420. Neudruck des Erstdrucks von 1529 mit Übertragung ins Hochdeutsche und Erläuterungen* ["The Artillery Book of 1420: New Printing of the 1529 First Printing with Conversion into High German and Explanations" by Josef Bujnoch] (Munich: Verlag der Deutschen Technik, 1941) [quotes are shown as: Hassenstein: Feuerwerkbuch].

Luther, Martin, *Gesammelte Werke: Lutherbibel, Predigten, Traktate, Gedichte, Biografie* [Collected Works: Luther Bible, Sermons, Tracts, Biography] (no place, 2015) [cite: Luther, *Gesammelte Werke*].

Palacký, František, *Urkundliche Beiträge zur Geschichte der Hussitenkrieg in den Jahren 1419-1436. 2 Bände.* (2 volumes) (Prague, 1873 [cite: Palacký, *Urkundliche Beiträge I&II*].

PRIMARY GRAPHIC SOURCES

Windecke, Eberhard (ca. 1380 – 1440/41), *Chronik* (Chronicle) (Eberhard Windecke, also Windeck, (born about 1380 in Mainz; died 1440/1441) was a German-Hungarian merchant and chronicler. He came from Mainz.

Windecke, Eberhard, *Geschichte Kaiser Sigismunds* (ca. 1438-39) See above.

Hartlieb, Johannes, *Kriegsbuch*. Johannes Hartlieb, also called Hans Hartlieb, (born ca. 1400, died 18 May 1468) was a German doctor and personal physician, learned councilman, diplomat, court poet and early Humanist translator at the court of the Wittelsbachs in Munich. In his early years, he participated in two wars, the first, sometime during the Hussite Wars (1419–1436) and the other during the so-called "Bavarian War" ("*Bayerischen Krieg*") of 1420–1422 on the side of Ludwig the Bearded of Bayern-Ingolstadt)

Jena-Codex (ca. 1490-1510). According to the Národí Muzeum (National Museum) in Prague, the Jena Codex "originated in the late 15th and early 16th century Czech Lands. The impetus for the drawing [sic] of this document came from the Utraquist Bohuslav of Čechtice. The manuscript bears rich and extensive illumination. In some parts, the pictorial decorations dominate the text. ... Almost the entire Codex is written in Czech, with only a small part in Latin".

Kyeser, Konrad, *Bellifortis* (1402-1405). Bellifortis ("Strong in War", "War Fortifications") is the first fully illustrated manual of military technology written by Konrad Kyeser and dating from the start of the 15th century. It summarizes material from classical writers on military technology, like Vegetius' *De Re Militari* and Frontinus' anecdotal *Strategemata*, emphasising the art of siege warfare, but treating magic as a supplement to the military arts.

Talhofer, Hans, *Alte Armatur und Ringkunst* (1459). This work shows illustrations of a variety of weapons and techniques for fencing and hand-to-hand combat.

SECONDARY LITERATURE

Bachmann, Adolf, "Georg von Podïebrad," in *Allgemeine Deutsche Biographie* (ADB). Band 8 (Leipzig, 1878) pp. 602–611 [cite: Bachmann, *Georg von Podïebrad*].

Beaufort-Spontin, Christian, "Das neue Antlitz des Ritters: Die Hundsgugel", in: Bloh, Jutta Charlotte von/ Syndram, Dirk/ Streich, Brigitte, *Mit Schwert und Kreuz zur Kurfürstenmacht. Friedrich der Streitbare, Markgraf von Meißen und Kurfürst von Sachsen (1370-1428)* (Munich: Deutscher Kunstverlag, 2007), pp. 60-62 [cite: Beaufort-Spontin, *Hundsgugel*].

Berger, Heiko, "Von der Kampfkraft der Hussiten" in Bloh, Jutta Charlotte von/ Syndram, Dirk/ Streich, Brigitte, *Mit Schwert und Kreuz zur Kurfürstenmacht. Friedrich der Streitbare, Markgraf von Meißen und Kurfürst von Sachsen (1370-1428)* (Munich: Deutscher Kunstverlag, 2007), pp. 100-109 [cite: Berger, *Kampfkraft der Hussiten*].

Bezold, Friedrich von, *König Sigismund und die Reichskriege gegen die Hussiten* (Munich, 1872) [cite: Bezold, *Sigismund und die Reichskriege*].

Bleicher, Michaela, "*Das Herzogtum Niederbayern. Straubing in den Hussitenkriegen. Kriegsalltag und Kriegsführung im Spiegel der Landschreiberrechnung. Inaugural – Dissertation zur Erlangung der Doktorwürde der Philosophischen Fakultät III*" (Regensburg: Geschichte, Gesellschaft und Geografie der Universität Regensburg, 2004) [cite: Bleicher *Das Herzogtum Niederbayern*].

Boeheim, Wendelin, *Handbuch der Waffenkunde*, (Leipzig: Seemanns, 1890) [cite: Boeheim, *Waffenkunde*].

Delbrück, Hans, *Geschichte der Kriegskunst Bd. III Das Mittelalter. Von Karl dem Großen bis zum späten Mittelalter* (Berlin: Nikol Verlag, 2000) [cite: Delbrück, *Geschichte der Kriegskunst*].

Demmin, August, *Die Kriegswaffen in ihrer historischen Entwicklung von der Steinzeit bis zur Erfindung des Zündnadelgewehrs*, (Leipzig: Seemann, 1869) [cite: Demmin, *Die Kriegswaffen*].

Dolínek, Vladimír and Durdík, Jan, *Historische Waffen* (Augsburg: Bechtermünz, 1996) [cite: Dolínek/Durdík, *Historische Waffen*].

Durdík, Jan, *Hussitisches Heerwesen* (Berlin: Deutscher Militärverlag [der DDR], 1961) (cite: Durdík, *Hussitisches Heerwesen*].

Ermisch, Hubert, "Zur Geschichte der Schlacht bei Außig", in *Neues Archiv für Sächsische Geschichte und Altertumskunde*, hereafter "NASG" Vol. 47 (Dresden: Verlag Ph. C. W. Schmidt, 1926), pp. 5-45 [cite: Ermisch, *Schlacht bei Außig*].

Feldhaus, Franz Maria, "Kyeser, Conrad", in *Allgemeine deutsche Biografie Bd. 52*, (Leipzig: Duncker und Humblot, 1906), pp. 768-769 [cite: Feldhaus, *Kyeser*].

Fiedler, Siegfried, *Taktik und Strategie der Landsknechte 1500-1650* (Bonn: Bechtermünz, 1985) [cite: Fiedler, *Taktik und Strategie*].

Grintzer, E., "Die Einnahme und Zerstörung der Stadt Plauen i. V. durch die Hussiten im Jahre 1430", in NASG Vol. 33 (Dresden: Verlag Ph. C. W. Schmidt, 1912), pp. 142-145 [cite: Grintzer, *Zerstörung der Stadt Plauen*].

Gundram, Ralph, *Döbeln und die Hussiten. Der hussitische Feldzug 1429/30 zwischen Elbe und Mulde in Legende und Wirklichkeit* (Oschatz: published by the author, 2007) [cite: Gundram, *Döbeln und die Hussiten*].

Harmuth, Egon, *Die Armbrust. Ein Handbuch* (Graz: Akademische Druck u. Verlagsanstalt, 1986) [cite: Harmuth, *Armbrust*].

Hilsch, Peter, *Johannes Hus. Prediger Gottes und Ketzer* (Regensburg: Friedrich Pustet, 1999) [cite: Hilsch, *Johannes Hus*].

Hönsch, Jörg K., *Geschichte Böhmens. Von der slavischen Landnahme bis zur Gegenwart* (Munich: C. H. Beck, 1997) [cite: Hönsch, *Geschichte Böhmens*].

Iselt, Gerald, *Tannenberg 1410. Die Belagerung der Marienburg 1410* (Berlin: Zeughaus Verlag, 2008) [cite: Iselt, *Tannenberg 1410*].

Jecht, Richard, "Der Zug der Hussiten nach der Mark im Jahre 1432," in *Forschungen zur brandenburgischen und preußischen Geschichte 25* (1912), pp. 29-50 [cite: Jecht, *Zug der Hussiten nach der Mark*].

Kejř, Jiří, *Die Hussitenrevolution* (Prague: Orbis, 1988).

Korowski, Franz, *Die Marienburg und ihre 17 Hochmeister des Deutschen Ritterordens* (Würzburg: Rautenberg Verlag, 2007 [cite: Korowski, *Die Marienburg*].

Korschelt, Johann Gottlieb, Kriegsdrangsale der Oberlausitz zur Zeit des Hussitenkrieges", in *Neues Lausitzisches Magazin* Vol. 44 (Görlitz: Oberlausitzischen Gesellschaft der Wissenschaften, 1868), pp. 173-186 [cite: Korschelt, *Kriegsdrangsale der Oberlausitz*].

Krocker, Ernst: Sachsen und die Hussitenkriege, in NASG Vol. 21 (Dresden: Verlag Ph. C. W. Schmidt, 1900), pp. 1-39 [(cite: Krocker, *Sachsen und die Hussitenkriege*].

Kroener, Bernhard R., *Kriegswesen, Herrschaft und Gesellschaft 1300 – 1800* (Munich: Enzyklopadie Deutscher Geschichte, 2013) [cite: Kroener, *Kriegswesen*].

Krzenck, Thomas, "Die Hussitenkriege, Sachsen und Leipzig", in Hehl, Ulrich von (ed.), *Stadt und Krieg. Leipzig in militärischen Konflikten vom Mittelalter bis ins 20. Jahrhundert*, (Leipzig: Leibziger Universitätsverlag, 2015), pp. 51-69 [cite: Krzenck: *Hussitenkriege*].

Lindau, Wilhelm Adolf, *Die Schlacht bei Aussig. Romantische Bilder aus dem 15. Jahrhundert* (Leipzig: Kollmann,1849) [cite: Lindau, *Schlacht bei Aussig*].

Lugs, Jaroslaw, *Handfeuerwaffen. Systematischer Überblick über die Handfeuerwaffen und ihre Geschichte, Band 1* (Berlin: Militärverlag der DDR, 1977) [cite: Lugs, *Handfeuerwaffen*].

Macek, Josef, *Die Hussitische Revolutionäre Bewegung* (Berlin: VEB Dt. Verl. der Wissenschaften, 1958) [cite: Macek, *Revolutionäre Bewegung*].

Machilek, Franz, "Hus und die Hussiten in Franken", in *Jahrbuch für fränkische Landesforschung 51* (Erlangen: Institut für Fränkische Landesforschung an der Universität Erlangen, 1991), pp. 15-37 [cite: Machilek, *Hussiten in Franken*].

-----,, "Jan Hus und die Hussiten in der Oberpfalz," in Machilek, Franz, *Die hussitische Revolution. Religiöse, politische und regionale Aspekte* (Vienna - Cologne – Weimar: Böhlau, 2012), pp. 181-222 [cite: Machilek, Hussiten in der Oberpfalz].

-----,, "Schlesien, Hus und die Hussiten," in Machilek, Franz, *Die hussitische Revolution. Religiöse, politische und regionale Aspekte* (Vienna - Cologne – Weimar, 2012), pp. 109-142 [cite: Machilek, *Schlesien*].

McLachlan, Sean, *Medieval Handgonnes. The first Black Powder Infantry Weapons (Osprey Weapons No. 3)* (Oxford: Osprey, 2010) [cite: McLachlan, *Medieval Handgonnes*].

Meinhard, Matthias, "Dresden und die Ketzerbewegung", in Bloh, Jutta Charlotte von/ Syndram, Dirk/ Streich, Brigitte, *Mit Schwert und Kreuz zur Kurfürstenmacht. Friedrich der Streitbare, Markgraf von Meißen und Kurfürst von Sachsen (1370-1428)* (Munich: Deutscher Kunstverlag, 2007), pp. 110-113 [cite: Meinhard, *Dresden und die Ketzerbewegung*].

Meinhardt, Matthias, "Im Dienste des Königs: Die Feldzüge Friedrichs des Streitbaren," in Bloh, Jutta Charlotte von/ Syndram, Dirk/ Streich, Brigitte, *Mit Schwert und Kreuz zur Kurfürstenmacht. Friedrich der Streitbare, Markgraf von Meißen und Kurfürst von Sachsen (1370-1428)* (Munich: Deutscher Kunstverlag, 2007), pp. 114-118 [cite: Meinhardt, *Im Dienste des Königs*].

Nicholson, Helen, *Medieval Warfare. Theorie and Practice of War in Europe 300 - 1500* (New York: Palgrave Macmillan, 2004) [cite: Nicholson, *Medieval Warfare*].

Palacký, František, *Geschichte von Böhmen. Größtentheils nach Urkunden und Handschriften, Bd. 3 Abt. 2. Der Hussitenkrieg, von 1419-1431* (Prague: Tempsky, 1851) [cite: Palacký, *Der Hussitenkrieg 1419-1431*].

-----, *Geschichte von Böhmen. Größtentheils nach Urkunden und Handschrifte*n, Bd. 3 Abt. 3. Böhmen und das Baseler Conzil. Sigismund und Albrecht. J. 1431-1439 (Prague: Tempsky, 1854) [cite: Palacký, Böhmen und das Baseler Konzil].

-----, *Geschichte von Böhmen. Größtentheils nach Urkunden und Handschriften, Bd. 4 Abt. 1. Das Zeitalter Georgs von Poděbrad. Die Zeit von 1439 bis zu K. Ladislaws Tode 1457* (Prague: Tempsky, 1857) [cite: Palacký, *Georg von Poděbrad I*].

-----,, *Geschichte von Böhmen. Größtentheils nach Urkunden und Handschriften, Bd. 4 Abt. 2. Das Zeitalter Georgs von Poděbrad. K. Georgs Regierung 1457-1471*) (Prague: Tempsky, 1857) [cite: Palacký, *Georg von Poděbrad II*].

Polívka, Miloslav, "Die Handelsbeziehungen zwischen Nürnberg und den böhmischen Ländern während der hussitischen Revolution (1419-1434)", in Machilek, Franz, *Die hussitische Revolution. Religiöse, politische und regionale Aspekte* (Vienna - Cologne – Weimar: Böhlau Verlag, 2012), pp. 163-180 [cite: Polívka, *Handelsbeziehungen*].

Poppolow, Marcus, "Militärtechnische Bildkataloge des Spätmittelalters", in Kortüm, Hans-Henning (ed.), *Krieg im Mittelalter* (Berlin: Akademie Verlag, 2001), pp. 251-268 [cite: Poppolow, *Militärtechnische Bildkataloge*].

Purton, Peter, *A History Of The Late Medieval Siege 1200-1500* (Woodbridge: Boydell & Brewer, 2010) [cite: Purton, *Late Medieval Siege*].

Querengässer, Alexander, "Triumph for the heretics. The Battle of Aussig 1426," in *Medieval Warfare Magazine No. 2* (2015), pp. 42-46 [cite: Querengässer, *Triumph for the heretics*].

Richter, O., "Ein hussitischer Spion", in: NASG Vol. 7 (Dresden: Verlag Ph. C. W. Schmidt, 1886), S.145-146 [cite: Richter, *Hussitischer Spion*].

Rieder, Heinz, *Die Hussiten. Streiter für Glauben und Nation* (Gernsbach: Casimir Katz Verlag, 1998) [cite: Rieder, *Die Hussiten*].

Rogers, Clifford J., "Tactics and the face of battle", in Tallett, Frank and Trim, David J.B., *European Warfare 1350-1750* (Cambridge: Cambridge University Press, 2010), pp. 203-235 [cite: Rogers, *Tactics*].

Royt, Jan, "Hussitische Bildpropaganda", in Eberhard, Winfried/ Machilek, Franz (Ed.): *Kirchliche Reformimpulse des 14./ 15. Jahrhunderts in Ostmitteleuropa* (Cologne: Böhlau, 2006), pp. 341-356 [cite: Royt, *Hussitische Bildpropaganda*].

Seibt, Ferdinand, *Hussitica. Zur Struktur einer Revolution* (Cologne: Böhlau, 1990) [cite: Seibt, *Hussitica*].

Seibt, Ferdinand, "Die Hussitische Revolution", in Seibt, Ferdinand, *Hussitenstudien* (Munich: Oldenbourg, 1991), pp. 79-96 [cite: Seibt, *Die Hussitische Revolution*].

-----, "Zur Entwicklung der Böhmischen Staatlichkeit 1212 - 1471, „Hussitenstudien* (Munich: Oldenbourg, 1991), pp. 133-151 [cite: Seibt, *Entwicklung der Böhmischen Staatlichkeit*].

-----, "Konrad von Vechta", in Seibt, Ferdinand, *Hussitenstudien* (Munich: Oldenbourg, 1991), pp. 241-252 [cite: Seibt, *Konrad von Vechta*].

-----, "Tabor und die europäischen Revolutionen", in Seibt, Ferdinand, *Hussitenstudien* (Munich: Oldenbourg, 1991), pp. 175-184 [cite: Seibt, *Tabor*].

-----, "Vom Vítkov bis zum Vyšehrad. Der Kampf um die böhmische Krone 1420 im Licht der Prager Propaganda," in Seibt's *Hussitenstudien* (Munich: Oldenbourg, 1991, pp. 185-207 [cite: Seibt, *Vom Vítkov bis zum Vyšehrad*].

Schmidt, Peter, *Die große Schlacht. Ein Historienbild aus der Frühzeit des Kupferstichs* (Wiesbaden: Otto Harrassowitz, 1992) [cite: Schmidt, *Die große Schlacht*].

Schmidtchen, Volker, *Bombarden, Befestigungen, Büchsenmeister. Von den ersten Mauerbrechern des Mittelalters zur Belagerungsartillerie der Renaissance* (Düsseldorf: Droste, 1977) [cite: Schmidtchen, *Bombarden, Befestigungen, Büchsenmeister*].

-----, "Karrenbüchse und Wagenburg. Hussitische Innovationen zur Technik und Taktik des Kriegswesens im späten Mittelalter" in Schmidtchen, Volker and Jäger, Eckhard (eds.), *Wirtschaft, Technik und Geschichte. Beiträge zur Erforschung der Kulturbeziehungen in Deutschland und Osteuropa* (Berlin: Verlag Ulrich Camen, 1980), pp. 83-108 [cite: Schmidtchen, *Karrenbüchse und Wagenburg*].

-----, *Kriegswesen im späten Mittelalter. Technik, Taktik, Theorie* (Weinheim: Acta humaniora, 1990) [cite: Schmidtchen, *Kriegswesen*].

Šmahel, František, "Prokop/ 3. Pr. d. Gr"., in *Lexikon des Mittelalters. Band 7* (Munich: Artemis-Verlag, 1995), p. 245 [cite: Šmahel, *Prokop*].

-----, *Die Hussitische Revolution*. 3 vols. (MGH-Schriften 43/I-III – MGH = Monumenta Germaniae Historica), (Hannover: Hahnsche Buchhandlung, 2002) [cite: Šmahel, *Hussitische Revolution 1-3*].

Stöller, Ferdinand, "Österreich im Kriege gegen die Hussiten (1420-1436)" in *Jahrbuch für Landeskunde von Niederösterreich 22* (St. Pölten: Verein für Landeskunde von Niederösterreich, 1929), pp. 1-87 [cite: Stöller, *Österreich im Kriege gegen die Hussiten*].

Toman, Hugo, *Das hussitische Kriegswesen in der Zeit Žižkas und Prokops* (Prague: Královská Česká společnost nau, 1898) [cite: Toman, *Das hussitische Kriegswesen*].

Tomek, Václav Vladivoj, *Jan Žižka* (Prague: J. Otto, 1879) [cite: Tomek, *Jan Žižka*].

Tresp, Uwe, *Söldner aus Böhmen. Im Dienst deutscher Fürsten: Kriegsgeschäft und Heeresorganisation im 15. Jahrhundert*, (Paderborn: Ferdinand Schöningh, 2004) [cite: Tresp, *Söldner aus Böhmen*].

-----, "*Markgraf Wilhelm I. von Meißen und Böhmen. Die Belagerung von Prag (1401)*", in Wilhelm der Einäugige, *Markgraf von Meissen (1346-1407)*, (Dresden: Sandstein, 2009), pp. 43-53 [cite: Tresp, *Die Belagerung von Prag 1401*].

-----, "Hussiten vor Bernau," in Bergstedt, Clemens (et al.) in *Dialog mit Raubrittern und schönen Madonnen. Die Mark Brandenburg im späten Mittelalter* (Berlin: Lukas Verlag, 2011), pp. 142-146 [cite: Tresp, *Hussiten vor Bernau*].

Turnbull, Stephen, *The Hussite Wars 1419-1436 (Osprey Men-at-Arms No. 409)* (Oxford: Osprey, 2004) [cite: Turnbull, *Hussite Wars*].

Verney, Victor, *Warrior of God Jan Žižka and the Hussite Revolution* (London: Frontline Books, 2009) [cite: Verney, *Warrior of God*].

Veszprémy, László, "The state and military affairs in east-central Europe, 1380 – c. 1520", in Tallett, Frank/ Trim, David J.B.: *European Warfare 1350-1750* (Cambridge: University of Reading, 2010, pp. 96-109) [cite: Veszprémy, *State and military affairs*].

Williams, Gareth, "The mace. Countering the armoured opponent", in *Medieval Warfare Magazine No. 4* (2014), pp. 34-35 [cite: Williams: *The mace*].

Winkler, Karl, *Die Schlacht bei Hiltersried* (Würzburg: K. Triltsch, 1939) [cite: Winkler, *Hiltersried*].

Wulf, Max von, *Die hussitische Wagenburg* (Berlin: (dissertation), 1889) [cite: Wulf, *Wagenburg*].

Zeune, Joachim, "Hussitenzeitliche Wehrelemente an Burgen der Hassberge," in *Burgenforschung aus Sachsen 17/2* of the Deutsche Burgenvereinigung e. V. Landesgruppe Sachsen (Langenweißbach: Beier & Beran, 2004), pp. 130-152 [cite Zeune, *Hussitenzeitliche Wehrelemente*].

Zimmerling, Dieter, *Der Deutsche Ritterorden* (Düsseldorf: Econ Verlag, 1988) [cite: Zimmerling, *Der deutsche Ritterorden*].